"Lift(s) the cover on the MacLean-Cherry dynamic—a life built 'around conversations over beers at night.'"
—*Winnipeg Free Press*

"MacLean has written a book that is consistently amusing and illuminating."
—www.canadianinterviews.com

PRAISE FOR **RON MacLEAN**

"I've known Ron MacLean for a long time. He loves the game of hockey, that's obvious, and I have a healthy respect for him."
—Mark Messier

"When I think of Ron, I think of the guy who is always one-upping Don Cherry. He's got a terrific wit and sense of humour and an analytic mind. Hockey's lucky to have somebody like him."
—Glen Sather

"Ron is a quick-witted professional, full of charisma and passion for our game. A true blue Canadian."
—Doug Gilmour

"Talking with Ron is so easy because he really knows his stuff. He makes all of the athletes feel valued. He is so real and grounded—I just adore the guy."
—Jamie Salé

"Legions of musicians are devoted to Ron because of his tireless promotion of Canadian bands. Having your song on *Hockey Night in Canada* tops every musician's bucket list. Hockey and music—got to love it!"
—Jim Cuddy

"Trying to keep up with Ron's amazing brain is like trying to change rotation in the middle of a quad jump, but the risk is worth it."
—Kurt Browning

CORNERED

CORNERED

HIJINKS, HIGHLIGHTS, LATE NIGHTS AND INSIGHTS

RON MacLEAN

WITH KIRSTIE McLELLAN DAY

HARPERCOLLINS PUBLISHERS LTD

HarperCollins Publishers Ltd
2 Bloor Street East, 20th Floor
Toronto, Ontario, Canada
M4W 1A8

www.harpercollins.ca

Library and Archives Canada Cataloguing in Publication
information is available upon request

ISBN 978-1-55468-975-0

Printed and bound in the United States
RRD 9 8 7 6 5 4

For Cari,
"And I want all the world to know, that your love's all I need.
And if we're lost, then we are lost together."
Blue Rodeo

CONTENTS

FOREWORD

I was sitting at the desk of *Hockey Night in Canada* alone before the Leafs game one Saturday night and in comes this kid. He sticks out his hand and says, "Hi, I'm Ron MacLean. I'm the new host." I almost said, "You've got to be kidding." He looked eighteen years old, and I'd never heard of him. I thought, "Oh boy, this is going to be fun." That first Coach's Corner was a near disaster. He had tears in his eyes, but I'm sure Ron will tell you all about that one.

I was not enjoying our time together on Coach's Corner. I could see we were not on the same wavelength. I'm a redneck from the East and he's a tree hugger from the West. Figure that one out. One time on the show we were talking about a guy, and I gave it to him pretty good.

MacLean tells me, "You can't say that!"

I said, "Why not?"

He said, "Think of the man's mother."

His mother? I looked at him and thought, "Is this guy kiddin'?"

I'd find a scoop for Coach's Corner and he'd say, "Good. We must share this with the rest of the crew working on the show tonight."

One time, just before we went on Coach's Corner, I heard that Lafleur was out with a bad injury. MacLean shared it with everybody! I could have throttled him. And then he tells me, "You must realize you are not bigger than the game or the story." Imagine, this snotty-nosed kid telling me how to act on TV. At that point it wasn't a question of whether Coach's Corner was going to survive, it was whether MacLean was going to live.

It came to a head in Calgary during a game between Edmonton and the Calgary Flames. I was wearing a red jacket and matching Stetson. He's from Red Deer. So as a joke, I turn to him on Coach's Corner and I say, "You should be wearing this red jacket and hat—you cheer so much for the Flames." After the show, he went nuts! He was throwing things in his bag and saying, "How could you embarrass me that way? It doesn't matter what you say anyhow, you won't be here next year."

I admit I have a hockey player's idea of humour—cruel. The more you can hurt a guy, the funnier it is. And when it's your turn, you have to take it on the chin. I only kid people I like.

I started to like Ron because he didn't back down. I appreciated his gumption. The problem was, he wasn't getting it. Instead of taking my kidding as a compliment, he was offended. He hadn't realized yet that TV is a tough business. There's no mercy. You screw up and a lot of people are happy and ready to take your spot. It's really not how good you are, it's how tough you are. You have to have tough skin. He was getting good reviews, but I knew his day was coming. I said to him one time, "Don't get too cocky, kid. You're just on a honeymoon. It's only a matter of time till you get yours."

And sure enough, it came in Edmonton, his home country

of all places. When he did his usual bang-up job at an NHL awards dinner (nobody does that emcee stuff better), the next day he was ripped to shreds in the paper. He couldn't understand it. I said, "Kid, the honeymoon is over. Now you are in my world. It's open season on us now, so toughen up! Can't you see it's us against them? Screw them all, we'll show 'em!" And he did toughen up, and that's when we started to click.

He started to get the hockey player's mentality—if you show weakness, make fun of it. If I showed I had a cold, a sore back, neck or knee, he would ridicule me just like the hockey players. It was pure joy for me, as I felt I was back in my hockey days. But with his puns, I opened Pandora's box.

I remember going out to drink with him for the first time. We were at the bar and he orders chicken wings. You don't eat when you drink, not even dinner—just ask the old AHL players. So I say, "What did we come here for—to eat or to drink? Now cancel that order!"

And now comes the hard part for me—compliments. I'm not good at giving them and he's not good at accepting them. At the end of the playoffs, we've been on the road together every day for two months and worked together every other day on what seems to be a zillion shows. Finally, after the last one, we head home. We only live fifteen minutes from each other, so the taxi drops me off at my house first. And it's just, "See ya." And then I always give him a shot, and he always shoots something back. No handshake or any of that phony stuff. And that's it, till next season.

We travel in different circles. He's a wine guy who likes sailboats, and I'm a beer guy in a rowboat.

Okay, anyhow, back to the compliments. First, let me say, I would not have lasted twenty-five years on TV without him. I feel he is like my defence partner on the Rochester Americans, Darryl Sly. He carried me on the ice for years. I had my strengths—tough in front of the net, I could fight and hit. But Darryl did all the legwork for me.

Ron is the same way. I have my strengths—sharp dresser, good-looking, charm, personality, I know hockey, and I'm humble. And he has his strengths. If he thinks I am going down the wrong path, he will steer things another way, which ticks me off. But that's what the game is. He tries to get to me on TV and I try to get to him. It's fun and dangerous and, yes, we've had a bit of trouble over the years. I'm sure Ron will tell you about that in the book.

He's good at picking things out in the game. For instance, this year in the third game of the Stanley Cup finals, I never noticed Shawn Thornton of the Bruins taunting Aaron Rome of Vancouver and then Rome coming out the very next shift and nailing Nathan Horton, knocking him out of the playoffs. Or Gregory Campbell of Boston yapping at Roberto Luongo at the end of the June 13 game. Ron is the guy who caught these things. And he is one of those rare birds who can do an update on air while in the middle of a conversation with somebody.

Another thing, as far as I am concerned: nobody does a better interview.

He has confidence supreme. When we are walking through an airport, a guy might holler, "Great show last night, Grapes!" And Ron will laugh. Or if we are somewhere and a guy hands him a camera and then asks him to take a picture of me with the guy, Ron thinks that is hilarious. Complete confidence.

Okay, enough of that. Ron, when he reads this, won't believe his eyes. But what the hell? After keeping the beer cold in hotel rooms after games for twenty-five years, he deserves it. Cold beer and nibbles and stories, that's what we do—and they are great stories. I'm sure you're going to hear them in this book. I can hardly wait to read it.

Donald S. Cherry
June 2011

ACKNOWLEDGEMENTS

A special thank you to Cari MacLean, who rode herd on the book—Cari was the calm in the middle of the storm. And we'd like to thank Kirstie's husband, Larry Day, for his balanced perspective, all his ideas and excellent edits. We'd also like to thank our amazing research assistant, Julie Folk, owner/editor of adrenalinereginasports.com, as well as Sonja Bloomer and Carol Morgan, who kept all pictures organized and on track. Thanks to our hard-working researchers and transcribers and facilitators from Pyramid Productions, Inc.: Carole Cottreau, Steve McLellan, Mike Banks, Carol Morgan, Arana Lyle, Justin Thomson, Shely Henry, Evan Adlington, Tyler McLeod, Sheila Rae, Geordie Day and Vittoria Walter. We'd also like to send a special shout out to Len Glickman from Cassels Brock, and to Alison Woodbury.

Thank you to HarperCollins Canada—Jim Gifford for his invaluable input and for pulling everything together, Noelle Zitzer and Allegra Robinson for their editorial expertise, Greg Tabor for the cover design, and our publisher, Iris Tupholme. Many others at HarperCollins rolled up their sleeves to make this book happen—Neil Erickson, Leo MacDonald, Michael Guy-Haddock, Sandra Leef, Norma Cody, Shelley Tangney,

Charidy Johnston, Cory Beatty and our publicity whiz, Laura Hughes. Thanks to Lloyd Davis and Sue Sumeraj for their copy editing and proofreading.

Kirstie expresses her love and thanks to her family for their ongoing support, in particular to her parents, Joan and Bud McLellan; her children and grandchildren, Charlie, Lundy, Paul, Geordie, Buddy, Kristin, Téa, Jaxon and Griffin; and her sisters, Jan Folk and Julie Sinclair.

We'd also like to thank the following people for their invaluable help and stories: Ron MacLean Sr., Don and Luba Cherry, Rodney Fort, Bob Goodenow, Dave Hodge, Craig Adams, Don Meehan at Newport Sports, Jim Byrd, Anne Wortham, Harold Bloom, Terry Ludwick, John Shannon, Charlie Macoun, Larry and Willy (JACK FM Vancouver), Kerrin Lee-Gartner and Max Gartner, Paula and Murray Brookbank, Dr. Matt Brown, Wendy McCreary (NHL Alumni Relations Manager), Marian Finucane, Todd Swanson, Ray Blair, Glen Sather, Brian Burke, Mark Messier, Marty McSorley, Jamie Salé, Jim Cuddy, Kurt Browning, Doug Gilmour, Trevor Pilling, Anne-Marie Maugeri, Kirstine Stewart, Jeff Keay, Dave Cutler, Heather A. Marshall, Mike Dodson, Paula Murrin, Kathy L. Harlen, Miragh Bitove (Archivist and Collections Registrar, D.K. [Doc] Seaman Hockey Resource Centre), Tyler Olsen (*Chilliwack Times*) and Jacob Bestebroer (Chilliwack Bruins).

Grateful acknowledgement is made to the following for permission to reproduce excerpts:

Lyrics from "Midnight at the Oasis," by David Nichtern, reprinted with permission of Notting Hill Music Inc., USA.

Transcribed excerpts from the audio interview between Marian Finucane and Nuala O' Faolain are used courtesy of RTÉ, Ireland's Public Service Broadcaster.

Lyrics from "Alive," by Edwin, reprinted with permission of David Martin, Stephan Moccio, and Edwin.

Lyrics from "The Wherewithal," by The Tragically Hip, reprinted with permission of The Tragically Hip.

Lyrics from "Lost Together," by Blue Rodeo, reprinted by permission of Keelor/Cuddy; published by Thunderhawk Music.

Transcribed text from Coach's Corner is reproduced with permission of the CBC.

Thank you to all who helped with photos:

Howard Elliott and Tammie Danciu from *The Spectator*; Andrea Gordon from *The Canadian Press*; Brenda Carroll, Simone Seguin and Peter Ogilvie of the CBC; Julianna Child of Fox 40

World; Patricia Desjardins from *The Gazette* (Montreal); Jillian Goddard from Sun Media; Reg Vertolli from Metroland Media Group; Jessica Tomao of the NHL; Clayton Didier, photographer; Wendy Watts from the *Toronto Star*; Louis Calabro and Judy Watt of the Academy of Canadian Cinema & Television; Paul Mason from the Jim Pattison Broadcast Group; Steve Poirier from the Hockey Hall of Fame; Sergeant Daren Kraus and Captain J.R. Noel of the Canadian Forces; Ted Pakozdi and Patricia from ICP Photography; Jerry Murphy; Todd Swanson; Marty Vellner; Terry Krushelnicki; Ben Flock, photographer; Brad Dalgarno, photographer; D.J. Wright, wedding photographer; Gary Kennedy, photographer; Gordon Phippen, photographer; Patrick Festing-Smith, photographer; Peter Bregg, photographer; Sherali Najak; David Sealy; Melanie McKinnon, Crown Copyright Officer, Public Works and Government Services Canada; Laurie Near from GetStock/*Toronto Star*; Barrie Erskine; Liesa Kortman; Frank Gunn; Nancy Ackerman; Chris Bolin; Doug Fraser; Cindy Gillies and Julie Chambers at the Calgary Stampede

1

GOOD GOD, IS THIS KID CRYING?

I'd been waiting in the studio since noon. The game was scheduled for 8 o'clock Eastern. I checked my watch—it was 6:30 p.m. An hour and a half to go. I could hear Mr. Cherry in the hallway, talking to a bunch of kids. I took a look. He was posing for photographs—thumbs up, the whole bit. My heart started racing.

Finally, he rolled into the studio and spotted me sitting at the *Hockey Night in Canada* desk. "Ron, me boy, you're from Red River, eh?"

Gee whiz, should I correct him? "That's right," I smiled, "Red *Deer* is my hometown. Calgary is where I've been working." My hand shot out from my side. "It's a real honour to meet you."

He ignored my hand. "Yeah, just great. You come down here to Toronto—from Red River—and we all say, 'What a wonderful fellow.' I go out to Calgary and Edmonton, tell them I'm from Toronto, and they call me a jerk. Did you know that?"

I chuckled and tried not to look at my hand, which was still frozen in front of me, unshaken.

"Anyways, don't be nervous, kid," he said. "There's only eight and a half million people watching you." He leaned over, pumped my hand and went off to say hello to Bob Cole, Harry

Neale and the rest of the *Hockey Night in Canada* gang.

I pulled out a Kleenex and pretended to blow my nose, but I was secretly patting sweat off my top lip. I didn't want everyone to see how nervous I was. Our producer, Doug Sellars, came up to me. He looked serious.

"Ron, when you do Coach's Corner with Mr. Cherry tonight, there are two things I'd like you to keep in mind." Doug started counting on his fingers. "Number one, do not let Don Cherry dictate the subject matter."

I nodded.

"Number two," he smiled, "don't be self-conscious about this, but there is something we need to point out to you."

Oh, God.

"When you're interviewing a guest, your eyes have a tendency to wander up and down your subject—from head to toe."

Head to toe?

Doug was still smiling. "You can't do that to Mr. Cherry. When two men are sitting side by side, it would be a little disconcerting for some of our viewership to see your eyes focused on his lap. So remember, don't look down." He clapped his hands, "Okay, everybody, let's go!"

The countdown into my first Coach's Corner, October 10, 1986, began. "Ten, nine, eight . . ."

I could hear the opening theme. Wandering eyes. I have wandering eyes. I told myself, "Whatever you do, Stupid, don't look below Don Cherry's neck."

"Seven, six . . ."

But what if I glance down? It'll look like I'm staring at Don Cherry's jock!

"Four, three . . ."

I won't blink. My eyes cannot wander if I don't blink.

"Two, one!"

"So, Don, who do you like for the Cup this year?" I looked into Don's big, bright blue eyes. I was fixed on them, concentrating hard.

He started talking, and I became a little uncomfortable. It was tough not to blink. My eyes were burning, filling up with tears. Suddenly, a huge tear the size of a Tic Tac slipped from my left eye and rolled down my cheek. Thankfully, the TV camera was to my right, so the viewers at home couldn't see it. I followed Don's eyes as he watched it splash off my collar.

He looked at me with his thoughts written all over his face. "Good God, is this kid *crying?*"

THE LONELY BOY

Both my parents were military. Dad was in the army, then the air force for thirty-two years, so I was a military brat. They met and married in France when Mom was in the air force. They were Cape Bretoners and had grown up only forty miles apart. Dad says Mom was a very pretty girl with a great sense of humour and really easy to talk to.

Mom's name was Catherine Sarah MacDonald. Her mother was only twenty-seven years old when she died of tuberculosis. Her father was an alcoholic, so Mom's Grandmother MacDonald raised her, along with a younger girl who was the child of another family alcoholic. This little sister couldn't say "Sarah." It came out sounding like "Lila," and that was the name that stuck with Mom for the rest of her life.

Mom had a wonderful sense of humour. She spoke Gaelic, like her grandmother. And she would use her extended vocabulary to tell Scottish jokes and stories.

Dad is probably one of the sweetest guys you will ever meet, but he had a childhood right out of a Dickens novel. Despite all his childhood hardships, he will be ninety years old this May (2012). I'm Ronald Joseph Corbett MacLean, he is Ronald Francis MacLean.

Dad was born Ronald Jacues Moulton. Moulton was his biological mother's last name. She was a housemaid in North Sydney. Dad's mother, Minnie, was twenty years old when she became pregnant by a very high-ranking military man. Grandmother Moulton forbade her daughter to keep the child. So Minnie gave Dad to an individual who grossly neglected him. He was five months old when the Children's Aid Society intervened. The court records show that Dad was "in a terribly wasted condition because of neglect" and his body "a mere skeleton." Under the Children's Protection Act, the court handed him over to the newly opened Bairncroft Orphanage on Kings Road in Sydney River, Nova Scotia.

Meanwhile, Mary "Esther" and Frank Corbett MacLean, a couple from Point Aconi, a little fishing village on the tip of the northeastern coast of Cape Breton, were having bad luck getting a family started. Their baby twins had died that year within three months of each other. Broken-hearted, the couple arrived at Bairncroft Orphanage and found my father, who was by then one and a half years old. The MacLeans didn't adopt him, but instead became his foster parents. Later, they went back to the same orphanage and adopted a daughter. Not long after, they were surprised when Mrs. MacLean became pregnant with a little girl. Baby Nina immediately became the darling of the family.

Dad wasn't very happy in Point Aconi. He felt like an outcast. Maybe it was because he was never legally related, but he was the child assigned most of the chores. The family treated him like a hired man. He'd wash the supper dishes, fill the bucket with coal for the night and work in the orchard, picking apples.

If he questioned why he did all this while his five cousins and two sisters played in the yard, he was spanked or given a hard whack across the side of the jaw. He would lie in bed at night wondering, "Why did they take me? I'm obviously not what they wanted."

When Dad was fifteen, he hopped a train and got as far as Edmundston, New Brunswick. But because he was a ward of the court, the police hunted him down. When he was caught, they brought him back to Sydney, where he was given a very strong lecture from an official who told him he was an ingrate and that he'd better do a better job of living with the MacLeans. As soon as he turned eighteen, Dad joined the army.

Mom and Dad went together for about three months, and then had a major falling-out over a simple disagreement. They were both so stubborn, they quit talking. Two months later, Dad broke the ice, and they were married right after, on July 18, 1959, in France. Dad was thirty-seven, and Mom was thirty-three.

At the ceremony, Mom was wearing a white suit, and her maid of honour, Ann Boucher, was dressed in pink. Dad's best man was Ann's husband, George. None of them could speak French except George and the priest. He recognized that Mom was the bride, but for some reason he figured that George was the groom. They all lined up in front of the altar, and the ceremony began. Partway through, George realized he was being married to Mom. He clapped his hands and said, "Father, you've got the wrong man!"

Mom found out she was pregnant with me at the end of November 1959, and when she told Dad, they were both excited. Dad figured I was a girl, but Mom said, "Oh, no, no. We are having a boy." Dad said, "Why are you sure it's going to be a boy?" Mom said, "Because all my aunts had a male child first, and I'm going to do the same."

Although they were stationed in France, I was born on April 12, 1960, in Unterm, Germany, on Zweibrücken Air Base, which is about thirty minutes by car to the French border. While Mom was in labour, they discovered I was breach, so they transported her over to the bigger hospital. Mom was in labour for forty-eight hours, until finally they tonged me out.

We lived in France for fourteen months before Dad was transferred back to the RCAF Station Gorsebrook in Halifax. While we were there, Mom and Dad decided to investigate adopting a baby girl so that I would have a playmate. They went to a Catholic orphanage, but were advised against it. The administrator told them, "If you are doing this only to please your son, we don't think that is a good idea." And so I grew up an only child.

In 1969, we were living in Hubbards, Nova Scotia, which is less than an hour west of Halifax. There were very few kids around, so I was alone a lot. Dad was driving home from Halifax one day and spotted a sign that said "Dogs for sale." My mom wasn't too keen on dogs, but my dad had convinced her a boy should have one. He stopped the car and went into the house and discovered they were selling dachshunds, complete with papers. He chose a male pup for me, a cute little scoundrel with long, floppy ears and a sausage body. He brought the dog home and I named him Snoopy. Snoopy and I hit it off really well. He was a funny dog, very high-strung. He piddled on the floor every time we came in the house. Snoopy loved to sit beside me in the bathtub and sleep on my bed. We were inseparable.

A week or two after we got him, he and I were outside playing. Dad was dozing, because he was working shift at the time, and Mom was busy in the kitchen. Snoopy started acting funny, walking around in circles on the grass. Then he squatted down and started pooping out live worms. The ghastly things were lifting their heads and squirming all over each other in a nasty pile. I ran screaming into the house, "Mom! Dad! Come see the awful thing that Snoopy's doing!"

That was the end of that. I never went near the dog again. I couldn't. I was convinced that there were more of those worms still inside of Snoopy, and I sure as hell didn't want them dropping all over me. Mom and Dad were very understanding. They didn't yell at me or try to force me to take care of the dog. They put an ad in the paper to find him a good home. We got a phone call from a lady in Dartmouth, Nova Scotia. She had three daughters and asked if she could bring the girls out to see the dog. Mom and Dad said, "Anytime, anytime." The girls loved the dog, and of course the dog loved them. Mom had taken me out to the store while they were there, because she felt so bad that we were giving up Snoopy. She'd grown attached to the little guy. We never had another dog while I lived at home, but we always had a cat.

When I was four years old, Dad was transferred to Victoria, British Columbia. We stayed there a year and a half, and then we were sent to Whitehorse, in the Yukon. Mom and Dad and I flew aboard a turboprop to our new home. I recall the wing lights strobing on the clouds as we flew through the turbulent night air. We moved into public married quarters called Steelox, which consisted of Quonset huts with two apartments per unit. In wintertime, frost built up on the inside walls wherever there were bolts or metal struts behind the drywall. In 1964, Dad was stationed in Alert on Ellesmere Island—83 degrees north, practically at the North Pole. He went up alone. It was a supply station, part of the Distant Early Warning or DEW line. Both Canada and the United States had a series of radar stations across the North that protected us from Russia.

I was a little bit fragile. I repeatedly fractured my collarbone. Whether it was a lack of calcium in my system or what, I don't know. I was a picky eater and didn't like much. I had a list of things I would eat: wieners, Kraft Dinner, peanut butter and honey sandwiches, or bologna. No veggies and fruit. Maybe that's why I was so hyper.

The first time I broke my collarbone, I was four years old. A friend and I were taking turns at a goofy stunt. One at a time, we would lie flat on our backs at the bottom of a hill near our house. The idea was not to flinch while the other came roaring down on a bike. He rode over my shoulder. I knew I was hurt, but didn't want to be grounded from playing on the hill again. I came into the house and didn't say anything about the accident. Three days later, Mom came in to wake me for school and I was crying quietly into the pillow. She said, "Ronnie, Ronnie, what is the matter?" and I 'fessed up. A couple of years later, I was skating backward at the public rink and I tripped over an Oh Henry! chocolate bar wrapper and dislocated my clavicle. I had a third shoulder injury in Mill

Cove, Nova Scotia. We were playing Red Rover, with locked arms. Somebody ran between me and the next guy, and *snap!*

I got into hockey in Whitehorse in 1965. Dwight Riendeau, who was a few years older than I was, was my next-door neighbour. His dad, Ed, was a real outdoorsman and a hockey player too. Ed taught me everything—how to skate and how to use my stick and how to drive the puck down the ice.

We used to play across the street at the Clementses' backyard rink, which had short boards and floodlights. We played shinny every day. It was a modest, small-town postcard rink surrounded by big, beautiful pine trees. The locals tapped the trees with tubes that ran into buckets collecting sap. On our breaks from shovelling the snow off the ice, we would chip the frozen sap from the bark and chomp on it, like gum.

But the real treat for me was the hard pink bubble gum that you got with hockey cards. I'd walk for miles to pick up a pack. I remember the excitement of carefully unfolding the wax cover and inhaling the sweet aroma, and then licking the powder off my fingertips. Trying to preserve the treat, I'd snap off the corners and soften them between my front teeth. And then, unable to control myself, I'd jam all the gum into my mouth at once. I loved the sugar burn at the back of my throat when I swallowed after the first good, long chew. After a quick look through the pack, I'd take the cards back home and sort them into my deck. Shuffling through them again and again made me feel so prosperous.

I always liked winning. I mean, that's why you play the game. But when I was very young, I learned that it isn't the ultimate experience. A feeling of effort and appreciation is enough. While we were in the Yukon, my folks, who loved the arts, explained to me that writers Pierre Berton and Robert Service were Yukoners. In "Spell of the Yukon," Service wrote, "I wanted the gold, and I got it— / Came out with a fortune last fall, / Yet somehow life's not what I thought it, / and somehow the gold isn't all." That one verse still sums up my take on life. In Grade 2, I bet my teacher, Miss McKenzie, that the Habs would win the Stanley Cup. I wanted the Leafs to do it, but I followed hockey closely and had made up my mind, based on everything I'd heard from Sunday night radio broadcasts (from 1965 until 1976, CBC Radio aired *Sunday Night NHL Hockey*) that Montreal was the better team. When the Habs won, I took the gold, but felt awful. I would have been happier as a loser.

In 1966, I asked Santa for the new Coleco table hockey game. On Christmas Eve, after we turned down the heat and went to bed, I lay there, overexcited, running my fingers over the frost heaves on the wall next to my mattress and peering out the window for a glimpse of Santa's sleigh. A few hours later, I heard footsteps coming down the hall. I squeezed my eyes shut, fearing that if Santa saw that I was up late, I would be stricken from the Good Boys List and risk losing that table hockey game. When I woke up Christmas morning, there was a miniature replica of the Stanley Cup on my nightstand. I knew right away what was under the tree. My parents never disappointed.

In 1967, the Anik satellites were not yet up, so the CBC's live television broadcasts didn't reach the Canadian North. I watched the Leafs win their last Cup on videotape, one week after they had won it. The game was still really exciting.

When you are military, you move a lot. So you are forced to make new friends over and over. It seemed I was always on my own again. When I think about those times, I didn't get a heartsick feeling until we left Whitehorse when I was eight. They closed the base and we were shipped back to Halifax. It was the first time I had to leave a pack of friends I'd known for a few years.

In Halifax, I signed up for a hockey division called squirt. I was quite a good skater because we had so much outdoor ice in Whitehorse. I loved goaltending, but I hated the pressure. When I played goal and we lost, I felt it too much. Playing out was a lot more fun.

The toughest move was after Dad's last transfer, to Edmonton. We left there for Red Deer when I was eleven years old, going into Grade 7. He was forty-nine and, like all military personnel at the time, he had to retire by fifty. Alberta was the land of opportunity. Dad retired as a sergeant after thirty-two years and found a good job in Red Deer as an RCMP dispatcher.

That first summer was a lonely one. I met nobody. Our street had no kids. I held a pity party for myself every day. Mom kept a poem I wrote that summer, and I ran across it in her things after she died. I called it "Lonely Boy."

Trying to make this city my home,
Is not an easy task.
There are many things I'd like to do,
But I'm kinda afraid to ask.
I'd like more friends to come to call,

And ask me over sometime,
To play some games or just gab a bit,
Or toss around a ball.
When winter comes and hockey's the thing,
I'd like to have friends for a game.
Most guys in organized hockey,
They don't even know my name.

Of course, once school started, I made a ton of friends and forgot all about being the Lonely Boy.

3

JUST SHUT UP

I was always the class clown. I couldn't help myself. Numerous times, I would have self-talks. "Take it easy, Ron, settle down. You don't have to be the class clown this year. You could just be a good student." Never happened.

I could be disruptive and hyper, and I loved to argue. I would challenge the teacher for the fun of it. Nova Scotia had the toughest disciplinary measures. When I was little, I would get the strap on my hand with a piece of fire hose. But from Whitehorse on, I spent a lot of time kneeling in the corner, which was the main punishment in the Catholic school system. Once in a while I was sent home for acting up. This would rile Mom up and she would chase me down the hall with a broom. There would be no television for a week, groundings, lots of different punishments. I didn't mind. I knew they cared.

Mom was mischievous, and funny as hell. When the occasion called for solemnity, she had a way of stirring it up. One time up in Whitehorse, Mom and Dad were getting ready for a dinner dance at the Sergeant's Mess. Dad had just got a new upper plate, but he left it in a drawer because it wasn't comfortable. Mom was in a fancy black cocktail dress. She wanted to accessorize, so she was rooting around, looking for something to pin to her shoulder. She grabbed Dad's dentures and shoved a safety pin through the gum, and away they went to the dance. When they were seated, Dad saw the other women at the table staring at Mom and looking confused. Finally, one said, "Lila, is your pin made of . . . teeth?" And Mom said, "Why, yes it is. I was waiting for someone to notice." And the whole table collapsed in laughter.

Two of the things that defined her were her humour and her ability to be a confidant. People really opened up with Mom. She was very compassionate, but God, did she have a wild temper. I loved her spit. Mom had a good job in Red Deer, but she felt she was being disrespected due to her gender. The last straw came when she was overlooked for a promotion that should have been hers, so she stormed out. Just up and left for good. Pride goes before the fall.

Sometimes when I am with Grapes and he loses it, it reminds me of her. When you crossed Mom and she got hot, it was funny. Later, she'd reel it in and then apologize. Mom could say, "I'm sorry." She would explode at me for something I probably deserved, and then she would say, "Look, Ronnie, I had a long day, you struck a nerve and I didn't mean that." She would never let me go to bed if she was cross with me. She would always come in and sit on the edge of the bed to make sure I felt good before I went to sleep. Where do you get that confidence to acknowledge that it's okay to be wrong?

Grapes can apologize in his own way, but in his household, "sorry" did not hold water. Don told me this story very early in our relationship. I think it was his way of letting me know where he was coming from. His brother, Richard, was playing midget baseball in Kingston. Don and Del, his father, went to watch. They were short a first-base ump and the home plate umpire asked Don to sub in. Del told him to do it, but Don said, "Well, geez, Dad, I don't know the rules." And Del said, "Donald, if the ball gets there first, then the guy is out. You know what to do, now get out there." Sure enough, in the first inning Don had to make a ruling at second base. He made it in favour of his brother's team. Well, the opposing manager fired out of the dugout onto the field and started tearing a strip off Don. He kicked dirt on him and called him all sorts of names. Don was mad. At the end of the game, as Don was walking off, he looked around for the manager so he could retaliate. Suddenly, the guilty manager popped up out of the dugout. Don came at him and brushed him with his shoulder. The manager stepped back into the dugout, fell, hit his head on the bench and was knocked unconscious. Don was kind of pleased with himself. It wasn't really a punch, but he was happy he'd done some damage.

Del and Richard headed home. Don followed behind with a stick he had picked up. He was running it along the picket fences. Suddenly, a car pulled up and four big guys, including the manager, jumped out. This was Kingston in the 1950s, a tough place to be. The manager walked toward Don and said, "Don, I just have to say I was a jerk back there. You were good enough to help us out at first base, and to tell you the truth, the call was right. I just wanted to set the tone for our team. You did a great job—I was a prick. Put 'er there." And they shook hands. Then the manager and his friends got back into the car and drove off.

Del stormed over to Don. He was just livid. He said, "Donald, if you ever shake the hand of a man who's crossed you again, you'll not live under my roof." And that became a code for Don. His dad was a fierce guy.

In 1996, we had probably one of our worst meltdowns on Coach's Corner ever. Usually, I am aware when I'm pushing Don's buttons. I'm playing with a bull, so if I'm careless, I deserve to get the horn. It was during the first World Cup of Hockey, which replaced the Canada Cup as the top professional hockey tournament outside of the Olympics. We were in Montreal at the Molson Centre. Canada had a best-of-three against the United States. In the first game, Canada won, but lost Mark Messier and Al MacInnis with elbow bursa injuries.

Canada lost game two and went to the rubber match. Game three was at the Molson Centre, now the Bell Centre, in Montreal. Canada came out and threw everything at the Americans. Canada outshot them by about 20 to 4, but the American goalie, Mike Richter, stood on his head. Don is always promoting tough guys, not finesse players, so he is a little anxious during international events. Canada always has the toughest team, so that means if we lose, it's his fault. Before we even started the Coach's Corner segment, I could see the sweat off his palms leaving marks on the desktop of the *Hockey Night* set.

The red light went on in the first intermission and Don said, "You know, Ron, a little something I have to get off my chest here. Really, really ticks me off. You know, I hear there are players, they're tired, they're sick, and they've played too many meaningful hockey games. Is that what you say?"

"Yes, Don."

"All these important hockey games they've played in their lives. It's just too much. They've given their all for their teams, for their country. They need a break. They need to have some time with their family. They need some quality time. It's just not possible to expect them to come and play for their country here in the Canada Cup, World Cup, whatever we're calling the stupid thing now. It's absolutely ridiculous."

I said, "Well, who do you mean, Don?"

"Never mind who I mean. I'm just saying there's some guys ought to be here for Canada. They wanted them to come and they didn't show up."

"I know, Don, but you're plowing a pretty broad swath with a statement like that. I mean, you don't think Mario Lemieux should be playing, do you?"

"No, of course not, with the cancer. What are you, stupid? I'm just saying there's guys who ought to be here."

I said, "I know, but you see what I—"

"Oh, I got it. I got it." And at this point, I could tell things were kind of going off the rails, but I didn't know why. "I got it," he said. "You just come back from the Olympic Games there in Atlanta, all the great write-ups in the newspapers . . . kudos? Is that what you call them? Anyway, gold medal coverage, CBC, 'Ron MacLean, Investigative Journalist.' Ron here is going to get to the bottom of this story—is that what you're doing?"

"No, Don, but if you're sitting at home with your family and you're being sort of charged with not being patriotic, that's a tough thing."

He said, "Look. Will you just . . . shut . . . up! Just shut up. I'm trying to tell a simple story here."

And I had to think quickly, because it was really tense to watch and to be a part of. I knew if I were aggressive in return, I'd be a bloodstain on the floor. In order for him to understand what I meant, I brought up an incident that had occurred eight months earlier. In January 1996, the Bruins' rookie coach, Steve Kasper, had benched his star players Cam Neely and Kevin Stevens after Boston lost to the Blackhawks. Neely was crushed and said of Kasper, who was also his former teammate, "I've been through a lot in nine and a half years to be treated this way." Grapes was furious and ripped Kasper on Coach's Corner. He said if he could reach through the TV screen, he'd take care of Kasper himself. So I was referring to that when I said, "Well, Don, I'm just doing what you did for Cam Neely when Kasper benched him in Toronto. I'm trying to stick up for anyone unjustly tarred by the same brush."

I could see Don was starting to feel a little bad. He said, "All right! It's Ray Bourque, if you have to know. Ray Bourque ought to be here. He lives five minutes down the road, for heaven's sakes. Matter of fact, Jeremy Roenick ought to be here for the Americans. The point I was trying to make, but you kept buttin' in, was Bobby Orr was the MVP in the 1976 Canada Cup. And Bobby did it on one leg, and now we're out of time, and that's that! You ruined the whole thing."

He folded his arms and glared at me. I felt a moment of regret, because I had obviously sent him down a path he didn't want to travel. Bobby Orr had chronic problems with his right knee dating back to the mid-1960s, when he risked his professional career to participate in the Memorial Cup. And in 1976 he did it again by helping Canada win the Canada Cup. Don was the assistant coach of that winning team, and he and Bobby are great friends. Grapes was Bobby's coach when he scored the most goals of his career—46 in 1974–75.

Don has superior radar about public perception, and the reason he had been reluctant to mention Bourque was because he was worried people might get the mistaken impression that Bobby had criticized Ray Bourque and sent Don out to throw snowballs for him. And here I was, stumbling along, thinking, "Geez, why is Grapes all riled up?" As television goes, it was wild and it was funny.

After blowing up on me and mentioning Ray Bourque on air, I wondered if Grapes would speak to me again that night. When Don and I are on the road, we have a routine. After the broadcast, we like to pull up a couple of chairs in one of our rooms and fill up the garbage pail with ice and cold water and light beers. (I know when Don reads this, he'll say, "Light beers? You told them we drink *light* beers? Why didn't you say Export, for Pete's sake? Make us look like men.")

Because it was the last game of the tournament, we were planning to have beers. I ran out to get something to soak them up. As I walked down the street toward the sandwich shop, a cabbie pulled up beside me, rolled down the passenger window and shouted, "You really had him going tonight."

We were both staying on the thirty-third floor of the hotel. When I got back, I stepped off the elevator, intending to knock on Don's door. As I made my way down the hallway, I spotted a rubber tree plant with a human arm extended from it, offering an icy beer. I recognized the arm immediately, because Grapes wears cut-off shirts all summer so the guns can breathe. That beer was his way of saying, "Sorry, kid, I got a little carried away tonight."

4

I WOULD PAY TO REFEREE

I was always happy, but secretly worried about life. I can vividly remember being nine years old and lying in bed thinking, "Rats! I'm going to have to grow up and life won't be easy like it is now. I really enjoy school. I love Mom and Dad. It's all so nice. It'll never be better than this."

I've had that thought a lot of times. In fact, to this day, when Don Cherry and I crack a beer in the hotel room after *Hockey Night in Canada*, it's kind of a line we say to one another—"Who could beat this?"

I worked hard at whatever I did. It didn't matter what it was, I put everything into it, and it sometimes made me really full of myself. During a class debate in Grade 12, I thought I was amazingly clever. I was the Mark Twain of Camille J. Lerouge High. My opponent knew nothing! I had this one in the bag. Then it came time to vote on who won, and nobody sided with me. I thought, "You're kidding. What is wrong with everybody?" I was superior in the debate, making all my points and absolutely burying my opponent. Then it dawned on me—my attitude had turned everybody off. It was a moment of clarity. I had communicated to my class all right. I had communicated that I was an arrogant twerp.

I liked to be a leader, and after learning to tone it down a bit I became class president and team captain in hockey, right up to the time I tried out for the Red Deer Chiefs in 1977. I definitely didn't like the rough stuff, so when I got to Red Deer there were a lot of kids with way more moxie than I had for that kind of play. I was scrawny, really scrawny, at five foot ten, maybe 140 pounds, but there were plenty of guys my size and smaller who were far braver than I was.

I'd made it to camp thanks to my skating ability, but I had horrible hands. So I played one level below Midget AAA, and by that time I was a left winger and centre. Sometimes I could see the ice, sometimes I couldn't. It was frustrating because once every ten games or so, it would magically appear. Most times when I played, I knew what I was missing. Wayne Gretzky always saw the ice, ten for ten. The only thing we had in common is that he credits fear for his awareness.

In 1978, I quit playing hockey and instead chose to referee. I've often equated broadcasting with refereeing. In principle, you are supposed to let your guest be the star. It's the same with reffing. Your job is to bring the players to a level of entertainment and honesty. I like the game to be exciting, with an edge. I use that same philosophy on air with Don Cherry or Gary Bettman or whoever I'm interviewing. I want a little anger. I want a little freedom of expression. I don't want to rein it in, constantly squeezing it so that it's deadly dull. I've had a few good experiences in both reffing and broadcasting that have helped me learn what works and what doesn't.

When I refereed, I didn't see everything, but I was a good communicator. As one of our supervisors used to say, "Some people referee with honey, some people do it with vinegar." I liked to try to charm my way through. That worked most nights, but not every night.

I liked to use the player's number, not his name, even if I knew it. I would say, "Look, Six, you're down 2–0. We all know that was a hook, but I'm not going to call it or you'll be down 3–0 and then we could all just go home. But I need you to help me out. Everybody in the rink knows you got away with one, so let's improve your chances of having a good night. You can't be hooking like that."

The guys would usually respect that. I think they enjoyed the dialogue, and I would feel confident I had the game under control. But for every five times that it worked, the sixth time a player would say, "Oh, screw off, just make the call." And I would walk away thinking, "Wow, that's interesting." Just when I was feeling like a wonderful manager of a game, I'd get shot down.

When I first started reffing, at eighteen, it was for atoms and pee wees. I moved up to novices, and within a year, bantams, midgets and senior hockey in central Alberta. Now, that was fantastic. I had some crazy moments. Early in my refereeing career, I was in Bentley, Alberta, reffing the Bentley Generals against the Sylvan Lakers. I was twenty years old and given a playoff game, which was pretty important. It went to overtime, and there was a collision between the Bentley goaltender and a Sylvan Lake forward as they both went for a loose puck. The goalie went down and glanced at me, so I knew he wasn't seriously injured. But he continued to lie there. We had a senior referee named Bruce Small working the lines. Bruce yelled, "The goalie's down!" and I yelled, "I know he's down!" I was mad at the goalie for peeking at me to see if I would blow down the play in order to save him from the risk he had taken. So I allowed the player from Sylvan Lake to shoot into the empty net.

Now, what I maybe should have done was blow the whistle. No one would have been upset, and I could have said it looked like the goalie was hurt. Later, I was driving home through the snow, trying to justify my actions and saying to myself, "Well, he wasn't hurt, and in fairness, the guy should have been allowed to score." But I knew I was wrong. The prudent move would have been not to allow recognition of the ploy to over-rule fairness. The whole basic essence of refereeing is conflict management. You're trying to adjudicate, just like the police. Sometimes they crack down, and other times they let you go with a warning.

So I allowed Sylvan Lake to score in overtime to win the game. The Bentley fans poured over the glass onto the ice. They were all around me at the referee's circle, which is in front of the penalty box. Everybody was screaming at me, but nobody louder than the mother of this goaltender. One of the Sylvan Lake players, an RCMP officer, stepped in to protect me because there was only one police officer from Bentley available. I think they thought the Bentley goalie's mother was going to kill me. She was screaming about how I had let her son get hit and he was hurt, and I shouldn't have let the play continue, and I was a fool and a moron and an idiot and had no idea what I was doing and should read the rule book. At that point I was still confident in my decision. I argued back,

"I'm sorry, ma'am, but your son gambled and I was sure he was okay."

She was pounding her fists into her hands and shaking her head violently in disagreement when suddenly the top plate of her dentures came flying out onto the ice. They began spinning around and around until they stopped suddenly in between my skates. Everyone was silent. There had been bedlam, and then her teeth were lying at my feet. It was the strangest thing. We all kind of skulked away, embarrassed for her.

Today, I would have given the game a chance to go on under fairer circumstances. Scoring into an empty net in overtime was too easy.

I was owed $75 for reffing that night. As I was changing into my street clothes, a gentleman from Bentley came by the referee's room and fired seventy-five one-dollar bills at me.

Half the time, I didn't submit my chits to get paid for reffing. I don't know why. I don't think I ever charged mileage. I loved it. Even when I made mistakes like I had that night, I would have paid to referee.

5

KICKING IT PURE

I wanted so badly to be cool. I wanted to be a jock, a high school sports sensation. I was such a sports junkie, and I loved to compete. We'd won the city baseball title in 1974— the Eastview pee wee community team. It may sound strange, but I play to win, and when I do, I don't really get a kick out of it. I like the competition for it's own sake. I was a second baseman, so my biggest job was to field ground balls, and I was determined to be good at it. I spent most of my spare time throwing golf balls against the wall to practise catching grounders or practising golf on the driving range. I practised so much I won the Balmoral junior golf title a couple of years later.

Like every other guy my age, I dreamed of making it to the NHL, but by Grade 11, it became clear that I wasn't going to make it in hockey. I was cut by the Red Deer AAA Chiefs after breaking my thumb in a game and refusing to fight. So football became my new focus. I love football for starters, and I always liked testing myself. Dave Cutler, the former Edmonton Eskimos kicker, was one of my early heroes. Dave had been a middle linebacker at Simon Fraser University in Vancouver, and he was always the first man downfield to make the tackle on kickoffs or missed field goals. And he was great in the clutch. He made the kick when it mattered.

The first football game I ever attended was at Clarke Stadium in Edmonton on September 29, 1971. It was pouring rain, with winds so high the stands were alive with flapping coats and hats. The Edmonton Eskimos beat the Montreal Alouettes 12–11. There were 13,346 of us in the crowd braving the elements. Dave Cutler came in and kicked a 50-yard field goal in that driving rainstorm, and I was won over that day. It was just fantastic for me. A kicker is supposed to be the ballerina on the team, not a tough guy. But he was both, graceful and tough. And funny. I remember hearing him interviewed, talking about his placeholder, quarterback Tom Wilkinson. "Wilkie has to stand on tiptoes just to piss on a flat rock!" Grapes is like that, the yin and yang. I admire that.

I would say that for about six years, from the time I saw Dave Cutler kick that field goal, I began kicking religiously through the uprights at Red Deer's St. Thomas Aquinas High School. You have to be certifiably insane to practise by yourself, because when you kick it, it goes 50 yards. That means you've got to run and get it, bring it back and kick again, over and over. In my head, I was kicking for the Grey Cup or the Super Bowl. I got so I could kick a reasonable distance, but I wasn't CFL material. A CFL kicker is good from 55 yards. I was good from 45 yards, which isn't too bad. I would kick every day during the season. So, my right foot became kind of dead.

I had lots of friends on my team: Marty Vellner, Jerry Murphy, Ray Blair and our quarterback, Pat Quesnel. Pat would place the ball for me. The fact that our quarterback was also a holder made him meat for the opposition. I was not known for fighting, but one time they came down so hard that I jumped in and threw a punch. Ironically, I still had that broken thumb from hockey. I was suspended for our next game, in Delburne. While I was out, a guy named Michael Watson, who at 130 pounds was an unbelievable player—he could run, catch, he could do anything—replaced me for a game during a big wind storm. He kicked it straight on barefoot. Today, everyone kicks soccer style. We called that a sidewinder back in the 1970s. I kicked straight on, like Cutler, with a modified kicking cleat—it had a square toe. But Michael gave it a nice high leg kick and drilled it through the posts. A 40-yard field goal into a hurricane. I was completely shocked by how good he was. I was on my best behaviour after that.

In Grade 11, the year I joined the football team as the kicker and cornerback, we won the championship. I didn't contribute much, other than to kick the converts and the field goals. But the next year, my big chance, the chance I'd played out over and over in my mind, became a reality.

In 1978, Don Sinclair was the coach of our team, the Camille Cougars. Don was a successful lawyer in Red Deer, and still is. We made it to the finals of the nine-man football championship of the Central West Alberta Schools Athletic Association at Great Chief Park in Red Deer. We fought hard, winding up in a 10–10 tie with thirty seconds to go. We had the ball on the Delburne Trojans' 27-yard line near the left hash marks. A 34-yard field goal would cinch a victory for us. I was called out onto the field. Even if I missed, it would likely sail through the end zone, which was 25 yards deep in those days. All we needed was a single point for the win.

I'd had a kick blocked earlier. One of our own guys ran from right tackle, behind the centre, to cover the left flank, and he wound up so close to our placeholder, Pat Quesnel, that the ball hit him. When I lined up that final kick, I thought, "Make sure you clear the line of scrimmage!" So I took a little power off to ensure a high kick.

And I kicked it pure. Struck it so sweetly, it soared. We were mesmerized, watching it go right over the right upright, 21 yards deep into the end zone. It was ruled wide.

We were all slow to pursue the Delburne receiver, who picked up the ball and ran back with it. Marty Vellner just missed tackling him in the end zone for a single, and the win. I had drop foot from practicing so much—I couldn't run him down. The Delburne kid ran it back 131 yards for a touchdown. There was nothing wrong with the hold, the snap or the kick. But I missed. It can happen.

It was one of those moments that would shape my actions forever. To this day, my bosses and producers are always all over me to be tougher in my questioning. I'm tough with guys like Gary Bettman, but not with athletes. When athletes screw up, I have no desire to ask them to review their performance. I know how badly they want it. Why make them squirm?

6

ROMMEL LIVES IN STETTLER

I had no ambition to get into the broadcasting industry. It wasn't something that I chose to go after. It found me.

I remember being in a lawn chair in our backyard in Red Deer in 1976, when I was sixteen, lounging in the sun, when my dad came out and said, "Ronnie, there's a Martin Smith on the telephone for you." Martin Smith was the program director at Red Deer's main radio station, CKRD. I picked up, and Martin told me that a pal of mine named Bernie Roth, who worked for him, was sick. He said Bernie had told him I had done some high school radio club stuff during noon hours, and he'd recommended me because I was the president of the students' union and the class clown. Martin said, "I need somebody to do some operating. It's a very simple procedure—you push a button at the top of the clock once an hour. You'll have no trouble figuring it out, and we pay $27 for a nine-hour shift. Would you be interested?" That was big money at the time.

CKRD-FM was a CBC repeater station. At the top of the clock they paused for station identification, and they needed a kid to flip the bar that took the network station offline and put the local station online. I would press a button to roll the cartridge with the voice-over—"This is CKRD, 99.9 megahertz in

Red Deer"—and then flip the lever back to rejoin the network. And for that I got three bucks every hour. I was like a kid in a candy shop, and totally in awe of the AM disc jockey who would occasionally walk by.

I had been planning to become a teacher, like Ed Shields, my Grade 7 teacher. Ed was a New Yorker, and he taught in Red Deer. On the first day of class, he laid out the curriculum. "We're doing this, this, this, and spelling . . ." We all groaned.

"What? You don't like spelling?" he said. "Well, I'll make you a deal. I'll give you a word and if you can spell it, we won't do spelling this entire semester." The word was Albuquerque. Fortunately, one of my classmates had been to Albuquerque that summer. Ed kept his word. I respected that, and was intrigued with how he grabbed hold of us. That moment was gold.

So that was my goal—finish high school and pursue an education degree. But after I finished my first shift at CKRD, Martin called and said, "Can you work every second Sunday, three to midnight?"

Five months down the line, CKRD found out they were shy of their Canadian quotient of news, weather and sports, so I was promoted to newsreader. I would rip headlines off the wire service (no rewrites) and stumble through them. In the winter of 1976, Lyudmila Pakhomova and Alexander Gorshkov of the Soviet Union won the ice dancing event at the World Figure Skating Championships. Trying to say their names was painful. I was already butchering every other word.

During my first year, a farmer from Stettler, Alberta, came in, opened up a briefcase and showed me two Lugers. He said,

"You know, Ron, Rommel lives in Stettler." I didn't know if the guy was crazy or what. He didn't seem crazy. He said, "What happened was the SS all got out of town and moved to different parts of the world, and Rommel ended up in Stettler. I'm his neighbour, and this is Rommel's gun." I didn't even know if it was an authentic Luger. I told my bosses, and they figured he was looney tunes. But I've always wondered about it.

I might have been awful at the job, but they knew I would always show up, so they offered me a chance to be a disc jockey on the weekends. Ken Nichol—a great guy, a broadcaster at the station—gave me some pointers while he walked me through the job. He told me how often to say your name and mention the call letters of the radio station, and how to announce the record artists. It was a formulaic format. Twice an hour, you would do a public service announcement and the weather, and right out of the newscast you were to run an old hit and a Top 30 hit song.

My first shift as a DJ was 11 a.m. on a Sunday. The newscast ran, then a commercial, then the weather, then, "Now back to more music on 85 CKRD."

Billy Joel's "My Life" came on, and I cued up Chuck Mangione's "Feels So Good." I sat there looking at the clock and practising what I was going to say. "That was Billy Joel with 'My Life' on CKRD. It's 11:08 and I'm Ron MacLean." "That was Billy Joel with 'My Life' on CKRD and I'm . . ." I was absolutely scared skinny. Billy Joel ended. I turned the microphone on and glanced at the clock. It said 11:10, not 11:08, and it threw me. "It's eleven o' ten . . . er, o,' . . . and that, er . . . that was Billy Joel . . ."

I was off to a roaring start. But I'll never forget the feeling of flipping the microphone on for the first time and thinking, "Well, now what?" There's nobody there, just a metal wall in front of you. So when I was on the radio, I always tried to visualize the listeners. You wouldn't know if a joke was funny, because there was no feedback. That was really awkward. For the first few times on air, after having the gift of the gab all my life, I had nothing to say.

During Grade 12, when I had my own all-night shift on weekends, my high school buddies would come down to the station. They were always a little gunned after partying. At two or three in the morning, they'd press the light at the back door and I'd let them in. We'd gather around in the little studio and I would try to keep them quiet long enough to introduce the next song. We had a lot of laughs.

I thought that the radio job would last just the summer, but my marks fell dramatically that last semester—not bad enough to prevent me from going to university, but I sort of lost the desire to go. I started to feel the radio bug. My teaching aspirations were kaput. I always thought teachers made your life, but I realized DJs make your day.

Besides, I was fixated on music. My favourite thing to do early in my career was to choose the music. Life was simple and happy when I did those overnight shifts. The sun would come up and I'd be playing nice songs on the radio.

From Grades 6 to 12, I spoke at just about every graduation, usually as the class historian or emcee. But I started to hate it because I was full of trepidation. I'd feel brutal about having agreed to do it. I worried about how I would do. It was probably normal apprehension, the kind of reasonable fear that we all have. Everybody wants to be loved.

By eighteen, when I entered broadcasting full time, I began having anxiety attacks. They would come at crunch time. I remember the old building where we worked, down on Gaetz Avenue in Red Deer. I would go down to the bowels of the basement, where the washroom was, lean over the sink and try to compose myself. I was nervous about my shift. I couldn't wait for the day when I would be confident about going on the air. I knew that time would come, but I was so scared. It was a tough time, due to all the internal churning. I'd tell myself, "You're eighteen years old, and you've made your choice. You're going to do this. You can't go on making $600 a month forever. So you'd better work at it and try to establish yourself." I sensed that this was my opportunity. I constantly told myself, "Don't blow it."

Fear would descend at the craziest times, and it could be crippling. One of the worst attacks happened during my first on-location broadcast in Red Deer. I was set up on the second floor of a plaza at a stereo shop. The DJ threw to me for a sixty-second live hit. "Here's Ron, live on location at . . ." and I couldn't get through it. I had to abort about thirty-five seconds in. I was breathless, my heart was racing, pounding so hard it was lifting up the fabric of my shirt. I was absolutely petrified. I thought, "Oh God, what am I going to do?" I was scheduled to do four sixty-second hits an hour for the next four hours. I had to fight my way through the rest of that day.

I moved to full time in June, just before graduation. I had a daily 8 p.m.-to-midnight shift, and the Saturday afternoon and Sunday morning shifts. I tried to improve the rapport I had with my listeners. I looked at it as if I were a doctor who works on his bedside manner. The disc jockey has the opportunity to entertain and to educate, but most of all he can give you companionship. Because I was an only child, I thought it was important for people to have company. If you do it right, you're good company. DJ-ing was a neat thing to do for a living. I loved it, but I wasn't very good at it.

I continued to study and work at it. Man, did I work at it. I took a little Johnny Carson, added a bit of Wes Montgomery from CHED in Edmonton and CFAC Calgary's Ed Whalen, sprinkled in a little Billy Joel and blended all of it into this new sensation—me! The result was brutal. I chirped like Beaver Cleaver sucking on a helium balloon. I had been a singer until I hit puberty, and then I had a terrible voice, very squeaky. Age and experience have managed to improve it. I don't smoke, which is too bad. It would have given me more resonance.

Mark Summers, the DJ who worked the shift before mine, would always turn over the mic and, off air, would set me up for my shift with the words, "All right, my friend, be great."

I cringe now, but, inspired by Mark's kindness, I used to end my show with "Thank you for being a friend." I figured no one would notice I'd stolen the line from the hit song by Andrew Gold. *The Golden Girls*, which had that song as its theme, was still six years into the future. In my mind, I was John Tesh meets Dan Rather, with a terrific signature sign-off.

I was totally oblivious to my limitations. By 1979, I thought I might be ready for the big time. I often listened to my favourite station in Edmonton, 630 CHED, which had a rock format.

The star of the station was morning man Wes Montgomery. I adored him. There was also a very good DJ named Bruce Bowie who did the noon-to-3 p.m. shift. I decided to send them a tape for feedback. I secretly hoped that once someone at CHED heard it, they would be so impressed they'd pass it on to the station manager demanding that I be hired at once. I was too intimidated to send it to Wes, but I respected Bowie and aspired to be like him, so I mailed it to him with $10 and a note thanking him and suggesting that he could use the money to buy himself a bottle of wine.

Bruce wrote back. He gave me a lot of great advice regarding connection, communication and brevity. He added, "Ron, your work is technically sound, but nobody in this world is that nice." And he returned the money, saying he did not drink. Bruce was right. In trying hard to engage the listener and sell myself with cheeriness, I came off as a phony.

Early in my radio career, I would pore over newspapers, trying to look for inspiration from stories. I needed song introductions, and I have never been very interested in pop culture, so it was a real struggle to create dialogue. I knew some DJs used the weather or "universals," which were what we called tidbits of information that we all connect to. So I would read the papers and see the headlines. I noticed that the headlines were often puns.

Throughout junior high school, I had a classmate named Ray Blair. Ray struggled with reading but was a masterful wordsmith. I always thought that was interesting. He was a guy who could barely read and yet had an amazing command of language. He loved toying with words. Instead of "drink," he would say "swig," and then turn that into "schwig." He had a relentless fascination with the sounds of words and their meanings. It became a huge part of my high school days, matching him stride for stride.

We both played hockey. We weren't always on the same team; he was an adversary and a really good one. Ray was a much bigger guy, stronger and tough as nails. I was captain and a blabbermouth. One time, I was going back to chase the puck while playing the point on a power play. Ray was right behind me. He could have killed me, but as I touched the puck, he didn't hit me—instead, he quietly said "Bang." It sent chills.

The way Ray played with words got me interested in puns. He loved to pun and was constantly punning—we called him the Prince of Puns. For example, we always used to talk about what to do on weekends. So he might say, "There's beerly anything going on." And I'd ask, "Rye not?" To which he'd reply, "Let's head to the liquor store, just in case." I'd say something like, "I can't give it a shot right now, my day is all bottled up." And he'd shake his head, "That's a foamy excuse." We'd go on and on, trying to top each other.

Ray's an oil field consultant today, but after high school he worked at an auto body shop. I asked him about it, and he said, "How hard can fixing a frame that's bentley be?"

7

ONE IN SIX BILLION

I made a good living at CKRD—7,200 bones a year—and I was living at home. I didn't need more money. I saved, and by the time I was twenty-four, I figured I could afford to move out and get married.

Cari Lynn Vaselenak (Vaselenak is Slovak) and I had been going out together for seven years, starting June 22, 1978, when she was in Grade 10 and I was in Grade 12. Cari was beautiful.

Before she even knew I existed, I used to sneak looks at her all the time. She had big, dark eyes and a smile that lit up a room. In 1983, when the movie *Flashdance* came out, I couldn't believe how much Cari looked like Jennifer Beals. Cari was cool and a really good basketball player. Even her dad, John, was cool. They called him "Hondo." He'd played baseball in the minors and scouted for the Cincinnati Reds and the Pittsburgh Pirates.

In the late winter of 1978, before we started dating, the boys' and girls' teams from Camille Lerouge High were at a basketball tournament in Drumheller. I was in Grade 12 and a point guard. Cari was one of two Grade 10s called up to sub in with the senior team. She played guard, too.

The guys were staying four to a room in two adjoining rooms. We'd smuggled in a bunch of beer. Our coach, Bruce Buchanan, knocked on the door and the beer was quickly stashed under beds, in suitcases, behind curtains and in the toilet tank. Later that night, we partied, and most of the players from both teams showed up, but we kept it down, so it was no big deal.

The next morning, we got up and the guys wanted to get rid of all the empties, but I said, "No, no. Let's put them back in the cardboard, stack them neatly on the coffee table, and the chambermaid can turn in the empties. It will be like a tip." So that's what we did, and then we went off to play basketball.

Unbeknownst to me, someone had gotten a little carried away and driven a headboard through the drywall. The hotel owner showed up after the game to claim damages. He said we had been partying up a storm and wrecked the room, and he had cases of empty beer bottles to prove it. So now we were in trouble. Our school decided to expel all team members from sports for the rest of their high school careers. In Cari's case, it was very bad news because she still had two years left.

I was student union president, so I went to our principal, Ray Killeen, and said, "Look, Ray, it's bad, no doubt about it, but let's make something positive out of this. To make amends, I'll apologize to the entire school at an assembly, and the teams will sell chocolate-covered almonds to raise money for charity." And I phoned every parent of every player, taking responsibility and explaining what and how it had happened. "This is Ron of the Camille Lerouge basketball team, and here's what happened. We were bad to do it, and we took advantage by wrecking the room, but we're going to make amends by raising money for charity, and I hope you'll forgive and support us." Cari's dad, John, took her out for a walk around the block and told her, "Don't worry about this, Cari. It was more important you were part of the group. It's good to be popular. It's good that you were included. I'm not mad at you at all."

In the end, we were allowed to finish the season, and in fact, we won the zone, the Central West Alberta Schools Athletic Association title, and Cari continued as a star player on the school team until she graduated. I can't believe we were able to weasel our way out of that predicament.

My nicknames were Thumper and Bunny because of my front teeth, and I was a member of the radio club, which in Cari's eyes was a step up from the debate club or the chess club. I thought about her a lot and wanted to ask her out, so I hinted around. I'd give her rides home from school and joke with her at parties, but I wasn't on her radar. My best buddy, Todd Swanson, has a sister two years younger named Val, who was one of Cari's friends. Val and Todd tried giving her the full-court press. They told her she should consider me as a potential boyfriend. But she had no interest.

I intuitively knew that this girl was for me. I'd go out of my way to spot her at school, and I used to estimate where she'd be and at what time so that I could intersect with her. She lived in a community adjacent to where I lived, and there was an ice cream store nearby on the corner of 39 Street and 40 Avenue. I had an innate sense of where she might go. For instance, about half an hour after her basketball practice I would stroll over to the corner for a cone and she'd be there. I'm not sure whether

I was plugged into her somehow or whether I was just good at calculating the odds, but I bumped into her a lot.

She seemed to like my company, but still did not look at me romantically. I kind of gave up and settled for hanging around her. Then, in the spring of Grade 12, I was recruited by the radio station to do this fashion show, modelling graduation suits. During the show, I met a lovely girl who went to another high school. I needed a date for graduation, so I asked her to go with me. This seemed to pique Cari's interest. She told Val that if I asked her out, she would probably say yes.

After a few dates, we were going steady.

Every time I hear the song "Music Box Dancer" by Frank Mills, I think of Cari. It was playing on the radio one night when I took her for ice cream at the local Dairy Queen. Prior to going inside, we sat in the parking lot, necking in the front seat. All of a sudden, we heard this loud revving. It was my car engine—it sounded like it might explode. People around us were staring. Turned out my car was running, and while we were occupied, my foot had landed on the gas pedal. That song always takes me right back to that moment.

I've never had a serious relationship with anyone else. I am Cari's first and only love, and she is mine. How often does that happen?

Cari was starting her third year at the University of Alberta in Edmonton, where she was pursuing a degree in Recreation and Leisure Studies. I was twenty-two and had been working for three years. I was wildly in love and remember the 160-kilometre-an-hour drives up to Edmonton with my foot all the way to the floor so that I could shave fifteen minutes off the trip.

I wasn't worried that Cari might be seeing someone else—I'm not possessive—but I thought I might lose her if I didn't tie her up. I was so nervous buying the ring. I went to Peoples Jewellers at the mall in Red Deer. I'm a very impulsive guy. I always regret it when I say no to impulse buying. I'll see something and kick myself later for not picking it up. I was making $750 a month, and the ring cost $600, which was a big-ticket item for me. I didn't have a credit card, so I paid cash. I forgot to ask her dad for her hand and felt bad about that afterward. You're supposed to do that.

I carried that ring around in my pocket for some time. I didn't tell anyone about it, but I had a plan. I worked conscientiously. I practised my ad-libs so they'd sound natural. I prepared for that proposal for a long time. I was going to tell Cari that we both had an apprenticeship to get through. Hers was schooling and mine was getting my feet under me in broadcasting. And that I was focused on that first, but I knew it was not fair to let her twist in the wind. I was going to say, "I want to show you some sort of commitment, and with you at university I think it would be a good idea to give you that promise of commitment, something to make you feel good about, so you don't feel alone." I envisioned taking her out to a nice dinner in Red Deer and slipping the ring to her under the table, Cary Grant–style, and then giving her my spiel. Thank God it didn't work out that way. She would never have said yes.

June 28, 1982, was D-Day. I picked her up and took her to the local Keg 'n Cleaver steak house. All was going well. She went to the bathroom, and I pulled the little velvet box out of my pocket, gripped it in my hand and rested it on my knee.

She sat back down and I found her knee under the table and tapped it with the little velvet box. She'd just taken hold of it when suddenly Joe McKenzie, a football teammate, came by the table to say hi. I have always had this philosophy that we are one in six billion, not one in two. Everyone is equally deserving of unconditional love, whether you are my wife or you are someone I just met. So even though it was supposed to be a big moment for Cari and me, Joe and I talked for about twenty minutes. From the corner of my eye I saw Cari peering down into the box in her lap. When Joe left, I forgot all about the speech I'd prepared. I nodded to the box and said, "Well, what do you think?"

She held up the ring and said, "It's beautiful. What's it for?"

8

ONE TO ONE

Life was busy. I was working six days a week, and on the seventh I would go on location to do a remote. I was determined to succeed. It was a total head-down, we're-going-to-make-this-work mentality. I was twenty-three and in the fifth year of my career when I was promoted to program director. Small towns, you move up fast, right? The first thing I did was dump the promotions budget, take the entire $10,000 and give it to our morning man, Danny Teed, bumping his salary from $1,300 a month to $2,300 a month. He had a great on-air presence. I figured if we had an amazing morning show we could capture listeners for the whole day.

Because I had no marketing budget, I went to Waterbed World and pitched a contest. I offered airtime to give away a $200 waterbed per day for an entire month. I said, "On the last day, we'll give away a whole bedroom suite!" Miraculously, they agreed. In the business, it's called a contra advertising arrangement. It was a hit with the audience. People started pouring into the store.

I really wanted to improve what we did at the station. I'd read a couple of books by Jay Trachman on the art of person-ality radio. He was the creator of an informative publication in the business called *One to One*. Today it would be like a blog on the subject of communication. Jay advised that in order to succeed, you had to be the best at being brief, believable and real. It was good advice. The problem with most on-air people is that they don't reveal themselves. You connect with listeners when you understand that they are like you, not who you wish to be. Talk to the listener who has the same ideas, same politics, same prejudices, same humour, same likes and dislikes, and hope like hell that's enough to win the day.

I called Jay in Fresno, California, and asked if he did seminars. He said he had never done one, but he had been thinking about it. I flew him up to Red Deer to consult for a fee of $500. I wondered what Jay would be like. I didn't even know what he looked like. I drove to Edmonton to pick him up at the airport. I waited and waited, but he didn't deplane. Then I heard an announcement: "Would Ron MacLean please report to immigration?" An immigration officer pointed to this older-looking gentleman with a slight build and asked me if I knew him. I was taken aback. I expected a studly type to go with his resonant, rich, mellow voice. I said, "Yes, I do know him. He is here to do a seminar at CKRD radio."

"Well, have you arranged for papers for him to work in Canada?" he asked.

That hadn't occurred to me. I told the officer that I didn't know about that sort of thing. And he asked, "What's he going to be doing exactly?"

I said, "He's going to be playing cassettes of each of the announcers, and then he is going to comment on them."

The immigration officers consulted and then told me they

agreed to look past my omission, but warned that you can't have people working in Canada without a work visa.

Jay seemed to take the whole thing in stride. On the way to Red Deer, I pumped him for advice. I was determined to go beyond good to great. "What's the best tip you can give me?" I asked. He talked to me about preparation. "For every hour you are on air, you should do ten hours of preparation," he said.

Our entire on-air staff gathered at the Red Deer Lodge, and Jay listened to each DJ's "aircheck" and offered his opinion on areas to improve. He was playing Danny Teed's tape and stopped it twenty minutes in to give Danny a tip. Danny said, "Geez, Jay, I've been in the business for twenty years. I can't change that now." And Jay slammed his fist on the table and said, "Danny! You're an adult. You can change anything you choose to!" That got our attention.

We had a manager in Red Deer we hired from Lethbridge, Alberta, where he was a popular morning man. His radio name was Wayne Barry. Wayne Heinrich is his real name. He was a godsend, because I was at the point in my career where I needed to home in. I was still trying to be all things—mostly Johnny Carson and Dave Hodge—a compilation of the best. Wayne dialled me in as to what to do to focus. I had an interview show on CKRD that was sort of like CBC Radio's *Definitely Not the Opera*. I managed to land interviews with a few newsmakers, including Senator Keith Davey, a former radio guy and sales manager for CKFH in Toronto from 1949 to 1960; Iona Campagnolo, president of the federal Liberal party in 1982—heavy-hitting politicians, artists and athletes. Wayne was a huge influence in terms of Radio 101.

One time, we were giving away two tickets to a Red Deer junior hockey game. A caller came on live, trying to win them. I was kind of being the hip DJ, Mr. Smart Ass, having fun at the caller's expense. The next day, Wayne pulled me into his office and he said, "You know, Ron, when you had that guy on, it was kind of funny. But the truth of the matter is you made him look stupid. The opposite would have been better. It's not you who should be the star of that conversation, it's the caller. The caller was good enough to listen to our station. And he was good enough to phone you and enter the contest. And what did you do? You turned on him with your skills. He was out of his depth, whereas you are comfortable on stage. You shouldn't work at making yourself shine—make your guest shine. Remember, if you make them look good, you'll look good." He was so right. I adopted that philosophy immediately.

Jay taught us "You be you," and Wayne was saying "You be you, but don't hog the limelight—let the guest be the star." These were really important lessons that shaped me, like the field goal.

Jay turned that first consultation in Red Deer into a whole career of seminars. He was very successful at it, one of the best in the business. Sadly, he died in November 2009.

Whoever did the noon-to-4 p.m. shift on CKRD-AM radio automatically did the weather on TV, so getting bumped from 8 p.m.-to-midnight to noon-to-4 was my big break. Environment Canada painstakingly explained the weather map to me. They told me about its features and the effects of different weather systems on central Alberta. I discovered that the number one information measure for Red Deer was not temperature, it was relative humidity, a critical factor for the farmers in the area.

For the most part, I loved the gig, but Red Deer was a small station, and so there was a series of equipment malfunctions. A clip wouldn't come up, and the anchors would throw to me. I was budgeted to do three minutes, and suddenly I had eight minutes to fill. The adrenalin would hit hard. I would turn my back to the camera, pretending to look at the weather map, gulp a few times and try to regain my composure.

Wayne Barry asked me to be the colour man/engineer on road games with the local junior hockey team, the Red Deer Rustlers. And we were such a team at CKRD that I didn't dream of saying no. As usual, my first attempt wasn't exactly smooth. At 5:30 p.m., during the warmup, we could not get a signal back to CKRD, so we unscrewed the mouthpiece on a phone receiver and wired the phone directly into the audio board using alligator clips. The next problem was that, although I knew all the Rustlers and their numbers, I knew only one player on the Fort Saskatchewan Traders—Sid Cranston. So I sweated it out every time Sid went back to the bench at the end of a shift.

For two years, I was host and colour man to Frank Ryan's play-by-play. As the bus hurtled up and down the Trans-Canada Highway, I'd look at the lights of the cities and farmsteads and wonder if the people in those homes could hear my work. I thought it must be cool to work on a network show.

Then the CKRD supper-hour TV news went from thirty minutes to a one-hour format. Maybe it was because I was long-winded and could help them stretch the 'cast, but they asked me to give up weather and do the sports. I had to be talked into it. I tried to make the weather interesting by drawing sports logos on the map, using them as locators and forecasting game outcomes. I tried not to be a sports guy. I loved sports and I was such an obsessive guy, I knew I'd develop tunnel vision like Cari's next-door neighbour Don Drummond, who was the sports editor of the *Red Deer Advocate*. He was a prototypical sports guy—beer in one hand, cigar in the other, talking sports 24/7. I remember one night in 1983, during the Progressive Conservative leadership race that pitted Brian Mulroney against John Crosbie and Joe Clark, among others. I mentioned that it would not be easy to choose the next leader. Don replied, "It has to be Gretzky, even if Messier is the true leader."

I was swamped. At the time, I was program director, the 9 a.m.-to-noon DJ, the TV weatherman and the voice of the Rustlers. I did a lot of commercials and promotions, plus, because it was a small community, I was the first guy they called to do speeches and emcee jobs—gratis, of course. On my day off, I did on-location broadcasts.

I didn't know it then, but I was six months away from hosting my first NHL game.

9

A LUCKY SIGN

I've always had this joyful feeling—"What a break! How in the world did you get to be alive? How did you get to be here?" Everything I've been given seems to be a really neat gift. But I'm conflicted. Part of me feels that I don't deserve it. I was bumbling along, DJ-ing on the noon-to-4 p.m. shift on CKRD radio in Red Deer, doing the sports on TV during the supper-hour news and then hopping the team bus to broadcast the Red Deer Rustlers. I was content, but juggling a little too much and wondering about my future, when I got a huge break.

In 1984, Jim Van Horne was the main sports guy at CFAC, Channels 2 & 7 in Calgary, when he accepted a job at a brand-new television sports network called TSN. They also hired Peter Watts and John Wells away from CBC Edmonton. Chris Cuthbert, Gord Miller and I were the beneficiaries of TSN's formation. Their moves opened the door for kids from smaller centres like Red Deer to move up to the big time.

I got a call out of the blue from John Shannon, the western producer for *Hockey Night in Canada*. The signal from CKRD Red Deer came in to Calgary, and he'd seen me doing the weather. He and CFAC news director Ted Arnold invited me to Calgary to apply for Jim Van Horne's position. The job was to host thirty Calgary Flames telecasts and to work as a sportscaster Wednesday through Friday at noon and on Saturday and Sunday evenings. I was so green I assumed I had the job. Why else would they call, right?

On August 20, 1984, I walked in and presented myself at the reception desk. "Hi, I'm Ron MacLean, and I'm here to see Ted Arnold and John Shannon for the Flames position." The receptionist was Lee Haskayne, the wife of Dick Haskayne, a very successful Calgary oil executive. At the time, Dick was president of Husky Oil and Gas. Dick and Lee were down to earth. Lee worked at the station because she loved the people. Lee said, "That's fine, Mr. MacLean, have a seat over there with the other gentlemen." I looked over at nine guys seated in the waiting area. I recognized "Mr. Ski" Mike Lownsbrough, CFCN's Doug Smith and CFAC sports guy Grant Pollock. My heart sank right through my chest. I felt complete panic. "Oh my God, they're considering all of us for this position!" I was shocked and worried. Grant had the great Lyle Waggoner hair and was dressed in a well-fitting black jacket and camel pants with a white shirt and pale yellow tie. He looked like he'd just stepped off his yacht. I felt confident in my light grey textured sport coat, but I started to second-guess the pink shirt and tie. I had sailed in, ready to start the job as this likeable fellow from Red Deer, and was instead trying to stay afloat in the deep end.

I knew it would be at least an hour before it was my turn, so I went for a drive down Memorial Drive, to the Dairy Queen by the base of Foothills Hospital. I lined up behind a guy with a freshly amputated arm. He had obviously snuck out of the hospital for a Mr. Misty. His bandages were blood-soaked, which made me feel kind of dizzy. This added to the surreal quality of the whole bizarre day. I drove back to 2 & 7, trying to talk myself down. "It's just a job. Relax. You're happy where you are in Red Deer. If you don't get the job, it's no big deal." But my chest was thumping. I could not get my heart to stop racing.

I went back and waited for another twenty minutes before I was called into the studio. I sat down and was given an IFB—an interruptible foldback earpiece. I could hear the director, Larry Brown, along with Shannon talking over the music and the effects. They had me do an opening to a Flames–Oilers telecast, a forty-five-second blurb about the Battle of Alberta, and Shannon said, "That's no good, Ron. You have to project. You have to pick it up. Yell a little! This is K-Tel hockey. We're *selling* the game here." So I did it a second time, and this time I was loud.

Shannon started to ratchet things up more. He was trying to replicate the tension and pace of a real hockey game so that he could gauge my response. We moved to hockey highlights. They gave me nine goals in forty seconds. You had to know your stuff, have an understanding of the game and get the names right. There weren't many things there that really threw me off. Next, I interviewed twenty-three-year-old Flames forward Jim Peplinski.

I powered through the Peplinski intro without taking a breath. "We're back live at the Saddledome in Calgary, where, after twenty minutes, the Calgary Flames, on the strength of a goal by Kent Nilsson at 18:12—a power-play marker, the Flames' first of the '84–85 season—enjoy a one–nothing lead over the Vancouver Canucks, a game reminiscent of the styles I'd expect the two teams to employ, and perhaps you do, too. The Flames coming off a year with high expectations, the semifinal last season against the Edmonton Oilers. Many people have already said that this is the year that the Flames will really get a chance to come on, and this is the gentleman [turn to Peplinski] that . . . can . . . perhaps . . ." Shannon was barking at me to stop. "No, Ron! Finish your thought over the scoreboard, come to a complete stop and then introduce the guest. Don't just come back with, 'Welcome back to the Calgary Saddledome, where it's 3–2 Calgary, and I'm pleased to be joined by Jim Peplinski." Start with 'Welcome back to the Calgary Saddledome. It's 3–2 Calgary after twenty minutes.' Pause. Let them get the graphic off the screen while we go to a two-shot, then, 'We are pleased to be joined by . . .'"

He continued teaching and explaining all during take two, but I plowed through, not letting it throw me. "We're back live at the Saddledome in Calgary, where, after twenty minutes, the Calgary Flames, on the strength of a power-play goal by Kent Nilsson, their first of the '84–85 season, enjoy a one-to-nothing lead.

"The Calgary Flames are coming off a year—and Jim Peplinski is my first guest this intermission—which, Jim, maybe you could attest, is a big one to the finish. The semifinals against the Edmonton Oilers led everybody to believe that 1984–85 just might be your year. Do you feel the pressure of a hot finish?"

Peplinski was smooth and we continued on.

Next, I had an ad-lib to camera. I needed to hit the two-minute mark. And suddenly my radio training kicked in. On every song, there's an intro or music bed for seven to twenty-seven seconds, and then the vocals start. The DJ talks over it. We called it "hitting the post" or "hitting the fade." Little did I know that learning to work with the clock was a great skill for TV. I managed to nail my ad-lib to the second. "All right, my name is Ron MacLean. For many of you, you may be getting a chance to familiarize yourself with me, as I am you. It's a great privilege and an honour to have the opportunity to work with a very competent and professional crew at Channels 2 & 7 CFAC and Canadian Sports Network, and that may sound patronizing, but as you sit in and watch the contest tonight, for me it's kind of a thrill to be part of the game action. We will look forward to the 1984–85 season and, I think, what are going to be some very high moments, particularly from a Calgary perspective. I've had an opportunity to work for CKRD radio and television in Red Deer the last seven years. And having monitored first the Atlanta Flames franchise and their start-up down south and then the eventual move to Calgary, where they aspired to put a team into the Corral, did very well with it and now, after a big season last year, the finish against the Edmonton Oilers, things are looking very hot. I might also mention, in terms of respect, Jim Van Horne, my predecessor, who has left to return to his hometown, Toronto. Should be a fun season; we're glad to have you aboard. We look very much forward to it. Eddie Whalen will be my guest when our hockey action continues in a moment."

The legend himself, Ed Whalen, dressed in a *Saturday Night*

Fever–inspired white suit, except for the striped brown and beige tie, took the seat beside me. He was easygoing and reassuring as the floor director counted us in.

We chatted about the Flames and Oilers, and I threw out there, "What do you think about Reggie Lemelin? Goaltending is a big issue in this division, obviously, because of the Oilers. Do you think this is going to hurt him?"

Ed said, "I don't know how much action he'll get due to the fact that Glen Sather sleeps with Grant Fuhr." What did he just say? Ed chuckled, "He's certainly in love with the guy."

I looked down at the papers in my hand. How should I respond? "Well, Ed, I know you have a lot of fans in Calgary who are glad to see you back and ready to go. Danny Gallivan retired." (Danny had just retired that year, after thirty-two years on *Hockey Night in Canada*.) "I heard you touch on that earlier this summer. He was a big man in your life, had a big influence. Now, maybe you're the man. Good luck with this year. Ed Whalen with the Calgary Flames. It's one–nothing Calgary after twenty minutes. Stand by for play-by-play we have more action for you in the third period."

Ed gave me a pat on the leg and said, "Good work, son."

I got back in my car and hit the highway, switching on the radio. The first song that came on was Rod Stewart's "Maggie May." That song was my all-time favourite song, so I thought, "Good, that's a lucky sign."

Two days later, I got a phone call from John Shannon. He was driving to Red Deer to meet with me. And my mom and dad said, "Oh Ronnie, you must have the job! He wouldn't drive all the way up to Red Deer to tell you if you didn't get the job." I told them I was doubtful. I wasn't going to jump to conclusions a second time.

I met John at the Capri, a hotel on the South Hill in Red Deer, right on the main drag. I pulled up in my 1983 Thunderbird. John is kind of gruff, not sentimental at all. He said, "You used to spice up the weather with little drawings of the Oilers and the Flames. David Letterman got his start doing weather, too."

I nodded, thinking I was pretty sure that was a good thing.

He said, "Okay, you got the job and you're going to meet with Ted Arnold on September 3, and you're going to ask for $40,000 a year." John says he got into trouble with station management for telling me that. They thought they could get me for twenty-five to thirty thousand. He got a phone call from Noel Wagner, the general manager at the time, who said, "Shannon, what are you doing telling my guys how much money to make?"

I was making about $22,000 at the time, so I just nodded. And he gave me my first instruction about the job. "For you, mister, no words bigger than 'marmalade.' We're selling beer here."

I nodded again.

He got up to leave, and I cleared my throat. "Excuse me, John, but could we possibly delay my start date in Calgary from the first week of September for a week or so?"

"Why?" he growled.

"Because I'm getting married on the first and I have to be there. We have 350 people coming."

10

IF I CAN MAKE IT HERE, SO CAN YOU

Cari and I had been married seven days when we moved to Calgary. Noel Wagner arranged to put us up at the International Hotel downtown while we looked for a place. Cari and I had never seen such luxury. I stood at the window on the thirty-third floor, listening to the silent streets. Calgary's a funny place in that the downtown empties out in the evening. All I could hear was the wind whistling through the giant skyscrapers, a haunting sound.

The first night there, Cari and I went for dinner at the Owl's Nest, and we were served one of those little sorbet palette cleansers between courses. I looked at it and thought, "What the hell is this? A little salad and then dessert already? Boy, that Noel is a cheap prick."

The next night, we went for dinner with Steve Lansky, who was John Shannon's producer. Lansky took us to an upscale steak house called Caesar's. I was so green, twenty-four years old and just chosen as the new Flames guy, and I didn't know what was what, but I was in this fancy place, so instead of a regular beer I was determined to have a cocktail. The waitress came by, and I said, "I'll have a Heineken, please." That was my version of a cocktail. Lansky looked at me and said, "We work for Molson.

If you ever make that mistake again, it will mean your job." And that's when it hit me—I was in over my head.

We rented a townhouse in Woodbine, in Calgary's southwest corner. Our house was next door to a 7-Eleven. I still loved junk food. I'd go in around 9 in the morning, stop and pick up breakfast on the way—a 7-Eleven coffee and a packaged Vachon chocolate square, topped with a little dab of caramel. Absolutely delicious.

Mom and Dad gave us what furniture they could—stuff they had in their basement, including coffee tables, end tables and a couch. Our only luxury item was a waterbed Cari's parents had given her for Christmas. By the time we bought all the staples you need to live, we were broke. It was neat. We didn't have much money that first Christmas, so we limited ourselves to $75 apiece. I splurged on two little plush Christmas mice by Gund. They were $20 each, which was way too much money when you only have $150 between the two of you. We still have them, and every Christmas I feel good when we bring them out.

I was lucky enough to do the Flames' broadcasts for two seasons, 1984–85 and 1985–86. Badger Bob Johnson was the coach. I got to interview some great players—Jamie Macoun, Joel Otto, Tim Hunter, Colin Patterson, Doug Risebrough, Perry Berezan and Al MacInnis. All the guys were just phenomenal interviews, but Lanny McDonald was the guy who took me under his wing.

On my first day, in 1984 at the Saddledome, before I had done a Flames telecast, I was walking down the hallway outside the Flames' dressing room, and there he stood with that big, red handlebar moustache. He was dressed like a hero from a Hollywood western—cowboy hat, blue jeans and a long leather coat that looked like it might be concealing a long gun. I was trying to decide what to say, but before I spoke, Lanny said, "Hey, you're the kid from Red Deer. I've heard many good things about you. Welcome." He reached out and shook my hand. "Remember this. I'm from the little town of Hanna, up the road. If I can make it here, so can you."

I've always loved Lanny for those words. I'd watched him from afar for many years. Edmonton had joined the NHL in 1979–80 as part of the WHA merger, and the Flames moved to Calgary the following year. By 1984 the Oilers had a beloved superstar in Wayne Gretzky, and the Flames had a terrific player in Kent Nilsson, but they didn't have what Edmonton had, which was a player that everybody in the city absolutely loved. Until, that is, Lanny McDonald got traded from the Colorado Rockies to Calgary in November 1981, and then the Flames had their guy.

Lanny grew up in Alberta and played junior hockey in Medicine Hat. After playing for the Toronto Maple Leafs and the Colorado Rockies for a number of years, he joined the Flames. In 1982–83 he had a remarkable 66 goals and 32 assists. It seemed like every time he shot the puck it went in the net. The fans loved him. He could have been elected mayor, premier, whatever. He was huge. In 1988, he was near the end of his career. It would turn out to be his last year, and most people thought before the season started that he should hang them up, it was over. But he had some unfinished business to take care of—to reach 500 goals and 1,000 points and

11

THE ROYAL VISIT

My first-ever home broadcast was my third show with 2 & 7, on November 7, 1984. Our broadcast team had just come home from games on the road in Washington and Detroit, and then we rolled into the Calgary Saddledome to cover the Flames versus the Blackhawks. I was nervous. In the second intermission, I was going to get the chance to interview Harold Ballard. He was in Calgary to promote the upcoming all-star game. I knew if I could just do a good interview with Mr. Ballard, I'd be on my way. The kid from Red River would have a chance. Whenever Ballard and his friend and confidant King Clancy—or the Canadiens' play-by-play and colour team of Danny Gallivan and Dick Irvin—came into town, it was like a royal visit.

Ballard was brought into the studio to be interviewed just before the puck dropped in the third period. He strolled into the room, bigger than life. The Leafs had a huge entourage. Jim Gregory was hanging around; Gerry McNamara, the GM at the time, was there; and Bob Stellick, who was the public relations director, came along, and of course there was Clancy. The whole thing, to me, was just surreal. Ballard sat down in the chair beside me, and I started the interview. I got the countdown and, straight to camera, I said, "Welcome back to the Calgary Saddledome. We are pleased to be joined by the owner of the Toronto Maple Leafs, Mr. Harold Ballard. Mr. Ballard, it's just wonderful to have you out here in Calgary. Of course, we're all wondering—while you're out west, who's running the country?" It was a really, really lame, wise-ass remark. I don't know what I was trying to prove. I was trying to be funny.

Mr. Ballard didn't even acknowledge it. He just said, "Here, I've got a letter I'd like you to read," and he handed me the letter. I glanced at it and saw a lot of writing. So I said, "Well, gee, Mr. Ballard, we're a little tight for time. Maybe you could give us the gist of the letter."

He said, "It's very simple, young man. I've written a letter to the president of the National Hockey League, Mr. John A. Ziegler Jr. It is regarding Marcel Aubut, president, CEO and co-owner of the Quebec Nordiques, who has come up with a cockamamie, hare-brained idea of bringing the frickin' Russians over here to play in the all-star weekend. Now, there is no way I'm letting the Toronto Maple Leafs participate. If you read the letter, it tells you how come."

I had lost control of the interview, and I realized that, after my stupid monologue, we were out of time. I said "I'm so sorry, Mr. Ballard, we're just really tight for time. They're about to drop the puck for the third period, but maybe you could just tell us your concerns."

He said, "Yes. It's very simple, young man. No way will I help with bringing the damn communists over here, giving them our money to fill their guns with lead to kill your kids and mine."

An electric shock went right through me. Did he just say what I heard him say? I nodded and smiled and thanked him for taking the time to join us, and then I threw to Ed Whalen and colour man John Davidson.

Despite Harold's feelings about Mother Russia, Aubut did go on to organize Rendezvous '87, the two-game Canada–Soviet Union hockey series played in February 1987. The Soviet Nationals played a team of NHL All-Stars in Quebec City. The NHL team won the first, 4–3, and the Soviet team won the next, 5–3, giving the Soviets the 8–7 win.

I enjoyed my time on air with Ed Whalen and John Davidson immensely. Ed was magic, and he was humble. He told me how he'd had to chide himself during his first hockey broadcast. He said he'd had to have a good talk with himself during the intermission, after an awkward first-period performance. He'd say, "Come on, Ed, pull it together here. Get mad! You're doing a horrible job because you're allowing your nerves and your fear to overcome you." That was his way of telling me, "Ron, you're going to go through that. Don't be discouraged. It happened to me."

Ed was a godsend as a mentor. He had a Gestetner typewriter from circa 1910, while the rest of us were on electric typewriters. Ed would sit at this old machine, thinking about what to write, and while he did he'd take his chewing gum and stretch it out arm's length in front of him. Visitors would always want to see the iconic Ed Whalen, the most legendary broadcaster in the west. And there he was, pondering his next verb with chewing gum dangling two feet between his mouth and his fingers.

In the autumn of '85, I was covering my first NHL training camp, in Moncton, New Brunswick, because I had been too green to go my rookie year. The Moncton Golden Flames were Calgary's affiliate from 1984 to 1987, as well as the Boston Bruins' farm team from 1985 to 1987. Gary Roberts had been Calgary's first-round draft pick the year before, in 1984. It was his first camp, and he was feisty.

We were treated very well. The front office held a little banquet for us, a little spread at somebody's home. It was lobster as far as the eye could see, and beer and champagne on ice. Here I was, a kid from Red Deer, in only my second year of broadcasting in the NHL. I was like, "Holy geez."

Al MacInnis came up to me and asked if I had heard any trade rumours involving him. Did I know anything? Was he going to be traded? I thought, "Wow! Here's a guy that couldn't be more of a star, and that's how unsure life is for these guys."

Being around the players in a setting away from Calgary and most of the media was a great opportunity to get to know them on a more personal basis and to understand things from their point of view, especially since there were only about five of us broadcasters on the trip. The main thing I learned was to give these guys their space. The very next year, Don Cherry's first instruction to me when we went on the road together was, "Don't go inside the dressing room and don't stand behind the bench at practices, because that's the players' sanctuary." He told me, "They will tolerate you and they will be cooperative and the whole bit, but they will resent you being around. It's much better if you're not up in their faces. Let them come to you."

One night in Moncton, we were all in a little bar called Ziggy's. Brian Burke was still a player agent at the time, and he was there as well. This was two years before he was made director of hockey operations for the Vancouver Canucks. A skirmish broke out in the bar, and Burke got up and took care of the troublemaker. It turns out he had worked part time as a bouncer when he was younger. He sat back down for a couple of beers, and he and I started talking about goaltending. I said, "I really find it ridiculous that Pete Peeters wears that long sweater down to his knees. I guess he thinks that will stop the puck from going through his five-hole."

Burke said, "Well, I appreciate your candour, but Pete Peeters is my client."

Twenty-five years later, Burke and I are still at it. Burke is now president and general manager of the Leafs. In December 2010, I texted him to invite him onto *HNIC*, telling him I'd love to have him rebut some of the reports about Phil Kessel, Nazem Kadri and Tomas Kaberle and to assess Dion Phaneuf's performance. I told him my angle was going to be, "Is Ron Wilson's attempt to toughen and battle-harden these kids on his team out of date?" I told him he was welcome to argue either way. Nothing mean-spirited, just edifying.

Brian replied that he had no interest. And that he'd had

a nonstop "rain of shit" from *HNIC*. He was referring to Coach's Corner, where Grapes complained about the way the Leafs' coach, Ron Wilson, was treating Kadri. Grapes said, "You had a kid last year with a swagger, kinda cocky, and he's got magic hands. You tellin' me this guy couldn't have played last year? . . . Lookit here, he got six goals here and he got one lousy game! And the guys they had on right wing . . . you coulda put the kid on right wing. He can't get into any trouble. He goes down to London, dominates, and then they brought him up here and he's gotta play on defence! I have never in fifty years seen a kid treated as a rookie like this guy. Why ridicule? Maybe knock him down a peg or two. Why go to the kid and rip him in the paper like that? I don't understand it myself. Terrible. Dumb move."

I texted back and reminded Brian of the positive things Don had said on the same show. Grapes had high praise for the fourth line. "Zigomanis, last game, five-for-five on draws. Terrific! Colton Orr, Brown, Zigomanis—that's my type of line!"

I told Brian he was either not listening, bullying or just worn down and venting. "Brian, that makes no sense . . . This is silly. I'd enjoy the chat and, obviously, so would the viewer."

Brian wrote, "Pass."

I let him know I was banking on him for the CBC blog I was writing. I told him not to be a fascist and said that Gary Bettman showed up on XM Radio each week. Brian answered that he had no obligation to come on the show. And that I could write and say whatever I wanted. We went back and forth some more, ending with him finally telling me, "I am not doing it. Methinks the lady doth protest too much."

I texted, "Huh?"

He replied, "Shakespeare."

That 1985 training camp was magical. Glenn Hall was an assistant coach for the Flames. Glenn, who was the first butterfly goalie, was one of my heroes. From Humboldt, Saskatchewan, Glenn won the Calder Memorial Trophy as rookie of the year in 1955–56, took home three Vezinas as best goalie, won the Conn Smythe Trophy in 1967–68 for most valuable player of the playoffs and made it into the Hockey Hall of Fame. The Flames were trying to figure out who was going to be the backup goalie to Réjean Lemelin. Donnie Edwards had moved on, so it was between Doug Dadswell, Marc D'Amour and Rick Kosti.

After practice one morning, the scouts and coaches, including Gerry Blair, Ian McKenzie, Al Coates and Al MacNeil, took off to eat while Glenn was in the washroom, so he was stuck at the rink. I happened to be there too. It was just me and Glenn Hall. We went to the little rink concession and had french fries and coffee. I was just thrilled to spend an hour alone with him.

The scouts all came back to watch the next session of practices. They all sat in a row behind Glenn, who was holding a huge black binder. I feel kind of bad about what I did next, but it's the truth. I was two rows back, and I tried to peer into Glenn Hall's binder so that I could get the inside track on who the front-runner for the backup goalie job was. I saw that

Glenn was working his Sharpie marker, and I figured I might be able to see who he was complimenting—Kosti or D'Amour or Dadswell.

I manoeuvred myself into a position where I was finally able to see what he had been writing and was now showing to the scouts. It turned out he was telling the guys what he thought of them for taking off at lunch and leaving him with me. In big block letters, he'd printed FUCK OFF.

I just loved that about Glenn Hall.

That trip to Moncton was a great education. Cliff Fletcher was such a presence, and he has never changed. He was with the team in the Soviet Union a few months before the communists relinquished power. I was there, too, covering the Calgary Flames just ahead of the 1989–90 season. Calgary, the Stanley Cup champions, played an exhibition series with the Washington Capitals. The games were played in St. Petersburg, Kiev and then Moscow. Calgary also played the Central Red Army, the reigning Soviet champions, in Moscow. It was kind of a big deal.

Don Wittman and Harry Neale were on that trip with me. The night before the Red Army game, Don passed a kidney stone. He was so happy he ordered a bottle of champagne. Don's not a big drinker, but he had forged through such pain and he wanted to celebrate. I was lying low because I had been partying during my days off. I wasn't going to touch a drop that night. It was the night before a game, and I'm disciplined that way. After Don ordered the champagne, in walked Cliff Fletcher with Boots, his wife at the time.

Cliff was frustrated because he'd lined up a big night out for the Flames. He'd booked thirty-seven seats for dinner, and thirty-nine people showed up. The Soviet system was very strict—you could not go into the restaurant with two extra people—so Boots and Cliff did the honourable thing and gave up their seats. Cliff was telling us this story, and he said, "To make matters worse, as I was leaving I bought a bottle of vodka, and I screwed up the exchange. It was six bucks and I paid sixty."

The champagne started to flow. It turned into a complete runaway that night, a really fun night, but we all had way too many drinks for a night before a game. None of us was feeling very crisp the next day.

The coverage was not live, because of the time difference. We had to tape two openings, one for Sports Channel America and one for the CBC. Harry, Don and I could not get the name of the American network right. Every time we were supposed to say "Sports Channel," we'd say "Super Channel." We were so punchy we'd start laughing, and that made us screw up even more.

We didn't manage to get it right before the first period started, so we agreed to tape the opening in the first intermission. We would still have time because, due to the tape delay, the game would not start in North America for another twenty minutes. At the end of the first period, Calgary had scored two goals, and it was time for us to tape the opening of the show. Harry went on and shamelessly declared, "I have a feeling Calgary's going to come out flying!"

12

CRASH EDITING

I learned early on just how seriously the CBC takes its news programming.

On April 30, 1986, the second-round playoff series between the Calgary Flames and Edmonton Oilers went to a seventh game. Edmonton had taken home the Cup the previous two years. They were the favourite and were hockey's glamour team, with Wayne Gretzky, who at twenty-four years old had 52 goals and 163 assists for a record-setting 215 points. And they had Jari Kurri, Glenn Anderson and Paul Coffey, who were all Wayne's age and had huge stats—68, 54 and 48 goals respectively. Add to that Mark Napier, Mark Messier, Charlie Huddy, Dave Hunter, Steve Smith, Marty McSorley and Grant Fuhr, and you have just an incredible team. Nobody on Calgary had the kind of stats the Oilers had—Dan Quinn had 30 goals and Lanny McDonald was second with 28—but they were a tough, tough team. Gary Suter, Al MacInnis, Hakan Loob, Joel Otto, Brett Hull, Doug Risebrough and Jamie Macoun beat Wayne and the boys 3–2 in the final game, and that was the end of the Oilers that year.

John Shannon thought the Oilers' exit was a bit abrupt. He

felt that the former champions deserved a proper send-off, so he elected to keep the show on past 11 o'clock Eastern time with a little video tribute to Wayne and the team. The network was livid. He caught hell for doing it and was fired by the CBC.

On May 24, the Montreal Canadiens won the Stanley Cup by eliminating Calgary in five games. That night, after the broadcast, we all went out to a bar called Three Cheers. Dave Hodge, Howie Meeker, John Davidson and Don Wittman were all there, and I had stars in my eyes. We all sat together talking hockey. I was too fascinated to leave—I stayed until 6 a.m. But I was pacing myself; I had only a few beers.

The following night, a Sunday, I was scheduled to host the 5:30 sportscast on 2 & 7. CFAC had a liberal union, so I could edit my own highlights. Nobody had computers back then, so we would load tapes into two Beta machines, which by today's standards would be like two DVD players with record, and simply cut from one to the other. We called it crash editing. I knew I didn't have to worry too much about the sleep deprivation, because the report on the Canadiens' ouster of the Flames was going to take up roughly eight minutes of the ten minutes scheduled. That meant I needed only two minutes of material for sports. The only other big story that day was the Indianapolis 500.

All afternoon, I edited the highlights of the seventieth running of the Indy 500. Looking at the tape, the action on race day started before the race even began. Kevin Cogan was placed in the middle of the front row between Rick Mears and A.J. Foyt, and as the drivers approached the start line, Cogan swerved right, bouncing off Foyt's car and then into the path of Mario Andretti. It caused confusion and collisions farther back, and four cars, including Cogan's, were too damaged to continue on in the race. Foyt's team made repairs to his car, and he was back out for the restart, which was delayed by forty-five minutes. Foyt said Cogan "had his head up his ass."

Foyt took the lead on the restart, but Mears took over. After ninety-five laps, a failed transmission linkage on Foyt's car forced him to pull out from the race.

Meanwhile, Rick Mears continued to lead. With twenty laps to go, Gordon Johncock took the lead. With a few laps left, Mears caught up, and with one lap remaining the cars were side by side. Johncock held off Mears to win by 0.16 seconds, which at that time was the closest finish ever. Considering how tired I was, it was a nice piece.

The sports started at 5:45 p.m., so at about 5:35, I decided to take one last look at my highlight package. This time, I noticed a graphic in the upper right-hand corner of the screen that said *Indianapolis 500, 1982*—and this was 1986. I thought, "Now, why would it say that?"

I checked and found out that the Indy 500, scheduled to be run on May 25, had been rained out. (They tried again the next day, with no luck, and finally ran the race on May 31.) In its place, ABC had aired a rerun of the 1982 race. I had edited the highlights of a four-year-old race!

With six minutes to go, I grabbed a feature off *The George Michael Sports Machine*, a syndicated sports show that CFAC subscribed to. The studio director began counting down to an empty chair. I managed to get the story loaded, then leapt across the room and landed at the sports desk in the nick of time. I had come very close to joining John Shannon on the unemployment line.

13

GET THE HELL OUTTA HERE

You always hear a lot of sports stories where people feel they were destined to become something. Mine isn't one of them. When I was young, I was really interested in *Hockey Night in Canada*, and for my eleventh Christmas my dad gave me a *Hockey Night in Canada* historical double record album set that I loved. But so did millions of other boys my age. My story is simple. I lucked out.

In addition to his role as host of *HNIC*, Dave Hodge accepted a job at CKNW Radio in Vancouver in 1986–87. It was a full-time position, but CBC wanted him to continue hosting *Hockey Night* on Saturday nights. He gave the CBC just one condition: whenever Vancouver had a Saturday night home date, he'd host from there instead of flying to Toronto.

There were ten Saturday nights in the 1986–87 season when Dave would be working in Vancouver, and the CBC needed a guy in Toronto to fill in. Dave had hosted the Leafs' Wednesday night telecasts on CHCH-TV in Hamilton, and he'd given that up, so they needed the same guy to be their studio host.

John Shannon, the producer for *Hockey Night in Canada* in Calgary, suggested I phone Don Wallace, the executive pro-

1. My dad, picking apples in Point Aconi, Nova Scotia, at age sixteen. Notice he's not wearing gloves—the original tough guy.

2. Three weeks old in Metz, France, May 1960. Mom held me with her eyes . . . and never let me go.

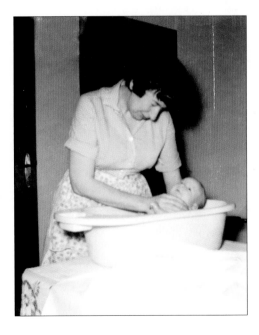

3. In thirty-six years of broadcasting, I've never taken a photo where I look as sincere as I do in this one.

4. At age six in Whitehorse, Yukon, in front of Steelox #102. It's where I first fell in love with hockey.

5. In Grade 2, at Christ the King Elementary in Whitehorse. My teacher, Miss McKenzie, used to tell us all we were special. She gave us great belief in ourselves.

Ron McLean
Being the 'core' of
Camille's school spirit,
Ron was involved in many
of the school's clubs and
activities. Despite his
unique word power, the only
arguements Ron ever won,
were with himself, as was
proven in Mrs. Atkinson's
Social 30 class. After
graduating, Ron hopes to
become a teacher and eventually dictator of the
world.

6. This is what my fellow classmates wrote about me! Teacher Eileen Atkinson prepared me for the critics she knew would come my way. I am grateful for the courage she instilled.

7. It's 1977, I'm seventeen years old and I am about to host "The Golden Wheel," my noon-hour show "broadcast" over the intercom at Camille J. Lerouge High School. No fear yet—it's still a lark at this point.

8. All dressed up for my high school graduation from Camille J. Lerouge in 1978. I delivered a speech during the ceremony but hadn't yet considered a career in radio or TV.

9. High-school sweethearts at Cari's house in Red Deer. I lived and breathed the Leafs.

10. At the old CKRD studio on Gaetz Avenue in Red Deer. I was nineteen, and rather scared. I had yet to figure out who I was talking to.

11. With Cari, celebrating Christmas 1978 at my house in Red Deer. Our first Christmas as a couple.

12. At the new CKRD studio on Bremner Avenue in Red Deer. I watched the sun rise outside the window and played good songs. It was a way to make someone's day.

13. My television career began as a weatherman at CKRD-TV in Red Deer, in 1981. One disgruntled farmer said, "Ron wouldn't know a warm front if he wet himself."

14. Ed Whalen was a prince of a man, a king of the business. Ed said, "The good thing about sports is that there is a winner. The bad thing about sports is that there is a winner." Amen.

15. I'm twenty-one and my ship has come in. I'm saved . . . With Cari, I will always be.

16. Cari and me on our wedding day, September 1, 1984, in Red Deer. A week later, I began a career that has seen me fly well over a million miles.

17. My wedding party (left to right): Todd Swanson, Marty Vellner, Jerry Murphy and me. One does not hit their stride without friends like this to walk with. We remain very, very close.

18. I've just been named MVP of a game at a Molson Slo-Pitch NHL event. Cari's dad was a semi-pro ballplayer, so my work at second was a home run with her family.

19. Reading a copy of *A Vintage View of Hockey* in the eighties. In 2011, Don and I wrapped up our twenty-fifth season together.

ducer of *HNIC* to let him know I was interested. "You should try to get your foot in the door," he said.

The front-runners to replace Dave Hodge were Brian McFarlane and Brian Williams. But on a tip from a producer named Jim Hough, Wallace agreed to give me a shot. Hough's argument was "Ron's twenty-six, just like Dave Hodge was when he started. I've worked with him. He's solid. And rather than try to replace a legend with either of two guys who are so well known, you're probably better off to take a young guy. If it doesn't work out, you can always come back to Williams or McFarlane."

It was the same principle that hurt Dan Rather when he replaced Walter Cronkite. On the other hand, if the CBC were to use some flunky or lackey for a couple of years, just to show how bad it could get, then Brian Williams had a much better chance to replace Hodge.

This was all shaking down at the end of September that year. The hockey season was a week away, so they were in a bind. I got the job.

Of course, it meant I would have to move to Toronto.

I went home and talked to Cari. We took a long walk around the neighbourhood. She had already given up a great job in Red Deer so that I could take the job in Calgary, and would now have to do it again. I didn't want to leave Calgary either. I loved working at CFAC. The job that the CBC was offering was just part time, and I'd also work part time at CHCH in Hamilton. The combined salary was $41,000. This was the same money I was making in Calgary, but the cost of living would be a lot higher in Toronto—for one thing, there's no sales tax in Alberta. We were going to be broke.

"Then why go?" Cari asked.

I said, "Because I think that if I don't, someday I will be watching *Hockey Night in Canada* and will wonder, 'What if I had gone to do those ten games? Could I have parlayed that into a career?'" She understood, and we both agreed I'd give it a shot.

Cari and I packed up and we moved east. I went ahead because I had two games to host on October 10 and 14. It all came together bang, bang, bang.

On the advice of Don Wallace, who lived in Oakville, I picked out a little place in a neighbourhood called Bronte. It was a beautiful little spot. When I first saw it on Thanksgiving weekend, it looked like Shangri-la. Paradise. For me, a kid from Red Deer, it was practically the Caribbean. It was a sunny day, and the blue sky reflected off a beautiful deep blue marina. There was even a little bit of beach. I called Cari and told her it was ridiculously pretty.

I flew home so that Cari and I could drive across the country together. I am not a car guy, but I had a new black 1986 Thunderbird that I really liked—it had a nice look. My first car was a Dodge—a big, black Polara with a push-button transmission that I'd paid $200 for with money I'd saved working at a Gulf gas station and car wash. It was huge—a big boat of a car. When I was sixteen or seventeen, I was at a farm party near Delburne and parked it next to a swamp. It was raining, so the ground was not as solid as I'd thought it was. The Polara slid down a muddy embankment and sank into the swamp on the LaGrange family's ranch, where I'd left it. It's probably still there.

My next car was a white Dodge Coronet that I bought

because that model and colour was all the rage with the police, especially the NYPD. It almost met a disastrous end as well. One night my best friend, Todd Swanson, dropped me off at home and we saw the Coronet parked up on the boulevard. I was surprised that I had parked it there. I thought, "Geez, Ron, what were you thinking?" And then we realized the back end was crunched. Todd noticed droplets of oil leading down the road and said, "Let's follow it." The trail ended only seven or eight doors down. I knew that there was a kid about my age who lived at that house, and I suddenly felt bad for the guy. I started thinking that I probably couldn't cobble together the money to fix the car, but maybe it was still drivable. But Todd, my buddy who had done the detective work, was ready to grab the guy and beat a confession out of him. So now I was in a bind. Should I call the police and get the insurance money? Or tell Todd to forget it? He was so pleased with himself for having done such a great job of sleuthing that I had to go with my best buddy. We called the police, they caught the kid, and my car was hauled to a garage and repaired.

My first new car was a 1981 Honda Accord. I got nicked for speeding in that car a few times. It wasn't as if I was tearing all over the place. I just had a lead foot when I wasn't paying attention. I'd be listening to something on the radio, because I was so into radio. When I got that absorbed, it led to trouble. And that's what happened to Cari and me as we toured across Canada in the Thunderbird.

I am not the best morning person, so we'd stopped for breakfast at Tim Hortons. Back in the car, I turned on the cruise control at a safe 110 kilometres an hour and, thanks to Timmy's donuts and coffee, I began to wake up. We were about seven hours northwest of Oakville, and Cari and I were talking about Blind River, which was to our right. I said to her, "Hey, Bug, do you know how to tell where the water is the deepest?" I'm not a fisherman, and I don't know why the hell I was making idle conversation at 9 a.m., but she feigned interest. And, feeling like David Suzuki, I turned and pointed to the river and said, "Wherever the land enters the water at the steepest is where the water is deepest. The topography of the land will give you an indication whether it's gradual or shallow."

I turned back to the windshield, and the glare from the bright sun in the eastern sky made me squint. I saw a car up ahead, parked in the middle of the highway. At that point, I had about a hundred yards to stop. I hit the brakes as hard as I could and continued to do everything you shouldn't do. I veered into the oncoming lane to try and avoid it. I might have cleared the car, but it turned left into me. It was a slow impact. The front of my car was crunched. I'd run into Sandra Tonelli, or she'd run into me. Sandra was a cousin of John Tonelli, the big winger who played for the Islanders and then the Calgary Flames.

The long and short of it is that, when I got to Oakville, the insurance company dropped me. I was twenty-five and had had too many demerits. I had to hire a lawyer to get off a careless-driving charge. I probably shouldn't have told the officer at the scene that I'd been pointing at the river before the collision.

Our car limped into town, and it was an overcast day, so the winds had shifted. All the emissions from the Petro-Canada plant in Burlington and the steel refineries in Hamilton had gathered over the area. It looked like something out of a dystopian movie like *Twelve Monkeys*. We were driving into the abyss. The smell was worse.

We made it to our little duplex—or semi-detached, as they call them in Ontario—and were surprised to find that the previous tenants had taken the appliances with them. When I signed the lease, I had neglected to notice there was no fridge, stove, dishwasher or washer/dryer in the agreement. The rent was $1,100 per month. We'd been paying $575 in Calgary. So we were shooting $15,000 out of $41,000 on rent. We were going to be up against it for a year or two. We slept on the floor for a couple of nights and woke up covered in flea bites—the house was infested. Thankfully, the furniture hadn't arrived yet. Fleas weren't covered in the lease agreement either, which meant we paid for the exterminator ourselves. Once again, we went through a Christmas with no money because we had to spend it all to get settled. On the positive side, the location was perfect. We were twenty-five minutes from Toronto's downtown core, straight down the Queen Elizabeth Way. We stayed in that semi-detached for three years.

I was just a part-timer flying under the radar for the first five months of my stint on *Hockey Night in Canada*. I did about six 'casts and worked the Toronto Maple Leafs games on Wednesday nights. It was relatively uneventful until the semifinal of the Brier (the men's national curling championship) that year.

On that day, March 14, 1987, something happened that would change my life forever.

That afternoon, the semifinal match between Newfoundland and British Columbia was tied, with two rocks to go in the tenth end, when the CBC in Ontario cut away to the NDP convention in Montreal. Two rocks to go in the tenth end of a Brier semifinal, and they cut away? In the west they joined an episode of *Star Trek* in progress. From a sports programming point of view, it was like, "You're kidding!"

That same night, Dave Hodge was hosting *Hockey Night in Canada*. After the Flames beat the Leafs 6–4 at about 10:45 Eastern, the CBC joined a nail-biter at the Forum. The Montreal Canadiens were leading the Philadelphia Flyers 3–2. There were five minutes to go in the third period when Hodge threw to Dick Irvin and Scotty Bowman.

Scott Mellanby of the Flyers scored on his own rebound in the third period to tie the game at 3, and the teams were headed for five minutes of overtime. The problem was that this would bump into the 11 p.m. news. In those years, CBC policy was that you could run over into the late news' time slot only if the original game went into overtime, not the bonus coverage. This meant that only the viewers in Quebec would get to continue watching the Habs game, because they had seen the game from the start. Hodge was told, "Let the viewers know that we're leaving the bonus coverage. We have to move to Knowlton Nash and the news."

Off air, Hodge said, "This is all wrong! It's crazy after what happened earlier. We cut away from the Brier semifinal this afternoon, and you know all the heat we took here. Now you want me to go on and tell our hockey fans we're not going to show them the overtime in Montreal? You can't do this."

And they said, "Well, we *are* doing this."

Hodge said, "Well, if you do, do not involve me. At the top of the clock, just cut to the news. Do not have me with egg on my face trying to justify this decision."

He was told, "No. Your job is to host the show and say 'Welcome' at the start and 'Good night' at the end."

Hodge said, "Well, if I must do that, please sit on a wide shot of the arena and let me do a voice-over so at least my face is not on camera and I don't have to suffer that indignity."

Again he was refused. So, in the heat of battle, with about ten seconds' warning, the red light came on. Hodge said, "Now, Montreal and the Philadelphia Flyers are currently playing overtime, and—are we able to go there or not? We are not able to go there. That's the way things go today in sports, and this network. The Flyers and the Canadiens have us in suspense, and we'll remain that way until we can find out somehow who won this game . . . or who's responsible for the way we do things here. Good night for *Hockey Night in Canada*." He flipped his pencil about half a foot in the air, and that was it.

Hodge returned home to Vancouver. He asked if he was suspended or fired, and the CBC didn't give him an answer. He asked, "When am I going back to work?" They couldn't tell him that, either. The CBC did suggest he fly back to Toronto and apologize to the head of sports at the network, Don MacPherson. Hodge replied, "I have nothing to apologize for. What I said, I believe." Hundreds of letters were already rolling in, supporting his position.

A few days later, Dave talked to the CBC again. He said, "If I'm not suspended and you can't tell me when I'm going back to work, then that must mean I'm fired." And he moved on.

John Shannon was now in charge of *NHL on Global*, a hockey telecast sponsored by Carling-O'Keefe Breweries. It was in competition with *Hockey Night in Canada*, which was sponsored by Molson. Shannon offered Hodge a hosting job, and Hodge took it. He kept his radio job at CKNW in Vancouver, as well. Radio is very much Dave's thing. He's an intellectual, a "theatre of the mind" over a "theatre of the obvious" kind of guy.

What it meant for me, a twenty-six-year-old kid from Red River, as Don called it, was that I got to roll in as the new host for *Hockey Night in Canada* and Coach's Corner. Ignorance is bliss. I didn't think too much about the opportunity. I was the backup goalie suddenly thrown into the game. I was supposed to be able to handle it. Right away, I got a call from the CBC higher-ups. "Listen, when you hear from the *Globe and Mail*, this is what we're saying about such and such, and when you do interviews, we're posturing it this way, and our position is this, and please don't say that . . ." Those calls started to make me feel a little anxious. I was to replace Dave Hodge for good, beginning with a game in Montreal, on March 21, 1987. Montreal and Toronto had the oldest rivalry in the NHL. The teams had faced each other in fifteen playoff series and five Stanley Cup finals, with Toronto winning three of them. During the 1960s alone, the Canadiens won five Stanley Cup titles while the Leafs took home four.

Don Cherry and I caught a flight into Dorval Airport on

Friday evening at 5 o'clock. If you've ever flown into Montreal on the weekend, you know it's very busy. All the tourists go up for a fun frolic, and a lot of business commuters are on their way back home. We landed, and there was a long lineup of people waiting for taxis to take them into the downtown corridor. Don was bigger than life again, posing for photos, signing autographs, and I was meekly watching all this. Finally, we made it to the front of the line and our taxi pulled up. It was a Lada, a Russian car.

Don looked at the car, and then he looked at the attendant, and he said, "You gotta be kidding me, right? What are you, in a fog or something? I've been standing here for a half an hour and posed for a million pictures and I signed a billion autographs. Do you wanna know why everybody loves me? They love me because I'm for Canada. You think I'd get in that Russian car and ruin my reputation? Now order me up another one!"

The attendant refused, and I stood there with my eyes like golf balls. I couldn't believe it. Don wanted to board the taxi behind the Lada because it was a Chev, but the attendant would not tell the Lada driver to pull ahead. The attendant said, "Well, Mr. Cherry . . ." Actually, he said "Monsieur Cerise," which did not improve the situation.

It escalated into a war between the two of them. Finally, Don said, "Never mind. I'll tell him myself." He opened the door of the Lada and yelled at the shocked driver, "I ain't getting in your communist dirtbox car! Now get the hell outta here." And he slammed the door so hard the entire car rocked on its tires.

I was mortified. My job was to replace the legendary Dave Hodge and to rein this guy in, and I couldn't even get him into a cab. It was all for the best, though, because there wasn't enough headroom for Don in the Lada anyway.

14

ALL THAT "EINST FREINTZ" CRAP

I got to the hotel all keyed up. I couldn't sleep that night. I'd done five previous shows as the alternate on Coach's Corner, but nobody had noticed them, nobody cared. This time, there was a lot of light shining on me due to the media brouhaha surrounding Dave Hodge's exit. "Who's this kid from Red Deer? *He's* supposed to be the new Dave Hodge?" I replayed the taxi incident and thought about how to handle Don. I couldn't let him intimidate me. I would step up next time, show him I was his equal. I was running on pure adrenalin by the time I got to the Forum.

During the first period, Don left the set for a little bit. When he returned, we were asked to tape a message to send to the Silver Broom curlers. Grapes said, "What do you mean? Silver what?"

Our studio director, Roland Saucier, was patient. "Silver Broom, Don. It's the World Curling Championships in Edinburgh, Scotland."

Don said, "Well, I like Scotland, but I don't know the first thing about curling. I'm not doing it." He crossed his arms and glared at all of us.

Roland said, "Don, it would really help out. We got a lot

of grief for the way we treated the Brier last week. It would really help to mend a lot of fences. The skip is Pat Ryan from Edmonton. Just say, 'Good luck to Pat Ryan and the boys, thumbs up, we're all cheering for you.' That's all we need."

Don sighed. "All right, for an Alberta boy I'll do it. I'll do it. It'll only take sixty seconds, right?"

He sat down on the chair beside me. Then Roland, standing by the camera, told us to stand by in fifteen seconds. He started the countdown. "*Dix, neuf, huit, sept, six—*"

Don held up his hands. "Hold it! Hold it. Hold it. Just a minute here, what the heck's going on? Roland? What is it with the 'einst freintz' crap? This is *Hockey Night in Canada!* It's bad enough I've got to do this thing for curling, but you're throwing me off completely here."

My upper lip was sweating again, and I was feeling weak and a bit panic-stricken. I forgot all about my resolve to take control. Thankfully, Roland remained calm. He started the count again, this time in English, and we finished the promo.

The first period came to an end, and it was time for Coach's Corner, live for the entire country. Don started before I could get a word out. He said, "You know, a little something here before we get rolling. Look, kid, I know you're scared to death, don't worry! Don't worry, kid, you just sit there. I'll carry you on this one. Okay, so anyway, folks, a lot of slings and arrows directed at the CBC this week. Everybody's hot because Dave left. First of all, I want you to know it was Dave's decision. He was not fired. He's got beauty contracts, I hear, like six-figure, multiple bones. Twenty-five-year thing he's got going on with radio out there. They already hired him at TSN to do that—

what do you call it?—investigative stuff. Anyway, Dave's happy. He was sick and tired after sixteen years of interviewing sweaty hockey players. It was his decision, so you people quit knocking the CBC for letting him go. That's not how it went down."

I opened my mouth to interject, but Don kept going. "Furthermore, all you people ripping *Hockey Night in Canada* don't know what you're talking about. I want you to get out there to Detroit. Everybody loves us. Go down to Buffalo. We're heroes. America knows *Hockey Night in Canada* is the greatest sports broadcast in the world, so leave it alone, all right?"

I lifted my finger to answer, but Don barely took a breath. "Anyway, during the first period there, Ron, I like to get a little feel for what's going on live in the building, eh? Midway through the first, I'm out there standing behind the penalty box—Montreal Canadiens are killing a penalty, right? Puck goes back to, uh, the rookie guy, the defenceman, supposed to be the next Chris Chelios, what's his name?"

My big chance. I looked at Don and said, "Mathieu Schneider?"

"Yes! That's it! Mathieu Schneider! That's good, kid. You got a bright future. The puck goes back to Schneider, he rifles a slapshot, trying to clear it down the ice, hundred miles an hour, goes over the glass by about this much, catches a fan flush on the cheek. Beauty cut, I got to admit. To you kids out there, I know you listen to me because I'm the expert here, if you ever get to an NHL game, please remember, you must keep your eye on the puck at all times. Right? That's good. What else we got? Before you start, I just have to say, Ron—you women are going to get mad at me out there . . ." He started jabbing his finger at the camera, and my bottom jaw dropped open. What now?

Don continued, " . . . but I was standing out in the hall in the first five minutes, and it was a tip shot. A guy tried to get it over the blue line, and it went over my head and it hit this poor lady in the face." He held his hand to his cheek, and I struggled for something to say.

Then Don started smacking the desk with the heel of his hand. "I'm telling ya, when you come to the games, keep your eyes on the puck. I've seen some awful smacks, and it's always a woman yapping away there. Look at the game!"

My job was to make sure this guy didn't offend anyone, and he just slammed 51 per cent of the population. I leapt in. "No, no! Lots of fans . . . What are you talking? . . . Both genders get involved in talking about the game!"

He swept my remarks aside with a pass of his hand. "Aw, c'mon . . . I'm just trying to help them!"

I remained indignant. "Don't blame women, men or anyone else for getting into the odd conversation when you get a ticket to come to the Forum."

Don shook his head, "What a twerp."

"It's an exciting opportunity for a lot of people," I continued.

"All right, all right. Ask some more questions." He shook his head and glared at me, "What else you got?"

I'd done about two or three editions of Coach's Corner that first season when we did one where Don came at me hard, which I loved but the CBC didn't.

Don started by going off on the league. Dave Brown of the

Philadelphia Flyers had cross-checked Tomas Sandstrom of the New York Rangers, for which he received a fifteen-game suspension. Don lashed out at the length of the suspension, saying that because Sandstrom was a New York Ranger, everybody saw it. But if it had been a late-night Los Angeles Kings game, no one would have cared or been the wiser. I argued that we could not tolerate cross-checking to the head. I said, "What about Mats Naslund?" Meaning that, if we allowed that kind of roughness, we would lose smaller players like Naslund and the game would lose thunder.

Don replied, "Mats Naslund, who cares? He's a Smurf. Don't worry about the kids in pee wee hockey [meaning Naslund was so small he was a pee wee]. That has nothing to do with it. This is the NHL."

Later, Bob Cornell, the CBC's deputy head of TV sports and a lovely man, pulled me into the Delta Chelsea hotel in downtown Toronto for a lunch meeting. Bob was concerned. He said, "Ron, when you're doing the Don Cherry segment, we can't have Don running roughshod over our CBC host. You are representing the network."

I sat there thinking, "They want me, a Junior B referee from Red Deer whose career ended after midget, to tell the NHL's coach of the year Don Cherry—whose two best friends are Bobby Orr and the winningest coach ever, Brian Kilrea—they want *me* to tell *him* what's going on in hockey? They must be nuts."

I thought there had to be another way. I simply couldn't argue with Don on everything. First, I didn't have the wherewithal. Don had a way better understanding of the game. Second, we had only six minutes, so there wasn't enough time. Don needed at least five and a half to cover just a couple of points. It occurred to me that puns might be a way to soften the blow. If Don went on a rant, I might be able to defuse the situation by cracking a joke.

I'd used puns earlier in my career as a DJ, and at CFAC I wrote openings with puns—too many, too often. John Shannon tried to break me of the habit. He sat me down and told me the viewer might groan or chuckle, but it shifted the focus from what I was saying.

When I threw one out, he'd say "That sucked" or "Stop it, it's irritating, you don't need them." His remarks fell on deaf ears. They were like a sickness. I was addicted to them.

In the end, he let me have me one a night. As soon as I said a pun in the opening, I'd hear him in my IFB: "Okay, you're done for the night. That's enough. You can't use them again." It forced me to be much more disciplined.

I hadn't yet used them in Toronto, but I felt they might work, so I dove in headfirst. And went overboard. After a few shows, Don pulled me aside and said, "You know, Ron, Richard—my brother—said, 'It's not a good thing for Ron to be doing those little wisecracks at the end of every Coach's Corner.' Richard thinks it makes me look bad, having this young whippersnapper mocking me with these puns. Maybe do it one in every three shows, but you shouldn't do it every Coach's Corner."

I think Don was trying to save me from myself. He realized the puns were lame and that it would be better for my sake if I cut back on them. But he wanted me to save face, so he gave me the impression that I would be doing it for *his* sake.

A few weeks earlier, Don had told me a story about Rick Bowness, who is now assistant coach in Vancouver. Before Al MacInnis or Brad Richards or Sidney Crosby, Rick was a real hotshot Maritime hockey player. In his rookie season with the Atlanta Flames, 1975–76, his coach, Fred Creighton, told him his skating wasn't strong enough for him to play centre, so they were going to put him on the wing. And that crushed Rick. It set him on his heels, and he never recovered. That's why, instead of telling me I was doing something bad, Don said, "Can't you help me out here?"

Don never so much as chuckled at my puns. Half the time, he wasn't listening anyway. He might roll his eyes. He didn't want the construction workers and the guys in the beer hall to think that he actually liked "the twerp." He'd be ruined.

But one time he couldn't help himself. He laughed out loud. It was the stupidest thing, too. He was talking about how it was funny to see Mike Keenan wearing glasses, and I said, "I thought you liked coaches who make spectacles of themselves." It was during the playoffs, so I guess he was really punchy.

In 2000, I got a call from Preston Manning, founder and leader of the Reform Party. His chief policy advisor was Stephen Harper. Manning was scheduled to host the morning show on radio station CFRA in Ottawa for a week and wanted to know about the art of the sound bite. Manning asked, "How do you manage to summarize Coach's Corner in ten seconds?" A politician's goal is to come up with an expression that people will remember. I told him that puns were a very effective method of doing that. They had the ability to be moralistic, funny and specific. You can pack a lot into one line.

15

PETER MANSFRED

Don and I were good on air, in a bad way for me. He would bully me, and I'd use the puns to soften the blow and break the tension. In the fall of 1988, I was twenty-eight years old and was in my third year. We were just at the point where we were starting to build a chemistry off air.

Wayne Gretzky had been traded to the Los Angeles Kings that summer—August 9, 1988. And his first game back in Edmonton was October 9. It was a Wednesday night, but *HNIC* decided we had to cover it. They felt Gretzky's homecoming was the biggest thing in television. So off we all went to Edmonton. The only problem was that the game started at 7:30 Mountain time, which meant 9:30 Eastern. We had edited a beautiful feature about Gretzky's glorious run in Edmonton, but there was no sense running it in the second intermission because that would be close to midnight in Ontario and Quebec—and even later in the Maritimes. So for this one time they decided to bump Coach's Corner to the second intermission. Gretzky's feature would get the prime-time slot.

We got the countdown for Coach's Corner, and Grapes started out by saying, "What time is it?" I said, "It's 9:30. Why do you ask?" He said, "That means it's almost midnight in the east. That's stupid. What are we doing here, anyway? Watching Gretzky in a Kings uniform is like watching Secretariat at a state fair. This is a brutal game, brutal team. He's going nowhere. I'll tell ya something, Ron, if he scores fifty without Jari Kurri, I will kiss your . . . hand."

After the show, the producers, Ron Harrison and Arthur Smith, cornered me. "Ron? What's with Grapes lighting into the Kings tonight?" The truth of the matter was that we'd bumped Coach's Corner and Don was mad. But I just shrugged. "What? I didn't notice anything particularly unusual."

I got back to my room and phoned Cari. I told her about Harrison and Smith. She said, "Oh, Grapes was great! He was hilarious!" So I phoned Don in his room and said, "Arthur and Ronny weren't too happy with you ripping the game tonight, but Cari said you were fantastic, and you were. Why don't you and I go for a couple of beers?" And we did.

The next morning, the *Edmonton Sun* had a review of the telecast, and the headline read, "CBC Offers Up Mundane Fare with the Exception of Vintage Grapes." And it went on to say how great he was and how brutal the rest of us were.

We loaded back onto the plane that morning, and as he passed by Arthur and Ronny in business class, Grapes dropped a paper on their laps. "There you go, Arthur, me boy. Just a little light reading for you. And Ronny, you might want to look at this." My call to his room was formative in our relationship.

In the spring of 1989, Montreal was playing Boston in the second round of the playoffs, the Adams Division final. Montreal and Boston have a great rivalry. By game five, Montreal had three close ones in the bag, so it was do or die. Our guest in the second intermission was Cam Neely of the Bruins. Don was standing over in the corner of the studio, gazing lovingly at Neely as he sat down beside me. Neely was sweating from exertion, and the crew brought over a towel and a glass of water for him as they pinned the microphone on his sweater.

Cam and I sat making small talk while a sixty-second CBC News update was running. Peter Mansbridge was talking about the *Exxon Valdez* oil spill, which at the time was the worst environmental disaster ever. On March 24, 1989, the oil tanker, on its way to California, struck a reef near Alaska and spilled between 260,000 and 750,000 barrels of crude oil. Then Peter talked about Lech Walesa, leader of Poland's Solidarity movement, being released from jail. Finally, he wrapped with a kicker about Mustangs. The gist of it was that a 1965 model in mint condition was worth a fortune. Suddenly, Grapes piped up. "When are you doing the interview?"

I said, "We still have ninety seconds of commercials left."

Grapes crossed his arms in disgust. "That's ridiculous, Ron! You can't keep a guy in the studio for all this time, a big game like this."

I said, "Well, unfortunately, there is nothing I can do."

He said, "Can't you tape it?"

At this point, we had only one more minute left on the commercial break. I said, "Not really, because we would barely have time to rewind the tape."

I did the interview with Neely, who seemed okay with it all, and immediately afterward Don hustled over with a poster for Neely to sign. He wanted to make copies for his Don Cherry restaurants. He and Neely left the studio. A couple of minutes later, our producer said, "Ron, you have to find Don! We've got a problem with the Zamboni, so you guys are going to fill for a little bit."

I hollered down the hall at Don, who had almost reached the Boston dressing room. "Don, come back!"

He said, "What?"

I said, "You and I have to go on and fill a little here. The Zamboni's broken. We have to go on for a couple of minutes."

He said, "What are you, nuts? I'm not going on again. Coach's Corner, I was sensational, that's it. You know I don't like to try to top a topper. No way. I'm not going on."

I pleaded with him. "You gotta help me."

He said, "Well, what'll we talk about?"

I said, "We'll talk about the game."

He said, "Awww, it's a nothing game."

I was getting kind of flustered. I said, "Look, I need you. It's game five of the Adams final!"

He said, "Okay, if you give me something."

I said, "I'll ask you how you felt about Cam Neely having to sit here and wait to do an interview."

We made it to air, and I said, "You know, Don, I know you were a little concerned that Cam Neely was in our studio for close to five and a half minutes when all was said and done because he had to wait for the commercials and the news. When you coached stars such as Phil Esposito and Bobby Orr, what was your policy on doing interviews in the second intermission of important games like tonight?" I don't know why I used the word "policy," but I did.

Don paused for a second and said, "What was my policy?

What was my policy? Well, I'll tell you what it was, Ron, and that is that you took advantage, and you people in the [production] truck." Then he started to ratchet up the intensity. "You took advantage! And you people at CBC, you took advantage! We've got to sit here and listen to some Peter Mansfred talk some schluck about Sloberderity . . . and '65 Mustangs, while Cam Neely of the Boston Bruins is waiting to be interviewed. It's absolutely ridiculous!"

I knew right away the CBC would be unhappy, because he'd brought the news into it. Although I was half chuckling to myself, I also realized I had to figure out how to get out of it. I don't recall coming out overly smoothly, but I threw it upstairs to Dick Irvin and Scotty Bowman, who had just joined us on the show.

As soon as we were done on camera, I looked over at Don, who was looking a little downcast. I thought, "Gee, he knows he crossed that politically correct line with the CBC by ripping the news division." I said, "Don, you look upset."

He said, "I am upset. You see what happens when you put me on and I wasn't prepared? There's no way, there's no way I would have said that."

I thought, "Good, he knows he shouldn't have said something negative about the news."

But he continued, "There is no way in the world I would have ever said a thing like that if I would have had time. I love '65 Mustangs."

16

STUARTT

Cari and I bought our first home in 1989, one we could afford in Ancaster, Ontario. The locals call the area "the Mountain." We paid $219,000. I remember that because we sold it for $189,000 three years later. It was a tiny little split-level, a really nice place, very modest. It is one of my favourite homes ever. The previous owners had done a lovely job of landscaping the property. When you stood in the kitchen, you'd look out over the Dundas Valley. In the fall, with the leaves turning, the view was spectacular. We didn't have a dishwasher. We washed our dishes in the sink, but we didn't mind because standing there, looking out—just Cari and me—was the most therapeutic time of the day.

We were trying to have a family at the time, and we considered that house a good starter home. We bought it in December, and Cari found out she was pregnant a month later. We were in the back bedroom of our new home and she said, "What do you think? Would this be a good room for our baby?" I took her hand, and together we slid down the wall beside the big dresser and sat together on the floor, smiling at each other. I felt such excitement. It was time. We discussed prenatal classes and how we'd set up the bedroom—

what colour to paint it, because neither of us wanted to know the gender. If it was a boy, would we call him Ron? Or John, after her dad? "How about Ron John?" I laughed.

On April 3, when Cari was three months along, I was in St. Louis to do the opening night of the 1990 playoffs, the Blues against the Leafs. I was at the desk in my hotel room, preparing for game one. Cari called to say she had cramping and spotting and was afraid there was a big problem. She was going to the hospital. As I spoke with her, I stared at myself in the mirror, but I wasn't there. My entire being was in the phone, trying to reach through it to be with her.

I couldn't get a direct flight back to Toronto. I got as far as Pittsburgh and had to overnight there. I told myself that as long as I didn't sleep, Cari and the baby would be okay. I arrived at Oakville-Trafalgar Hospital, where Cari had been admitted. The baby hadn't made it, and she was crushed. I tried to console her in my clumsy way.

I missed one game and then went back to work. Cari said there was nothing I could do.

We wanted kids. Cari's parents inspired us that way. Cari's mom, Bev, was young and hip. She used to buy cigarettes with coloured filters and tobacco sleeves that matched her lipstick or her outfit. She was always very kind to me. The Vaselenak home was full of music, laughs, food and drink. Bev was always hinting that while she loved John and the life she'd led, she wanted Cari's husband to be the kind of supporter who'd provide well for her. She wanted so much for Cari to be happy. One night, while John was barbecuing in the backyard, I was sitting back with a beer, basking in their companionship, when

Billy Joel's "Just the Way You Are" came on the radio. John smiled at me and said, "Never forget it, Ron."

We tried again, and after a couple more failed pregnancies, followed by fertility treatments, we sort of wore ourselves out. Finally, we just gave up on the idea of thinking it might happen. We hadn't applied to adopt, but by then we were in our early forties, so it was too late. Obviously, it was, and maybe still is, a hole, wondering how you would have evolved as a person, and what the joy of a child might have brought.

For Cari, who was very accomplished and orderly, getting her undergraduate degree and then her master's degree to set up a life for herself, it was very tough. She is my business manager, and she's great at it. Everybody loves her, but her job is handling "Ron's life."

Cari runs marathons, plays hockey and is very involved in several charities. She sits on the board of directors for SOS Children's Villages Canada, an organization that rescues orphaned and abandoned children around the world, so she does have her own thing going. But I wonder if that is rewarding enough for her. It doesn't help that I live by the credo that we should love all of mankind equally. I do not distinguish between different types of love. Love is love. Love for the human race, love for your fellow man, love for your wife. Cari and I have had conversations where I try to explain that I love my dad, my friends and her all the same. Grapes once told me that when you are on board a big ship, you can't trust and depend on four hundred guys. Instead, you must always make sure you find one mate. He said, "Every guy has to have someone who's gonna notice if he goes overboard."

Grapes was talking about the buddy system. I struggle with that.

Although I am not a Buddhist, I keep coming back to the philosophy that each of us is only one in six billion. We are all interconnected and, consequently, deserving of equal love and compassion. Whether you're my wife or best friend or a person I just met, I feel I should treat you the same. That bothers most of my friends, and it's not a quality you look for in a husband. I've had a few breakables and shoes fired at my head for reminding Cari about it on the wrong day. But it doesn't mean she's not my girl, because she's the one.

I sometimes feel that without children to sort of rein me in and give me responsibility, I've never really grown up. I've been able to play hockey, go out with my buddies and become obsessive about work. I'm selfish in a way that children don't allow you to be. I'm not saying that is a good thing or a bad thing. It's just the way it is.

On the plus side, Cari says it has made her a strong, independent individual, but it has come at the expense of some intimacy. She says she can't imagine spending twenty-three hours a day with anybody else. I guess somewhere along the line, she has accepted the way I feel about love. In any case, we've somehow made it work.

Our dog Stuartt helped us through tough times. We got her in 1987, the year before we bought the house. Cari has always had dogs. Her family had a nice dog when we were going together. Her name was Tasha, short for Natasha. She was a mutt, some kind of poodle–terrier cross. Cari's mom, Bev, was the main caregiver for Tasha. She boiled stewing beef or liver for her every night. She also gave the dog Almond Roca at Christmastime.

I picked Stuartt out at a pet store in Oakville's Hopedale Mall. We had nice neighbours who owned the store. I used to pop in to say hello and look at the animals. This one time they had a schnauzer, and I melted. They explained that the original owner could not keep the puppy, so the store had taken her to sell on consignment. I couldn't pull out my wallet fast enough. I bought the dog, a kennel, a blanket and two toys. Then, leaving her at the store, I took the other items home and set them up in the back bedroom. Cari worked for the Town of Oakville Parks and Recreation department. She walked in the door just after 5 p.m., and I was waiting for her. I said, "You know how Mom and Dad are coming down here at Christmastime? You should see what I got to surprise them. Go have look in the back bedroom and tell me what you think."

Money was scarce and we were trying to save for a house. I knew Cari was a little tired of me spending what we had. I was always coming through the door with stuff—bathrobes, Hudson Bay blankets, wine, chocolates, you name it. Cari rolled her eyes and trekked back to see the "surprise." We had been thinking about getting a dog. Neither of us wanted a small dog. We didn't want a mastiff, either. We had talked about a Scottie or Westie, for no real reason except that we were both crazy about the little beards on those breeds. Schnauzers have them too.

Thankfully, Cari was tickled about my surprise. We went to Hopedale and retrieved our miniature schnauzer. We loved the name Stuartt. We added an extra "t," and gave her the middle name Louise to make it more girly. We leashed her up and proudly led her away. She had never been on a leash, and she decided to lie down on her side. So unbeknownst to us we were dragging her behind us. She weighed maybe three pounds at the time.

To celebrate what would be her new "birthday," we picked up some Gino's Pepperoni Pizza and Molson Export on the way home. Buying Export made it an occasion. Export cost more than regular beer and had more kick in the taste. We poured it into frosty mugs and toasted our new addition. I decided to give Stuartt a swig out of my glass so that she could properly share in our celebration. Within minutes, she was acting strange. She curled up on the floor and started whimpering. We rushed her to the vet. X-rays showed she had a gas bubble. A hundred and fifty bucks to solve the problem when a burp would have sufficed. Stuartt went on the wagon after that.

Stuartt was terrified of bubble gum. Maybe dogs have an inventory of fears based on traumatic sights and scents. She'd had her ears and tail bobbed. Maybe the vet or assistant was chewing gum at the time. Even the smell of it got her shaking. The sight of a bubble sent her cowering. I don't usually chew gum anymore, but when I was in my late twenties I still loved it, so this was a problem. Thank God she never met Ed Whalen.

Schnauzers are either chewers or zoomers. Stuartt was a chewer. In the days before computers, I kept back issues of *The Hockey News*, sports sections of newspapers, magazine articles and anything and everything written about hockey. It was all stacked neatly beside the desk in our bedroom. One evening,

Cari and I came home from a movie and Stuartt had shredded about five years' worth of research material. There were bits of newsprint covering our entire bedroom. I grabbed a magazine off the desk, rolled it up and started to whack the floor next to Stuartt. I was yelling about her misbehaviour. Lord knows it had probably been hours since the crime, so the connection for her would have been sketchy at best. But she never touched a thing near my desk after that.

Stuartt Louise grew to thirteen pounds. Every day for her was a bad hair day, and like Fiver in *Watership Down*, she was brilliant. However, she did have a bad leg-humping compulsion. When Todd Swanson, the best man at our wedding, was visiting us in Oakville, we had a great party at the house. We were all gathered in the TV room, and Stuartt started wooing my shin. Before I could shoo her off, Todd took a picture. A little while later, I was booked to give a speech in Red Deer, and when the emcee introduced me he mentioned that I was a dog lover. At the same time, that very photo appeared up on the screen behind me. Todd had sent it to one of the organizers.

Despite that one unbreakable habit, Stuartt was a great watchdog and companion. She loved to snuggle close between Cari and me. We had her for almost fifteen years, and then, as old dogs do, she got very sick. The most merciful thing to do was put her down. Cari made the appointment.

On her final day, November 25, 2003, I wrapped my dear old friend in her favourite blanket, picked her up and carried her outside. Before we got into the car, I held her face up to feel the warmth of the winter sun. I stroked her ears reassuringly and she licked my cheek. I sang softly to her an Edwin song that I'd first heard at the Olympic Games in Sydney, Australia: "It feels so good to breathe the air, another spin around the sun . . . Let's find a star, a star to call our own and make a wish, maybe we can make it home . . ."

We stayed there for a long time, taking one last spin around the sun.

17

BLUE CHIFFON

We were in our little house that overlooked Dundas Valley until 1992, and then we sold it because the one-hour commute to Toronto was getting to us and we'd got a good deal on a house in Oakville. We bought it for under $500,000, although it was worth more.

In April 1991, for game one of the playoff series between L.A. and Edmonton, Don and I cooked up a slapstick routine in which Don dressed up like a gay pimp. We thought it was hilarious. There is a bit of a history to it. This faux interview stemmed from a remark Wayne Gretzky made the previous year on Roy Firestone's ESPN television show *Up Close*. Wayne said that if the game were going to grow in the United States, we might have to eradicate fighting in hockey. And Grapes was upset at that, but it's not easy to tug on Superman's cape, so he used this pimp bit to respond.

On April 18, we were live at ice level at the Forum in L.A., just ahead of the Kings game. I had a hand-held mic and I was "interviewing" Grapes. He was wearing a fitted black jacket, with his signature big-collared white shirt and a black and white polka dot tie, a black fedora ringed with a white band, huge sunglasses and a large gold ring. A pirate earring dangled from his left earlobe.

In a soft voice and with a discernible lisp, Don began, "I'm out here and I've been reading the papers, and I can see how people say they really don't want fighting here. And I can see that—the hot weather, the people, I can see why we shouldn't have hockey here with fights." He played with his tie and started waving his hands around. "Yeah. I can see that."

I could see the Kings coming down the hallway toward us, ready to step onto the ice. Playing it straight, I said, "You want to talk about any of the players involved in this classic?"

Don gave a delighted little jump. "Yes! I want to first of all talk about Kelly Hrudey. Here comes Kelly right now. Here's Kelly. He's coming in right now." As Kelly walked past, Don pointed to the blue headband covering Kelly's mullet that stuck out from beneath his helmet. "I love the little blue string that hangs from the back, don't you? I love him. You can see the little string there. I think it's blue chiffon."

At this point, it was all I could do not to break up. "What's with the earring on the left side?" I asked.

Don lifted his hand to his ear and gently held the earring up to the camera. "Well, when it's on the left side, that means I'm available. And not only that, hockey without violence is like a . . . silver ballet."

I said, "Who are you pickin'?"

Don erased that idea with his hand in the air. "I'm not picking. Let the best team win." He looked at me and chided, "Why keep score?"

Alan Clark, the head of CBC Sports, was in Victoria. He

was not happy with us. Alan's nose would get purple when he got mad. Some of us get flushed, but the blood from his face channelled to his nose. The darker the purple, the madder he was. He saw the skit, and he and Ron Harrison, who was now the executive director of CBC Sports, boarded a plane to Los Angeles. We had planned to plant Don in the crowd for the next game. Grapes had rightly predicted the winners for six of the first eight series and for game two of the L.A.–Edmonton series. In order to brag about it, he was planning to sit in the crowd with a sign that said, "Cherry picks 6 of 8 first-round series!" And then, when the camera shot the sign, he would lower it to reveal himself holding it. But when Alan showed up, we gassed that plan. Alan told us to stop goofing around, and get serious.

I would tell the pimp story sometimes during a speaking gig, and I would always end with this joke: "When they saw the segment, head office sent us a fax asking, 'What kind of drugs are you guys on out there?' I went to find Don Cherry to tell him that we were in trouble, and found him in a hot tub with ten gorgeous California blonds . . . all really good guys."

As a rule, the gay community has always gone to bat for Don, and if I objected to his shenanigans, we got emails and calls from the community telling me to mind my own business. They understood that Don has good command of camp, and what he does is no more offensive than *La Cage aux Folles*.

Don's "silver ballet" crack was inspired by the hot water he got into in 1990 when he did a Sports Select lottery commercial, in which he's running hockey drills and accuses a player of dogging it by saying, "What do ya think this is, a ballet practice?" The Royal Winnipeg Ballet invited him out for a lesson to shine a little sun on their upcoming season. He was good about it. We showed clips on *HNIC*, and my punchline at the end of Coach's Corner was, "Until now, the closest you'd come to *The Nutcracker* was blocking shots in Hershey." It was a little bit risqué. Alan's nose held only a hint of purple when he heard it.

I was now making six figures, and Cari was still working for the Town of Oakville and making good money—we were doing well. But a watershed moment for me, financially, came in 1994 when Don Cherry went in and demanded to be paid what he was worth, which was over the half-million-dollar mark. I had been thinking of asking for a raise when my contract was up. It wasn't like he and I were in lockstep. Neither of us was aware of what the other had done.

I knew that Don was dealing with a really nice guy, Jim Byrd, from Newfoundland. Jim was vice-president of English television networks at the CBC. He had been very good to Don, and he was good to me, too. He had our backs.

When Grapes and I went to Nagano to cover the 1998 Olympics, Don had a terrible cold he couldn't shake. He was sick as a dog. We were seconds from going on air on February 21 when we started discussing Jean-Luc Brassard, a French-Canadian freestyle skier who'd won gold in 1994 at Lillehammer. Brassard had carried the flag at the opening ceremonies in Nagano, and then failed to win the gold medal the following day. He said that carrying the flag the night before the race had affected his performance.

I told Don this and that there was a storm brewing back home in Canada because Suzanne Tremblay, a member of the Bloc Québécois, had lashed out at the Canadian Olympic Association for having too many Canadian flags at the athlete's village. She said they caused the Quebec competitors so much distress that they underperformed.

Suddenly, *whack!* We were on the air and Grapes went ballistic. He said Brassard was some French guy, some skier that nobody knows about, who cried because he didn't win. And he said Quebec nationalists "don't like the Canadian flag, but they want our money. We bail them out. I've never seen such a bunch of whiners in my life."

Byrd began getting all kinds of calls from the press and members of Parliament, trying to find out if Don was going to be fired. Byrd feared that if the matter were left in the hands of Ottawa, the momentum to do something to Don would steamroll. He told head office, "Put out a press release and say it's not CBC policy and it doesn't mean that we agree with him, but we respect Don Cherry's right to say these things. That's what we hire him for."

There was a great write-up in an American paper about it. The article said that you had to love Don Cherry's CBC Olympic coverage because while most critics are woodpeckers, he carried a sledgehammer.

Two months later, Bell Canada, who had been sponsoring us for the past two seasons, pulled their ads from Coach's Corner during our broadcasts in Quebec. The next September, Bell announced they would no longer be sponsoring Coach's Corner at all. They said they had done focus groups with some of their customers and found that some Ontario customers were also unhappy. Canadian Airlines stepped in and sponsored us instead.

I was at an event the night Bell announced they were pulling out, and Jim Byrd pulled me aside and said, "Ron, don't even worry yourself about it. I've got it under control." And that was it. He was an upstanding guy and a great leader.

I'm not into the concept of "stars," but Byrd supported the idea that CBC should build recognizable personalities to represent the network. There were so many channels coming on stream at that time, so the CBC decided to sell Rick Mercer, Peter Mansbridge, Don Cherry and me, among others, because the network needed stronger identification than just its content. It was all part of a plan to make the CBC more personal to the public. Each year, our late-spring launch usually opened with a big fanfare and a video, but that year we opened with our on-air people all across the country, both local and national, introduced onstage, one at a time.

And that recognition is how I got to a higher level of salary. Whereas, my thinking was, "You're going to get the best out of me, and I don't need fame. So if you want me, this is what it's going to cost you."

In 1994, I started negotiating with Alan Clark. Labatt had just come on as our title sponsor, taking over from Molson. I handled my own negotiations. I had kind of an understanding of what players make and about market royalties. I'd read various reports of what different radio personalities were making around the country. For instance, I'd read that the average salary of on-air talent at CKNW was $300,000. I assumed that if CKNW, a local radio station, was paying $300,000, surely to God CBC television, on a national level, could afford at least that.

Alan and I met about it while I was anchoring the Commonwealth Games in Victoria in August 1994. He brought a bottle of wine to my hotel room and we sat down. I asked for a salary of $400,000. I picked the number out of the clear blue sky. I was totally talking out of my hat and was nervous to be asking for that kind of money.

Alan said, "Well, Ron, the president of CBC doesn't make that kind of money."

"Well, do you think the president of the Edmonton Oilers makes what Wayne makes?" I replied. I wasn't comparing my talents with Gretzky's, but that was the parallel. I really didn't care about the figure. I did care that the CBC thought I was worth it. It felt like Monopoly money. I was going to throw out a number, and if they fired me out the door, I'd had a good run. I expanded on my reasoning. "Labatt is buying Ron and Don. It's easier for CBC to go in to the advertiser and say, 'Would you like to have Ron and Don and *Hockey Night in Canada?*' than to say, 'Would you like to have some guys they never heard of and *Hockey Night in Canada?*'"

It was a simple argument. We had unscientific data to back it up. We'd been getting a lot of street feedback. Another thing that shored up my case was that, during a seminar we'd had at the start of the season, a senior producer for NBC named Glenn Adamo, who was now in charge of broadcasting with the NHL, came to speak to us. Glenn said, "Coach's Corner is a rather interesting phenomenon. *Hockey Night in Canada* is the only property in all of sports television where the ratings go up [during the] intermission."

I had noticed that whoever hosted *Hockey Night in Canada* became famous by default. The show gave you that. So a chicken-and-egg argument could be made. Alan could have said, "You're only famous because you're on *Hockey Night in Canada*." The other thing I thought he might do was give me hell again for something we had done toward the end of the playoffs between the Rangers and the Canucks that year. Don and I were in Vancouver, and we were getting a little punchy. Try drinking light beers sixty nights in a row after games during the playoffs. Trust me, it puts hair on your chest. It led us to say something impolitic.

There were three big issues in the news. Americans were fighting with British Columbia over fishing rights to Coho salmon in the Strait of Juan de Fuca, which is the outlet to the Pacific Ocean for the Georgia Strait and Puget Sound. B.C. fishermen were catching the salmon returning to Alaska, and United States fishermen were catching salmon as the fish made their way through the Strait of Juan de Fuca. Both countries blamed each other for depleted stocks and endangering the fish. Between 1992 and 1998, they were not able to reach an agreement on it. At the same time, there was a spat going on off the Grand Banks of Newfoundland between Canada and the Portuguese about overfishing of turbot. While all this was happening, there was outrage and controversy over a human-rights story in which a war veteran, Lieutenant-Colonel Pritam Singh Jauhal, tried to enter the Royal Canadian Legion in Vancouver with five other Sikhs for a Remembrance Day celebration, and they were forbidden to do so because they wore turbans. The Legion rules did not allow headgear. They do now.

Bob Cole, Don and I were all at a morning skate, talking about the turbot situation, and, being a wise guy, I said, "Well, I asked Don about the turbot and he said he didn't mind that the Mounties were wearing them, but no way they allow them in the Legions." They rolled their eyes, and nothing else was said.

During Coach's Corner, I squeezed it in. "One last thing—what about the turbot?"

Don replied, "Well, I don't mind the Mounties wearing them, but there's no way they should have to have them in the Legions."

We have such an understanding of each other that I knew he'd jump on the set-up line like a dog on a bone. We were being raunchy and belligerent. I knew it would cause trouble. I'm not proud of it. It's a silly joke, but every so often you just get in a mood.

Alan's nose was blinking when he talked to us after the show. He said, "Don! It's the sixth game of the Stanley Cup finals! This is the best series we've had in twenty years, and are you telling me you can't find something in that hockey game to talk about? Instead, you have to talk about the Legion turban policy?"

"Nope, there was nothing more important to me, Alan," Don replied. Poor Alan. We always tormented him because he was such a sweet man and he wanted so much for us to behave. That just seemed to make us worse. Grapes was really happy that Alan, who was usually unflappable, was so mad. He loved it. Don would never do a thing to hurt Alan Clark, but when he thought it was harmless, he would have fun.

I thought maybe Alan might bring that incident up in my salary negotiation. Instead, he agreed to the money. I was stunned.

The first time Don and I got into political hot water over the Middle East was also in 1991. During the first war in the Persian Gulf, Prime Minister Brian Mulroney sent Canadian troops over to support the Americans in the war.

That year, the NHL All-Star Game was in Chicago. Chicago is always amazingly patriotic. During the singing of "The Star-Spangled Banner," everybody held these sparklers and cheered throughout. Everywhere you looked, you saw a celebration of America.

We were back in Chicago a week later, on January 26, 1991, to cover a game between the Leafs and the Hawks. Just before we started Coach's Corner at Chicago Stadium, Grapes pulled out this enormous Canadian flag and draped it over our little travelling set. He stood there, looking like General Patton. "You know, Ron," he said, "just a little something before we get rolling here. Just have to say, Brian Mulroney, me boy, you've ticked me off with a couple of things you done. You said you're going to get rid of the GST. It hasn't happened, I don't know how come. But I have to say, Brian, you're coming up absolutely roses right now with me, and I'll tell you why. You're the only guy that would have the nerve to stand up and send our military over there to help the Americans. Who do you think is going to be there in a time of need for us? It's the USA. The whole world depends on them. Oh no, the big old left-wing communist media in Canada . . . everybody's giving them a hard time for fighting over there. Where is it they're fighting again? Lower Slabovia or something, but they're doing a great job. The Americans are our friends, and you always stand by your friends. Brian Mulroney, thumbs up in my books. All right. What's next?"

I said, "Geez, Don, I don't know if a hockey game is the best place to be espousing our views on the war." Why I would say that, I don't know. I guess I wanted to get him going. But he let it ride and we continued with the show.

When we got back to Toronto, we got called onto the carpet at head office for having talked about the war.

Alan Clark's nose was a new shade of purple. He said, "Geez, you guys. It's not whether we agree or disagree with what you said, Don, but this is *Hockey Night in Canada!* It really isn't the forum to be talking about the war. The board of directors are upset, everybody is upset. That wasn't premeditated, was it?"

And Don said, "No. Hell, Alan, of course not. I always travel with a 100-foot Canadian flag stuffed in my pocket. Believe me, it's not easy."

But the war was a taboo subject. A conversation in March of 2003 about the American invasion in Iraq almost got us both fired. We had an unbelievable Coach's Corner. It is still so unpopular with the CBC that it has been stripped from the website. I must have had a death wish.

When I was in my forties, I became interested in political science. I read everything I could get my hands on—Noam Chomsky, George Steiner, Anne Wortham and many others. My favourite writer, former *Harper's* magazine editor Lewis Lapham, had asked, "Why would you attack Iraq unless they have attacked you?" He said you couldn't go on hearsay about weapons of mass destruction. You needed conclusive proof. I thought he was right. The events of 9/11 forced us to step back and wonder about our world. And when the U.S. broke the rule of law and walked into Iraq, searching for "weapons of mass destruction," I saw an opportunity. I thought it was too important to let pass.

I was an honorary colonel for 1 Air Movements Squadron at 17 Wing Winnipeg. I'd recently spent time at CFB Calgary, speaking at a mess dinner. Afterward, we all retired to a bar downstairs, where I met the pilot who had landed the first Hercules aircraft that went into Kandahar. Although he couldn't discuss details, his eyes were wide when he described how hairy it was there. He'd been on a joint forces mission—Russians, Americans, all these different allies—and said there was a lot of confusion. For instance, Canadians were well schooled at working on aircraft for just about every fleet in the world, but no one else was. The Russians didn't know how to deal with American aircraft, and vice versa. This led to concerns about sending the airplanes off when they were not properly loaded. Loading, balance and everything to do with weight distribution on an aircraft is vital. The impression I came away with was that all these countries were there and the left hand didn't always know what the right was doing. That's the state of mind I was in.

Historically, we hadn't avoided hot-button topics. We'd certainly touched on politics all through the evolution of Coach's Corner. I was ready to fall on my sword to make sure this subject was addressed.

Don is Sir Francis Drake, Lord Nelson, Winston Churchill. People tuned in to the Gospel of Don to see how to live an honourable Canadian life. I thought, "You can't have a guy that goes on every Coach's Corner and pays tribute to all these fallen soldiers, and then when war breaks out, puts the mute on. You just can't." It was important for the viewer to hear from Don on that matter. And I was ready to fight him on this one.

Don was aware. I wouldn't cold-cock him, but he wanted to make it look like it was off the cuff to save us from ourselves. The CBC had asked us to give them the heads-up if we were going to debate any subject other than hockey, but we were sure if we did they would have forbidden us to go there.

On Saturday, March 24, 2003, we were set up on location at the Air Canada Centre. U.S. Ambassador Paul Cellucci was in the crowd to see the Leafs play the Bruins. At the end of the first period, the score was 2–1 for Toronto. Time for Coach's Corner.

Don was stewing about an incident on March 20, during a game against the Islanders in Montreal. The crowd had booed the American anthem. It was a political hot potato, but not all that surprising. Two hundred thousand Montrealers had demonstrated the previous Saturday to protest the war.

He brought it up, and it was the opening I was looking for. "Where do you want to go with this?"

He said, "I don't want to go anywhere."

"Everybody'd like to hear what you think about this."

"All right. I want to start off by apologizing to all of my American friends. I feel so bad about what has happened. If you watch the news down there, that *Crossfire* and *Hardball* or whatever they call it, all they do is talk [say negative things], those two jerks. They call him [President George W. Bush] a moron and bastard and things like that. And now [they're talking about] this here booing in Montreal. And I guess there's no comeback [because] we don't go over there and support them over there. And it's a tough situation when you think . . . God love England. God bless them. England and Tony Blair and Australia [are all sending troops]—and we're not there. Fifty years of pride down the drain, as far as I'm concerned. But let me ask *you* one question. If we had a catastrophe up here, or God forbid somebody [attacked us]—who'd be the first ones in line?"

I said, "That's the first thing I wouldn't do it on, Don. I wouldn't base it on our security. I wouldn't base it on commerce. These are our great trading partners. Friendship I understand. But I'll say this about our air force. We're in Afghanistan—"

But Don didn't want to hear about Afghanistan. "Just a minute. Let's lay the cards on the table. The troops went over there because the fighting was going to be in Iraq. Let's get that straight."

"You are absolutely not—" I began, and then, in my IFB, I heard our producer, Joel Darling, saying, "Okay, Ron, move on."

Don was adamant. "Let's get that straight. Yes, sir."

I looked at him. "No, Don, that's ridiculous."

Don said, "We have a country that has been—has come to our rescue—and helped us—"

"That's . . . you're selling our soul." I was getting heated.

Don said, "We're not selling our soul."

Joel was in my ear again. "Get off the topic, Ron."

I said, "Well, maybe—"

Don said, "These guys are over there, they're over there giving it all."

I said, "Wait a minute." I had to interrupt my argument with Don to argue with the truck. "It's okay, Joel, we've got this. We're fine."

I just felt there was nowhere to go. There was no point in getting off it. My mind was awhirl. I couldn't just leave it at "You're selling our soul"—something I said in the heat of the moment. I had to clarify my thoughts. I was also thinking, Okay, you're probably hanging yourself here. You are going to lose your job over this. There were a lot of things I was juggling.

Don said, "We're over there, riding their coattails."

I said, "No, we're not."

Don said, "And when all they needed was a little moral help—if we didn't want to send anybody, at least have some moral help to help them . . ."

I said, "Well that's where the prime minister got into trouble. The day the war broke, or began, when he was trying to back off because he realized that you want to be a help—"

"You don't know what you're talking about. Everybody knows what I'm talking about. I'm not getting mad, I'm just—"

I could see where he was going. I said, "It just hurts you to see them go it alone."

Don said, "I hate to see them go it alone."

At this point, I wanted to bring up Lapham's argument that we should not be there because there were no confirmed weapons of mass destruction. Just two years earlier, the United Nations Security Council passed Resolution 1441. UN weapon inspectors went to Iraq to verify that there were no weapons of mass destruction and cruise missiles. They were given access and they found nothing. I didn't want to attack George Bush—I was reckless, but not suicidal. I said, "But what if it's the wrong thing to go?"

Don said, "Who says it's the wrong thing to go?"

I said, "I think it is."

Don said, "Well, *you* think it is . . ."

Hating that I'd made it sound like I thought my opinion was important, I said, "Yes, not that that matters."

Don said, "The people that think it is—like you—are walking out on the streets with signs." I tried to interject, and he said, "Wait a minute! And the people who think that it's right are over there laying their jobs and their lives on the line."

I said, "That's ridiculous."

Don said, "No, it's not ridiculous."

I said, "I would go and fight on, you know—the basic question—"

Don said, "What are you saying? What are you saying? Say it."

I pulled out Lapham. "Why attack Iraq if Iraq hasn't attacked you or your allies?"

Don was born five years before the beginning of the Second World War, so he spent his formative years during the war. He equated what was happening in Iraq with Nazi Germany. "You know, that's the same thing as Hitler. Hitler never attacked us."

I said, "And they voted Churchill out two months after Hitler surrendered."

Don said, "So you're saying if they don't attack us—I've heard that before about the Second World War—then you're saying that the United States is wrong?"

I felt we were complicating the issue by bringing up the Second World War. I didn't want to get trapped there, and I wished I hadn't responded with the remark about Churchill. "Well, I don't have every bit of information."

Don said, "Are you saying they're wrong?"

I said, "No, but I understand Prime Minister Chrétien's concern about not going in. And I understand it's good sometimes to step back from the herd and, as a good friend, you might say once in a while, 'I don't know about this action.'"

Loyalty and team are very important to Don. He said, "So if I ever get into a fight in a bar, you'd—"

"I'd be there with you—that's just what I've been saying."

"What if I were wrong, and you'd say, 'Well, he was wrong.' You're with your friends, right or wrong. Either you're with us or you're against us."

I said, "And that's why the prime minister got in trouble for trying to back off on the day the war began. Because now he was betwixt and between. And I think, as I say, Canada *is* helping the United States."

Don said, "How?"

I said, "In Afghanistan. Our troops are in Bosnia. Don, listen, Don."

"Wrong."

I said, "You don't know how—we don't have enough—you know our military is underfunded—America is—"

Don said, "There was forty countries backed the coalition." He was alluding to the forty-nine UN countries that voted to support the U.S., including Britain, Australia, Singapore, Japan, the Netherlands and ten eastern European countries.

I said, "Right."

Don said, "And we didn't."

I said, "That's right, and we made a decision. I think you have to stand by it. You're Canadian. I love the Americans, and I wish them Godspeed, of course, and I wish the Iraqis all the best in getting out of this as quickly as possible, but as a Canadian, we have to stand for ourselves sometimes."

Don said, "You actually are saying you don't back the United States in this war."

"Right."

Don said, "In this war."

"Right."

We were winding down when Don said, "What more can I say, folks? We'll end it right there."

Then Joel was in my ear again. "Nancy Lee's on the line. This is coming right from the top. You have to get off the topic!"

Cari always says I'm a total rebel. She says I like to fly in the face of the establishment. Cari knows me well.

I said, "We do have a couple of minutes. Why don't we

show—and you know, Don, that's democracy. I've always felt America . . . you know, they had an awful tragedy, of course [with 9/11], but they had an opportunity to showcase their appreciation of democracy. But listen to me. In a democracy, you and I can have a difference of opinion. And if I hear things like 'Good versus Evil' or 'Wrong, Right,' 'You're with us or you're against us,' that's not necessarily a democracy. That's tyranny."

Don shot me a look. He had just paved the way for a clean ending. A beautiful out. And this is where trust between partners comes in. Don puts his money where his mouth is. This was the bar fight he'd just been talking about. Right or wrong, you stand by your friends. His contract was up at the end of the year, and this could be used as ammunition against him. He could have earned copious brownie points by holding his hands up and saying, "Enough, Ron, let's move on to something else, okay?" Instead, he stood at my side and took another swing.

"So you're saying the United States is wrong?"

"No, I'm saying it's our right. Our right. Canada's right to make a decision that goes against them. That's all."

Don said, "Well, if you're against them . . ."

I said, "I'm not against them, I'm just—"

"You're against them. You just said you were against them. If you're against them, then they must be doing something wrong."

I said, "We're not supporting . . . We said let's give it more time, we took a tack and now that the war is on—"

Don threw his hands up. "See, folks, what I have to put up

with here. He actually means this, that our best neighbour, who's always been there, all the time—and if we get the chips down, and we get in trouble again, they will be there—and when they needed us, and all they said, all they needed was us to say, 'We back you.' They didn't want any troops. Just say, 'We back you.' When the chips were down, we turned our back on them."

We were close to time, and I thought that was a good exit point. "All right, we'll leave it at that. Peter Mansbridge is out there—"

"Oh, well, Peter'll tell it, he'll have something to say," Don said sarcastically. "He'll be neutral." Once Don is on a roll, it's easier to stop a freight train. I had to give him a chance to cool down.

I said, "Don't knock this. That's the thing, don't knock any of this."

Don said, "Come out for it one way or another!"

I said, "I am."

"Don't sit on the fence!"

I said, "I am."

Don said, "And you're wrong."

"And I'm a Canadian. But you're a Canadian guy. I don't get it."

Don said, "I'm a Canadian and I'm with the United States because they're always with us."

I said, "All right. You have ties with the United States and that's your comment."

Don said, "Got it."

"And that's the way it should be in our democracy."

By this time, it was dawning on us there might be serious consequences to what we had just done.

Don said, "Anybody who's got a job for me Monday, I'll be happy to—"

"You'll be fine."

Don said, "What?"

I wrapped up. "You'll be fine. That's good stuff. It's what we're all worried about. You know that. Don Cherry, on the Coach's Corner. *Hockey Night in Canada* on CBC."

We were off the air, and—crickets. You could hear a pin drop. Don picked up his empty Tim Hortons coffee cup and started tapping it slowly on the desk in front of him. There was complete silence in the studio except for that cup.

Finally, Grapes said, "So you took a chance. Huh? You took a chance."

The immediate fallout was fairly minimal. Nancy called me in. I wasn't worried, but I was kind of excited. I'd fallen on my sword and was ready to face the consequences. She and I sat and talked it through. It seemed the CBC brass were mad, but not furious.

Nancy told me how I was to position it in the media. "I/we went too far. Coach's Corner is about hockey." She said that I was not to refer to the incident by word or gesture on any upcoming Coach's Corners. Nor could I talk about any war issues. In fact, going forward we could not talk about anything not related to hockey without her signing off first. All in all, it seemed reasonable.

I had a speaking engagement that week in Kenora, an event for former player and coach Bob Murdoch, and almost everyone who came up to me sided with Don. Then I had an event in Winnipeg, and former Jets fans felt the same. Apparently, I had taken an unpopular position.

18

THE NINETY-NINE ALL-STARS

On September 16, 1994, the NHL's collective bargaining agreement expired, and negotiations on a new deal reached a standoff over the owners' desire to introduce a salary cap. Owners were claiming that, for every dollar of revenue, teams were paying $1.14 in salaries, and they wanted players' pay pegged to a percentage of revenue. Gary Bettman had been commissioner of the NHL for less than a year, and his claim to fame had been to bring the cap to the NBA.

In return, the NHL Players' Association suggested a tax on payrolls exceeding $50 million and offered a reduction in rookie salaries, a 5 per cent reduction in existing contracts, and annual revenue sharing—but no cap. For the second time since 1991, hockey was stopped.

Several players went to Europe to play on different teams, and in December 1994, I went on a trip with Wayne Gretzky. With the International Ice Hockey Federation's (IIHF) permission, he formed a team of close friends and called it the Ninety-Nine All-Stars. The roster included Al MacInnis, Rob Blake, Kirk Muller, Mark Messier, Pat Conacher, Brett Hull, Steve Yzerman, Tony Granato, Charlie Huddy, Todd Gill, Russ Courtnall, Steve Larmer, Marty McSorley, Paul Coffey,

Sergei Fedorov, Rick Tocchet and Wayne, with Kelly Hrudey and Grant Fuhr in goal. Travelling with the NHLers was and is one of my favourite things to do.

The Ninety-Niners were booked to play seven exhibition games in Finland, Sweden and Norway. The CBC decided to broadcast two of the games, on consecutive Saturday nights, to hockey-starved Canada. The first game was in Helsinki, Finland, and the second was broadcast from Stockholm, Sweden. It was kind of a *Hockey Night in Canada Presents.* The players made about $4,000 per game, but the profits went to charity and the NHL players' pension fund. Wayne chartered a plane, and most of the guys brought their fathers.

The day we took off, the team played an exhibition game against the Detroit Vipers of the International Hockey League. Bill McSorley, Marty's father, came to watch. As the plane was loading, everyone was telling Bill to get on the plane. He hadn't packed anything for the trip, but he came along anyway. The trip was magical.

On the first Saturday, we did a broadcast in Helsinki, Finland. Next stop was Tampere, a town north of Helsinki. Theo Fleury was playing there at the time. After the game, our group spent the night at a nightclub, drinking double sambuca shooters with beer chasers. I got up in the morning feeling kind of fuzzy. We were leaving for Oslo, Norway, that day, so I started to pack, but could not find my passport. I ran down to the lobby and spotted a Finnish newspaper reporter. He told me that the next day, December 6, was yet another Finnish holiday—they have fifteen a year. This time, it was Independence Day, celebrating Finland's separation from the Russian

Empire in 1917. He suggested I hustle back to the Canadian consulate in Helsinki to get a new passport. I scrambled to finish packing and to leave a message to let the guys know I would meet them in Oslo, and then I grabbed a taxi to the airport so I could hop the next flight to Helsinki.

I got to the consulate in Helsinki before it closed and managed to get a new passport. Early the next morning, I caught a flight into Norway.

The rest of the guys were late in getting there because they'd had a problem with their charter. It was karmic justice, because it turned out that my passport wasn't lost. Rather, somebody had snuck into my room and taken it as a joke. I can't confirm it was Gretzky, but I heard rumours to that effect.

Wayne's brother-in-law Kip, Brett Hull, Rob Blake and I went to a house party an hour north of Oslo. It was about 3 a.m. and we were walking around the neighbourhood with our hosts while they introduced us to their friends, calling us the "NHL people from Canada." Brett Hull was the life of the party and the last man standing. He was great. I really enjoyed everyone's company that night.

We headed for Stockholm for our next broadcast, and I decided I'd had enough partying. I was going to pull myself together so I'd be ready for the rest of the shows. I took it easy on the Friday night, and on Saturday we did the broadcast. After the show, we were at the bar again. I headed off to get Bob Cole a rum and Coke, and a beer for me. Bob is a very interesting drinker. He would drink an entire tumbler in two gulps—shooting half, pausing for fifteen or twenty minutes, and then shooting the other half.

Bob had a lot of wisdom. His stories were fascinating, and he was a good sounding board. He always had time for me in my young career. During my rookie year I'd done a Friday night game for CHCH, and Bob said, "Don't change a thing." That's all he said, and it meant a lot.

Mark Messier had captained the Stanley Cup winners in two different cities, Edmonton and New York, which no one had ever done before. Wayne had tried to win a Cup in Los Angeles, but he couldn't get it done. While we were on the road, I asked Messier, "Do you think Wayne envies the fact that you were able to win in New York?" He was quite angry with me for even hinting at that idea. He said, "No, no! We're family. There would never be an element of jealousy in all that."

That night in Stockholm, as I returned to our table with Bob's rum, Messier was sitting at a little cocktail table with two drop-dead beautiful blondes. The girls said, "Hello, Ron!"

I said, "Oh, you must be from Canada."

They both started laughing. "No, Ron, you were partying at our house in Oslo two nights ago!" Mark Messier smiled. "Every man for himself, right, Ron?"

The players started to get sick of the media, but I think I started to build a bit of a rapport, which was cool.

Before we left for Europe, I had been doing some professional reffing for the Colonial Hockey League, which had teams in Ontario, Michigan, Ohio and New York, and I was reffing for the Ontario Hockey Association (OHA) at the Junior A, B and C levels. It was complicated to referee in two different organizations. I'd send the OHA a list of eight dates per month, which left six for me to work in the Colonial league. Depending on the year, I'd ref fifty to seventy-five nights. On top of my *HNIC* job, it got a little insane.

When I returned home from the trip to Europe with the Ninety-Niners, I quit professional refereeing. I just couldn't keep up with the schedule. I knew I was going to miss it. I had some interesting and rewarding experiences in the Ontario system. When I first moved there, I officiated a game between the Newmarket Hurricanes and Richmond Hill Dynes. Everybody came to see the game—there was a full house. It was a rough game, fast and furious. Richmond Hill was known to have a pretty fiery team, and pretty fiery fans, too. Six players were ejected for fighting in the second period. In the third period, with twelve minutes to go, a brawl broke out between the fans and the players. I looked up and saw fans spilling into the players' bench, fists flying. Jamie Macoun's dad, Charlie, a director and general manager of the Newmarket franchise, was standing behind the glass. Charlie ran everything. He paid the refs, organized the 50/50 draws, and recruited the PA announcers. I went over and said, "Charlie, I'm going to have to call this game because it looks like deep trouble. In fact, we've got to bring in the police." Charlie said, "We're fighting for a playoff spot, and if you call the game, we'll still have to finish it at one time or another." People were getting hurt, so I called the game and called the police, who showed up but said they were not in the business of policing hockey games.

The crowd was in shock. Calling a game was unheard of. Later, the OHA said, "Ron, what the hell were you doing? You can't call a game. It's a black mark for hockey." I wrote a letter back explaining that you have to have security at the benches if you're going to have those kinds of wild nights. I was judge and jury that night, but there were no hard feelings. Afterward, Charlie and I went out for a beer.

Don Cherry would have killed me for calling off a game like that. He would have looked at it as a black eye for the OHA. I don't think he ever knew about it. I reffed a goalie who used to say to me all the time, "You know, you should listen to Don more. You really should."

One time when I was reffing a game, the crowd got out of hand *before* it started. We were in Port Colborne, Ontario, which is a half-hour south of St. Catharines, right on the northern shore of Lake Erie. I was the head referee. A veteran official named Steve Stasiuk was one of my linesmen. We were going into a playoff game and could hear bedlam in the arena as we got dressed. It sounded like a riot.

Someone started pounding on our door, and Steve got up and locked it. We could hear the person shouting, "Ron, Ron, you've got to get out here, there's a fight in the pre-game skate! There's a war going on out here."

Steve calmly continued to get ready. He said, "Awww, don't worry about it, Ron. They'll settle it."

And by the time we'd finished lacing up and opened the door, sure enough, the donnybrook had subsided. As we walked toward the rink, one of the coaches came up to me and said, "Nothing here, Ron. There was nothing going on here."

19

WITH A CHERRY ON TOP

The first Stanley Cup final I worked on was in 1987. I received a last-minute request to speak at the NHL's Stanley Cup luncheon on Tuesday May 19. It was a real honour. I had never done anything like that before, and certainly not in front of a thousand people paying $50 a plate and with the entire Toronto media in attendance. I only had a little over a day to prepare. I got up and told my jokes and got a few friendly barbs in return. For instance, when I introduced Scott Morrison, who was president of the Professional Hockey Writers' Association, he said, "Ron was born in Red Deer, but his parents moved to Calgary. He found them two years later." But the next day, I got carved in the newspapers. They said I was horrible. John Short wrote a column for the *Edmonton Journal* and said that I "tried hard to impress [my] new bosses at *Hockey Night in Canada*." He called it embarrassing and said, "No luncheon could have been long enough to give MacLean time for all the stroking he directed at his bosses.

"When MacLean aimed a couple of verbal barbs at [Edmonton Oiler president and general manager Glen] Sather, Sather fired back, 'Where's Dave Hodge?' Nobody laughed because Sather was right on. Not kind, but right on."

At the morning skate, Don pulled me aside and said, "Look, Ron, those guys were just gunning for you. You were just great up there." He was very good to me, and he said something else that day that resonated. It was something along the lines of "it's hard to be a prophet in your hometown." He got it from the gospel of Matthew. I tucked it away.

Grapes says that, in Canada, we build people up, and when they reach the top, we tear them down. This really bugs him. Me? I don't usually care. Refereeing was the greatest experience for thickening the skin. I knew there were times when my decisions would be unpopular. I knew there were times when I would be wrong. I knew that things happen fast and you can't be perfect. I was conditioned to understand that we all say and do stupid things, the media included.

Don was kind. I appreciated his remark, but I honestly didn't care one way or another what they said. And I told him that. Don replied, "Ron, bums don't care." It was an expression his mom had used.

I thought, "There is a part of me that is like that." I don't sweat it. I really don't. You have no control over respect. Lots of people earn respect, and then it goes away. It's one of those qualities I love and admire, but I don't trust it. I knew I wasn't great, I knew I wasn't horrendous. I was a twenty-six-year-old doing the best I could. I didn't overthink it by any stretch.

I can recall only one time where open criticism from the media got to me. Larry and Willy were a morning team on a Vancouver radio station. (They are now at JACK-FM Vancouver.) In 1992, they did a song parody called "He's a Crotch-watcher." It was to the tune of the O'Kaysions' 1968 hit "(I'm

a) Girl Watcher": "He's a crotchwatcher, he's a crotchwatcher, Don Cherry's thighs . . . my, oh my." You get the drift. That one hurt. I've never had an easy ride in Vancouver. But I think it was a good thing, because it put the period on the end of the sentence for me. After that, I was able to tune out criticism altogether. I can't recall ever being upset at anything like it since.

That is the kind of guy Grapes is. He will always, always go to bat for the underdog. I did an opening for the Toronto Maple Leafs during my first season. I used the phrase "the hapless Leafs" because they had just lost about four in a row. Don looked at me and said, "The *hapless* Leafs, Ron? You don't kick them when they're down. Kick them when they're up!"

I learned from Grapes early on that it's important to bring something that no one else has. And he will protect this information like a Cerberean hound at the gates of Hades.

On December 10, 1988, while playing for the New York Rangers, Guy Lafleur broke a bone in his left foot. He was hit by a Bruins shot midway through the second period. We got the news early in the third. I said, "Wow, we have to hurry upstairs to report that for the sportscast."

Don said, "Bullshit. I found it out. I'm telling that story."

I said, "Don, people aren't tuning in to Coach's Corner to find out if people are injured. We don't do news bulletins." But I couldn't talk him out of it. It was his story and, like all of us, anytime he was on, he wanted it to be interesting. And if he didn't have something interesting, he wasn't afraid to hang me out to dry.

In 1994, the New York Rangers had just beaten Vancouver in a big, big Stanley Cup final. It was the most watched hockey series ever. We had time left after game seven, so we asked Don to come on at the end to help us wrap.

He said, "I have nothing. I have nothing to say. What am I supposed to say? You've been on for half an hour kissing up to the guys. I don't want to be on, gushing like all you other guys. You have nothing to say, but you're blabbering anyway about how wonderful everything is. Keep me off."

I said, "How about you talk about the fans? You've had a lot of interaction and feedback here."

He said, "All right, I'll do that. Leave that for me."

Then, at the last minute, unannounced, they brought Arthur Griffiths, the owner of the Vancouver Canucks, into the studio. So what the hell was I supposed to talk to *him* about? I had to talk to him about how the fans had been great during the run. Meanwhile, Grapes was in this little washroom in the studio. He always hides. He doesn't want to see the players because he has too many enemies.

I was desperate to fill time, and Grapes had his head around the washroom door, watching me do the interview with Griffiths. He was in my eye line, and he gave me a look that said, "Don't you mention the fans."

I knew this, but I was stuck. I didn't know what else to ask Griffiths. So I asked about the Vancouver fan support. That sealed my fate. No way was Don going to come on now. I finished with Griffiths, and I threw to Bob Cole and Harry for their final thoughts, but they were not available. It was going to be me for two full minutes. We went to a commercial, and I begged him, "Don, come on, you've got to help me out."

"And talk about what? The fans? Forget it."

I filled the two minutes without him, bluffing something that was brutal. We finished up and I was hot, really mad at him for leaving me out there. There was a pail of iced beers in the room, and Grapes was passing them out to everybody. He was smiling and joking because he hadn't had to make a fool of himself.

He said, "Ron, aren't you having one?"

I continued packing my stuff. I wouldn't even look up at him. I said, "No, because I have to do the NHL awards show open tomorrow morning." (I was scheduled to tape the opening with actor Leslie Nielsen.) I added, "Some of us actually work, you know."

Don said, "Here! Have one!" And he fired a beer at me at about a thousand miles an hour from about five feet. I downed two and called it a night.

Don always seems to run into the guys he's ripped. In 1996, at the World Cup of Hockey, Canada was leading 2–1 with less than five minutes to play. Claude Lemieux came from the right wing down into the left corner in his own zone, and shot the puck around to the right point—a giveaway. Don climbed all over him. He said there was no way Claude should have done that, and he just ripped him. The next morning, we were at the airport and there was only one other person in the Air Canada lounge. Claude Lemieux. But he was cordial.

And Don had a funny night in Vancouver with Donald Brashear in 2000. It was not long after Marty McSorley had taken Brashear out from behind with a stick to the head with three seconds left in a game between the Canucks and the Bruins. Don said, "[Brashear] ridicules an old warrior—I'm not saying what Marty did was right—it was wrong . . . [but it happened] because he ridiculed Marty. You don't do that . . . if he hadn't ridiculed him, it wouldn't have happened."

A couple of games later, when we were back in Vancouver, Brashear walked into the studio. He was not dressed for the game that night because he was still out from the McSorley hit. He laid into Grapes, and Grapes challenged him. "What do you want to do about it?"

Brashear said, "What am I gonna do? Hit an old man? You're nuts!" And he left. Grapes started down the hall after him, yelling, "Yeah, just like you ran on McSorley!"

During the 2010 playoffs, Grapes was pretty hard on Dan Carcillo of the Flyers. Before game one of the final in Philadelphia, we walked down a hallway in the arena and there was Carcillo, riding a stationary bike. I thought, "Uh-oh, here we go. Dan's going to say something snarky to Don for all the criticism." But it was the opposite. He was kind—"Hey Grapes, how's it going?"

Later, Don came to me and said, "Can you believe that? I was hoping he'd say something nasty, and I was ready. Instead, he charmed me to death. I feel really bad now." From that day on, he never said a bad word about Carcillo.

Then there was Matt Cooke of the Pittsburgh Penguins. Grapes had carved him for a dirty knee-on-knee hit against Erik Cole of the Carolina Hurricanes in the 2009 playoffs. Cooke came up to Grapes in the bowels of the RBC Center in

Carolina and said, "You had a lot to say on television. I wonder if you'll say it to my face." And Grapes said, "You're damn right I'll say it to your face!" They stood face to face, and Grapes said, "You're a chickenshit, back-stabbing, no good rat! There! What do you want to do about it?"

I don't have a quick temper, but it's a bad one. When I go, I go. Grapes says the only time he remembers me going wild was after a 1989 Coach's Corner. We'd just been discussing a Calgary–Montreal game during the final, and Don was wearing this red coat he had been given. I defended a Flames player, and he said to me, "You should be wearing this Calgary Flames jacket, you being from Red River, you're such a Calgary Flames fan."

I know I was probably too sensitive about it, but when we got off the air, I said, "You can't say that! That's very unprofessional. Now everyone is going to think that I am a Flames fan, and that does me no favours. I have to be impartial, I'm a sports journalist."

Don said, "What're you talking about? Everyone knows I'm in the Bruins' corner."

I was such a jerk about it. I said, "It's different, Don, you belonged to the team. Ah, what does it matter, you'll be off TV in two years anyhow." I don't know why I picked two years. Just wishful thinking, I guess.

He loved that, of course. I learned it the hard way. The more defensive I got, the happier he became.

Meanwhile, back in Red Deer, Garnett Eastcott, who was the father of a kid I'd grown up with named Kenny Eastcott, sent City of Red Deer souvenirs along with a note to Don saying, "Look, Don, I know you're just having some fun with Ron, but just like in Kingston, we have a proud hockey heritage. We in Red Deer have the Rustlers and a history of talented players. We'd appreciate it if you'd get the name straight. It's Red *Deer*, not Red *River*."

I presented the souvenirs and the note to Don on the next Coach's Corner. Even though he thought my remark about him being off TV in two years was funny, inside he was also mad and hurt. He just looked at me deadpan and that made the whole thing fall flat. Don was a grump for the next three shows, which didn't improve my quality of life. But he wrote Garnett Eastcott back and said, "Garnett, my boy, you're right. I was just having some fun with Ron, but from now on it will be Red *Dear*."

20

I'M SICK OF YOUR THEORIES

Despite his tough exterior, Don is soft-hearted. He reminds me of my mother that way. We'll be walking along and there'll be a dead bird on the road, and he'll start singing that old hymn, "God Sees the Little Sparrow Fall." And he's very well read, with an unbelievable knowledge of trivia.

In 1996, I was refereeing a hockey game in Streetsville, which is a little community within the city of Mississauga, Ontario, when a guy came into the officials' room to make small talk before the game. He started talking about Don Cherry's wife. He said, "Rose is really sick."

I said, "Oh, no. She had breast cancer three years ago, but I think everything is good now." And he kind of looked at me as if to say, "My God, Ron doesn't know." And just like that, I knew.

The signs were everywhere. I mean, they should have clunked me over the head earlier. Don was mentioning Rose more, and was fanatical about wearing the rose in his lapel. When we were on the road, I'd watch from my hotel window as he'd go for long early-morning walks by himself.

I'd been to their house a few times when she'd been wearing a wig because of the chemo treatments, and I didn't even notice. I had sat at the kitchen table across from Rose and I didn't even pick up on it.

Rose was great. She would get angry with Don if he interrupted me or put me down on the show. He'd go home and she'd say, "You are the most ignorant guy I've ever met." A writer out of Edmonton used the phrase "Bambi eyes" when he described how I looked when I was slighted by Don. I thought that was so funny. Sometimes it did appear as if Don was being rude to me. I loved it, and Grapes delivered the lines with such perfect cruelty. One time, we were in Anaheim for an Oilers–Ducks game, and just before we went on, I told Don that Marty McSorley and I had been discussing how the Ducks were chasing the Oilers behind the net. It's usually a no-no in hockey to chase a player behind the goal on a forecheck, but the Ducks did it to force players like Jason Smith to move the puck faster than they wanted to. I said to Don, "I'll say, 'I have a couple theories,' and you say, 'Shut up, I'm sick of your theories!'" Our boss, Richard Stursberg, was watching, and told Grapes he loved how he nailed me good.

A lot of times, I got slapped down when I would try to help Don remember a story. And even though I knew he was completely lost, he'd say, "Will you just shut up? I'm the one telling the story here." One time, an interviewer questioned him for telling me to shut up, and he said, "I go too far sometimes, but he should know better than to interrupt me when I'm on a roll." There can be only one wolf with his tail in the air on the show. I understood that going in.

Rose was the greatest. She gave Don his comeuppance at every turn. One time, we were at a Christmas party and I drank way too much and was kind of making an ass of myself. Don kept it going by telling the bartenders to keep running me beers. Rose was furious at Don for having them overserve me. She was protective like that. She was very protective of Don, too, but sensible about it. She wasn't starstruck at all. She didn't want this high-profile life. She was a really nice, strong lady.

On Monday, May 26, 1997, Don and I were staying in Windsor, getting ready for the Detroit–Colorado game. The series was three games to two in favour of the Wings (who went on that night to win 3–1 and advance to the Stanley Cup final). Don called me up and told me, "Ron, I have to leave in the morning to be with Rose." But nobody else knew she was dying.

I went on to the Detroit–Philadelphia series alone. It began Sunday, May 31. A couple of minutes before the show went on the air, Bobby Orr, who had been looking for Don, came up to me at the Zamboni entrance and asked, "Ron, what's going on?"

I decided to let Bobby know what was actually shaking down. I said, "Here's the situation. Rose had stem cell surgery and things aren't working." As I talked, I started feeling bad. The floor manager called out, "Ten seconds to air."

Bobby said, "Look at this. Some idiot got mustard all over my pants!"

He was feeling as tough about it as I was, but he made the remark to distract me from the sadness so that I could concentrate on work. It was incredibly unselfish.

On Coach's Corner that night, I said that Don was away

to attend to a family matter and, "As is the Cherry way, he wanted me to say, 'I'm all right. Don't worry about me.'"

Rose died the next day, June 1. I flew home and missed game two of the series. I rejoined the crew on June 5. Don did not. Don was done—he was done.

Grapes would be the first to tell you he went a little crazy during the stretch after Rose died, but I thought he held it together remarkably well. Eating became a problem. Rose's death had broken his heart and his rhythm. Don still lives by a strong circadian rhythm—a twenty-four-hour cycle that's most prevalent in dogs and the plant kingdom, where everything repeats itself exactly to the minute from day to day. Dogs will come for their food at the exact same time every day, and they like to go for their walk at the same time each day. Don had a morning ritual. Rose and he would sit in the solarium and have coffee. She was his sounding board. He wouldn't even pick up the papers. (He never reads the paper in front of anybody. He considers it bad manners.) Sitting with Rose kick-started his day. So not having her there ate away at him horribly, and it killed his appetite. He started looking a bit frail.

However, his desire to work remained, and the first show that he did when he came back the following season was a pre-season game out of Japan. Mark Messier and the Canucks played Paul Kariya and the Anaheim Ducks. That first show was a tough one, but he got it back on the rails.

Don had lots of women coming by the house, bringing apple pies and trying to offer comfort. But he didn't bite. He figured some of them were just gold diggers who were after his money or fame. I wasn't sure he was right, but he's like a finely tuned athlete—way too aware of everything. World-class athletes, like Don, get into a bubble where their focus narrows.

Don had gone from pro hockey player to TV personality, yet he'd maintained that same regimented lifestyle. That included his appearance, his diet, his exercise, his preparation. After Rose's death, he was worried about his performance and how some of the things he was supposed to do to get ready for the show were gone. Most of all, he was sad. Really sad.

In the spring of 1998, I was emceeing a dinner to honour former Leafs Stanley Cup legends, and Don came with me. His daughter, Cindy, and son, Tim, and I were all trying to think of things to do with him. He was still grieving Rose and seemed sort of lost. Don hates dinners. He cherishes the time he spends in his basement, so I kind of forced him to come. But I knew that guys he knew, like Gerry Cheevers, would be there. During the dinner, a nice-looking woman in her forties came up to me and introduced herself as Luba. She said, "Ron, would you sign this card for my brother Ihor?" I did, and she said, "Do you think Don would sign it?"

I said, "Luba, you go over and ask Don. He will be happy to do it for you." She hesitated a little, and I said, "He won't bite."

Later that night, she came back to the table. "I bet you get this all the time, but I just want Don to know that I've spent a lot of my career in the hospitality industry, organizing professional dinners, and if Don would ever like help with an event, or company to have lunch or dinner with, this is my phone number. You can do what you want with it . . . you probably think I'm a crackpot for even suggesting it."

But I didn't think that at all. On the car ride home, I said to Don, "I got a phone number from a woman named Luba. She mentioned that she's done a lot of organizing and such in her life, and if you need any help with dinner—"

Don said, "Look, I'm not looking for anything right now in the way of companionship, for sure. But hang on to the phone number. When you get home, put it on the fridge in case I need her for something. Don't let Cari find it in one of your pockets!" I guess Don didn't realize I do my own laundry.

A few miles later, he asked, "What did she look like?"

For some reason, I remembered that she wore bright pink lipstick and I remembered that she was attractive and blonde, but that's about all I knew.

During the playoffs that year, he kept asking me questions, "Well, was she tall? Was she short? What was she like?" But I couldn't remember those details. Finally, he said, "Well, do you still have the phone number?" I did, and I brought the number with me to the third round of the playoffs—Washington was playing in Buffalo. Don went to the morning skate. He was dressed in a suit and, at sixty-four years of age, looking good and feeling pretty confident that day. So he went back to his room and called Luba.

He had the phone receiver just inches off the hook, with his head down and his mouth close to the top of the table. He identified himself and then said, "Luba, is the situation still the same as you described it to Ron at that dinner at the Inn on the Park?'"

He decided that if she hesitated even a second, he was going to slam down the receiver. He couldn't stand the rejection.

But she was cheerful and said, "Absolutely, Don. I'm certainly available and would be glad to meet you for lunch if you like."

He said, "I've got to finish the playoffs, but after the playoffs I'll come out to . . . where is it you live?"

She told him she was in Caledonia, which is a town down by Hamilton. They set a date, but he didn't know what to do. Should he take her to lunch? Take her to dinner? Take her to a movie? We talked a lot about it, but I was very little help. My expertise on dating ended in high school.

Finally, he drove down to Caledonia in his big white Lincoln. Meanwhile, Luba had told all the neighbours, "Don Cherry's coming, but when you see him, please don't make a fuss. Don't run out and bother the man when he gets here."

When he arrived, most of the neighbours were sitting on lawn chairs in the driveway two doors down, drinking beers. And as he pulled up, they were yelling, "It's Grapes! Hey, Don! Over here!"

Grapes got out of the car and went to the door and saw that she had a really nice figure. He was happy about that. In fact, upon first meeting her, he was quite smitten. He called our house that night and left a message on the machine saying, "Ron, I have only two words for you: knock out! You don't know much about hockey, but you sure know about good-looking women." A year later they eloped to Vegas.

I love Luba. She has a good heart and seems to see the best in everyone. She's so agreeable that Don's pet name for her is Absolutely Luba. But she's not a pushover. Grapes always tells her to just keep away from him during the playoffs because, when he gets home, he's not a very nice guy to be around.

Afterward, he asks for five days of total solitude. He's tired. During the 2011 Vancouver series, he said to her, "You're happy I'm leaving again. It's okay, be honest. You won't miss me. You'll be relieved."

I told him he could change all that with a page from my book. "Clearly, if you did all the laundry, made all the meals, walked the dog and did the ironing, Luba would miss you more. Just ask Cari." Don looked at me and said, "You know what? I always thought you were kidding until I saw you fold hockey sweaters."

Whenever we go on a trip, I do the driving, and Luba makes us these amazing sandwiches. Don's a happier guy now that she's around.

21

THE OWNERS SMELLED BLOOD

Don has a scathing wit and temper, and whenever I ride too high he cuts me down. When I interviewed Gary Bettman in April of 2002, during the seventh game of the Eastern Conference semifinal between Ottawa and Toronto, I was hard on Gary. Cari watched from home and told me Gary had placed his hand on top of mine fourteen times to try to interrupt me. I had no idea he was doing that. We were deep into the conversation, going toe to toe. Sometimes, instead of patting me, he said, "Ron . . . Ron . . . Ron . . ." I was pleased with the interview, but Grapes felt sorry for Gary. Afterward, he pulled me aside and chastised me for sticking it to the NHL boss. He said, "C'mon, Ron, that's not your style."

In his book *The Rise and Fall of the Press Box*, Leonard Koppett, one of the twentieth century's most famous sportswriters, wrote about commissioners. He said they are the agents for the owners and should be treated with respect, and that the pitfall in challenging the boss is that although people will admire you for standing up to authority, you have to be careful to make sure that's not your motivation.

In 2002, when Grapes admonished me for my contentious interview with Bettman, that's what he was talking about.

Gary and I have had several interesting on-air chats. I look forward to them because the dynamic in our relationship is kind of like two bantam roosters with their chests puffed out. I like him, I really do, but he becomes so defensive when I get after him. Bettman's awkward in a way that reminds me of Dustin Hoffman in the movie *Rain Man*. It's interesting that he ended up representing the establishment, because guys like him make great advocates for the underdog.

Gary is a fast-thinking guy with lots of nervous energy. He travels at 100 miles an hour. I remember meeting with him when he was just appointed commissioner in February 1993. He said, "I'll take you for lunch." We went to this Chinese restaurant, and we were in and out in about ten minutes.

His job is so secure. He did the owners the ultimate service by breaking the players' union, so he deals with them from a position of strength. Essentially, his job is to try to modify and coordinate the interests and demands of thirty owners, and he's done an amazing job of that. He is very smart and always ensures that he approaches the right people so he can divide and conquer. He has enough protection now that he maintains control. And you have to respect him for that. His job involves law and politics, and he is brilliant at both. He doesn't need to know hockey. His forte is the *business* of hockey. He wants the standings tight so that every fan in every city believes that their team has a shot at the Cup. The 2004 lockout and the resulting salary caps achieved that, and a lot more, for the owners. To this day, what happened is still a contentious issue.

On September 14, 2004, the ten-year-old collective bargaining agreement between the league and the players was due to expire. Negotiations began early in 2003, and Bettman, on behalf of the owners, was determined to do what he had failed to achieve ten years earlier—implement a salary cap. Bettman argued that the owners' biggest expense was player salaries, which accounted for 75 per cent of their budgets.

Their primary issue was cost certainty, so that they could plan for future expenses. But there was much more at stake. A cap would increase the value of their franchises overnight.

Bettman faced off against Bob Goodenow, the executive director of the NHL Players' Association. Goodenow was smart, tough and cunning, which made him perfect for the job. He was determined to let the market decide what players should make. He felt hockey stars could not achieve their full earning potential without a free market.

Both Bettman and Goodenow were educated at Ivy League schools. Goodenow graduated from Harvard in 1974 and from the University of Detroit Law School in 1979. Bettman studied industrial and labour relations at Cornell and got his law degree at New York University in 1977. The two fought hard, but as September 2004 rolled around there was still no deal. On September 15, the league announced it was locking the players out.

Bettman claimed cost certainty was essential to the deal. Just prior to 2004–05, the owners' public report claimed the league had lost almost a quarter of a billion dollars. Goodenow offered a 24-per-cent rollback on player's salaries for one year. He knew that if the PA could avoid a salary cap, the players would eventually make up the rollback money. But with Goodenow's softened position, the owners smelled blood.

My favourite source in these matters is Rodney Fort, who at that time was an economics professor at Washington State University. He's now at the University of Michigan. He wrote, "First, the NHL accepted the NHLPA's 24-per-cent rollback offer. They have announced it and it is built into all of the subsequent calculations they do at the NHL web page.

"Second, in addition to that rollback, they now demand a 'floating limit' proposal that really is their previous cap demand, to the dollar, in a thinly veiled disguise."

Bob Goodenow really had his work cut out for him. He kept asking, "Why should labour accept a system that doesn't permit management to pay an individual as much as it wants?"

Leonard Koppett also wrote about labour strife and pro sport commissioners. "Whose ultimate influence counts most, for a settlement before or after a strike actually occurs, is seldom obvious. Usually it comes from someone, or some factors, outside the formal bargaining." And with respect to the lockout, that was absolutely the case.

Several of the players' agents were the primary outside force pressuring for a resolution. During the lockout, they had a powerful voice. The agents who pushed the hardest were cash-constrained—they had lines of credit with the banks that payments had to be made against. They knew players only want to play. "Listen, you may only have five good years. Are you sure you want to sit out for one or two of them?"

Goodenow said this was short-sighted on the part of those agents who supported the cap, because in a capped environment agents provide zero incremental value and their commissions are tied to the cap. The players cannot make a dollar more or a dollar less. Instead, there is a formula that determines how much is spent, and it's just a matter of who gets what. The only decision is, how much do the first-line guys get? How much do the second-, third- and fourth-line guys get? It's an allocation issue. The formula just spits out the number. "Player X, you're worth $15 million a year, but we're going to get you $8.5 million. I'm going to negotiate less, but not too much less than what you really should get. Then I'm going to charge you 3 per cent, because even though I'm not going to get you as much as you should get, it's not as little as it could be."

Second, some of the wealthy players with seniority didn't hold the line. There were guys who'd earned $50 million to $100 million in their careers. When they risked losing up to $10 million to sit out a year, they buckled. And at the end of the day, all players paid the price.

On February 15, Bettman put his "final offer" on the table—a salary cap of $40 million. Goodenow agreed to a cap of $49 million that would grow with revenue. Bettman made another "final offer" that would expire the next morning for a set limit of $42.5 million. The deadline came and went, and Bettman cancelled the season.

Rudyard Kipling said, "If you don't get what you want, it's a sign either that you did not seriously want it, or that you tried to bargain over the price." The deal Goodenow offered was their bargain price, and the two sides could have agreed on the fluctuating revenues and saved the season, but the owners locked the players out anyway. Was it because they were bent on breaking the union and serving up Goodenow's head on a platter?

Goodenow, on the other hand, thought the length of the lockout was helping the NHLPA gain a stronger negotiating position. He misjudged the players' resolve and the agents' influence. For at least four years ahead of the contract negotiations, he had warned the players that the owners would be willing to lock them out for a season, and maybe even deep into a second, over the salary cap issue. He told them that if they weren't willing to hold out, then they might as well negotiate a cap up front. He told everybody to start tucking money away, and promised them that, in the end, it would be worth it.

Either some didn't believe him, or they weren't paying attention, but as the lockout continued past the cancellation of the 2004–05 season, problems arose. Players knew the start of the next season was also in jeopardy, and they lost composure and faith. Certain players felt Bob was not the guy to get the deal done, and they derailed him.

On February 19, 2005, Trevor Linden met alone with Harley Hotchkiss, part owner of the Calgary Flames who was also chairman of the NHL Board of Governors at the time. Sometimes, smaller sessions can lead to breakthroughs, but in this case the meeting aided the owners' position.

The players requested that Goodenow's second-in-command, Ted Saskin, sub in and deal with Gary's lieutenant, Bill Daly. The two met in Niagara Falls, and the players lost even more footing. Daly and Saskin agreed to a 24-per-cent rollback on existing contracts, a $34 million cap with a $21.5 million minimum, and that was the end of Goodenow. He wanted no part of the deal and resigned. We will never know whether Goodenow's strategy of continuing to sit without cracking would have worked.

The formula consists of multiple caps. There is one that is specific to rookie salaries. There is another on individual players' salaries—no guy can make more than 20 per cent of the team cap. There is a cap on each team—how much a team can spend on player payroll. And there is a leaguewide cap—the cumulative total that all teams spend on player salaries. The owners have an insurance policy in case the leaguewide cap is breached. It's called escrow—a percentage of players' salaries is held back, and if the owners stay within the leaguewide cap, the players get the money back. If they go over, the escrow is used to make up the shortfall. In other words, the players subsidize the owners.

The league calculates the sum total of all hockey-related revenues (HRR), and players, as a group, are assigned a share of this. In 2005, it was 54 per cent, and it's now 57 per cent. All player compensation—not just salaries, but also signing bonuses, amounts received by injured players and contract buyouts—must come under this limit. There's also a salary "floor"—a minimum amount that teams must spend. The floor is set at $16 million below the salary cap.

At the start of 2011, owners thought they were going to overspend by 17 per cent, so they withheld 17 per cent of the players' salaries. This rate is adjusted every three months as the owners look at revenues. The final calculation for 2011 was down to about 6 per cent. So if a player's contract gave him a $2 million salary, the league kept 120 grand. A guy like Crosby gave the league back almost a half million dollars in 2011.

The current collective bargaining agreement gives players absolutely no input into decisions that affect revenue. This means where teams play, which franchises should be moved, which payrolls are out of whack. The players can't say, "Gary, we think you should move the Phoenix Coyotes to Hamilton. That way, the league won't lose money on that franchise, and we won't have to pay back 17 per cent of our salaries to make up your losses." Owners never have to engage—it's strictly a one-way street. They can do a poor job of managing the revenues, but no one can call them out on it.

Goodenow told me that one owner informed him that, every time the owners discuss the escrow provision, they enjoy a hearty laugh. This owner was truly astounded that the players agreed to hand over total control over operating and labour costs while also providing sufficient funds to cover overruns.

Owners told the public that if they couldn't get salaries under control, fans would have to pay higher ticket prices. I don't see it that way. Even with a salary cap, owners can continue to charge whatever they want for tickets, concessions, beer, sponsorships, parking, and television and radio rights. Games in Toronto, Vancouver or Calgary are not a cheap night out. Prices are set by supply and demand. The truth is that some teams used to spend much more on salaries. Before the lockout, the big-budget teams like the Rangers, Philly, Toronto and Detroit were each spending $80 million. Was it so expensive that they had to take out loans to cover payroll? Of course not. They all made money.

Today's top players all take less than market value, for the good of the game and for the good of their teams. The Sedin brothers took hometown discounts. They had to. Otherwise, the Vancouver Canucks would not be Stanley Cup contenders. Since the collective bargaining agreement, rather than working out a dollar figure with the owners, it's now a fight between twenty-three guys on each team to divvy up the amount allowed under the cap.

The multimillionaire owner can sit out until the cows come home. The players are in a gunfight, armed with a butter knife.

For the next go-round, players only have a chance if their union leader is extremely tough and principled. Goodenow was, but the members didn't understand it. They got fat.

One more point. I think the cap does the game a disservice. Toronto has missed the playoffs seven years in a row. Limited in how much they can spend on players, the Leafs have fallen off the face of the earth.

I loved the dynasty teams in the pre-cap days. When you had the Oilers in their heyday, they were loaded with talent and just a joy to watch. I understand fans were unhappy when suddenly Paul Coffey, Mark Messier and Wayne Gretzky moved, or when Calgary traded their Stanley Cup team away, trades motivated by contract issues with Hall of Famers Doug Gilmour, Al MacInnis and Joe Nieuwendyk, among others.

The cap lowers the quality of the top teams. Which is better: a powerful Cup dynasty, or the suspense created by contrived competitiveness? Teams now have a better chance if Toronto, Detroit, Philly and the Rangers can't hire away all the top talent. The Blackhawks blew apart, trading players after winning the Cup in 2010. They couldn't keep everybody and stay under the cap, so *pfffft!* they were gone. If you build a winner, you have to tear it down. And it used to be that players stayed together for years, building a fraternity and ties with their fans. Now it's a mercenary culture, like all the other athletes in capped sports—"Win or lose, drink the booze, who cares? We win, we don't stay together as a team. There is no family anymore. I'm here for today, gone tomorrow."

Lots of people think that's great. I can't convince them it's not. They love the standings where, with two games left, nine teams are four points apart, still in the playoff hunt. They think it's terrific. I sound like a nut trying to explain that it's bad. I really do. I don't lose sleep over it, but it does grind me that the Blackhawks were gutted and that it's going to happen to Edmonton again in a few years.

Bottom line, I want to see John, Paul, George and Ringo. Not John and Paul and two guys they can afford.

22

IF YOU DON'T WANT ME TO TELL
ANYONE, DON'T TELL ME

During the 1999 Stanley Cup run, Don and I covered the Eastern Conference final between Buffalo and Toronto, and when that ended, Colorado was still playing Dallas in the Western final. We were sent to Dallas to do the seventh game on June 4. They were having a real problem at the Reunion Arena. It had been built in 1980, and apparently they had never contemplated that hockey would be played in the summer, so it was not equipped to deal with 80-per-cent humidity and 90-degree temperatures. They were having a tough time maintaining quality ice, so the NHL flew in its ice expert, Dan Craig.

I had been a weatherman, so I knew all about the humidex (known in the States as the heat index), which is an indicator of what the temperature "feels like," based on how hard the human body has to work to cool itself. The humidex was a story because it affected the play.

We had been covering the story of the bad ice in Dallas, and that night I took the humidex device and went on the air. "Good evening. Welcome to game seven, the dramatic conclusion to the series between Colorado and Dallas. Obviously, one of the questions on our minds here on June 4 is, 'Will the ice be okay for this big game?' Then I pressed the button, and the humidex reported 98 degrees Fahrenheit.

The ice was slushy. I reported that Dan Craig had been flown in and had put ventilation ducts in the ceiling to cool the ice to minus-6 degrees Celsius, about two degrees colder than normal. I also pointed out that the Zamboni doors were being left ajar to help get rid of some of the humidity. I talked about all these things they were doing to try to ensure that we would have decent ice for the important game. And then I said, "And now, here's a feature on the great Rocket Richard." And as soon as I threw to the item on Rocket Richard and we were off air, Gary Bettman came running over to me. "Ron, why do you have to talk about 'bad ice conditions'? Everybody understands that we are in Dallas, Texas, and there is bound to be hot weather. This is a big game, and it's not fair to the players and it's not fair to the game that you are so negative. We're all looking forward to this game."

I said, "Well, Gary, if it weren't the first week of June, we wouldn't have to worry about it, would we?" There's not a human alive who wouldn't like to see hockey end earlier in the season. But the truth of the matter is that we play in June because the major American networks won't allow the playoffs to end in May, which is one of the "ratings sweeps" months that they base their advertising rates on.

During the entire half-hour of the pre-game show, Gary and I continued to take swipes at each other behind the scenes about my negativity and the heat and playing in June. Colin Campbell was standing there, his eyes as wide as saucers. Then I went over to the dressing room that we were using as a studio for Coach's Corner that night. Don was in there having a coffee, and I vented a bit. I said, "Gary Bettman wasn't too happy with me talking about the relative humidity and the possibility that the ice would be a concern tonight."

Don said, "Oh, is that right?" He didn't say another word about it.

Later that night, at the beginning of Coach's Corner, Don said, "You know, Ron, this is really something. We flew in, we're very lucky guys, we fly in for the seventh game between Colorado and Dallas. Do you know, Ron—this is true, I just found this out, my buddy Dave works for *Sports Illustrated*—there are more professional hockey teams in the state of Texas than anywhere in the world? They've absolutely gone crazy for hockey. They love it here. I just come out of Denver the other night there. They had their 350th consecutive sellout. They're going crazy in Colorado. You've got the Stars and the Avalanche. Mike Modano and Joe Sakic have never been better. You got Eddie Belfour against Patrick Roy. It's the seventh game, Saturday night, everybody is in a good mood. Except you. You've got to stand out there with your stupid thermometer trying to ruin it for everybody. Can't you just give it a rest? This is a hockey show. We're trying to have a good time here. All right?"

After the Coach's Corner segment ended, Gary Bettman came hustling into the room, wearing a wide smile. His hand was out to Don. "Thank you, Don, thank you! Absolutely great show."

The season after the lockout, every arena had signs painted on the ice, just inside the blue lines at either end, that read, "Thank you fans!" And I could hear Gary's voice all over again.

Gary always tells me what the viewers want. He came into the studio one time and said, "You know, Ron, you should keep your interviews to three questions on the same subject. It's very boring for the interviewee and the viewer when you go back to the topic over and over again." In New Jersey, in 2003, he said, "Ron, I've come to the conclusion that you think it's a good interview if I look bad." Of course I denied it, but inside I was chuckling. I told him I would take it easy. That night, I did the interview and asked just a couple of questions per subject. No arguments. In the cab back to our hotel, Bob Cole said to me, "That interview was nothing."

My mom worried whenever I interviewed Gary. "Geez, Ronnie! Did you have to be so ignorant to Mr. Bettman? I would paste you for being so rude if you weren't my son!" Paste me. She was always threatening to paste me. "Oh, Ronnie, you looked so smug on stage at the NHL awards. I just wanted to paste you."

My dad says it got to the point where Mom wouldn't even watch if Gary was on the show. She'd say, "Either turn it down or I'll just go down to the bedroom. I'm not going to watch. I can't watch." Mom was scared that Gary could have me removed from the job—not fired from *Hockey Night in Canada*, but from being the host. Dad would try to reassure her. "I don't think that's right. I don't think he can do that, because Ronnie's not working for Gary Bettman, he's working for CBC. And Gary Bettman doesn't run the CBC." Whenever they would ask me, I would say, "I can't worry about that,

Dad." Mom continued to lose sleep over it. She worried about me being like her. She didn't want me to storm off and quit my job the way she did when she felt disrespected. She knew that I had inherited her trait of challenging authority and feared it would come home to roost at some point in my career. Mom felt it was in our DNA to act too proud.

On June 2, 2010, I got into it again with Bettman. We were in Philadelphia for game three of the Stanley Cup final, the Flyers versus the Chicago Blackhawks. I planned to discuss franchise values. I had done my homework. Bloggers are incredible. Many are now experts on almost every facet of the game. From statistical analysis to labour law, you'll find a blogger who keeps journalists honest. And as a result of the availability of information via social media, even casual viewers have a deep knowledge base.

I didn't even want to do the Bettman interview. I was sick of beating my head against the wall. Why arm-wrestle with Gary in the middle of a great Stanley Cup final? Who needed it?

I elected to go ahead because I knew it was good TV. I was conflicted because I felt it was cheap of me to put him in that position.

I wanted to have a foundation for the interview, so I decided to focus on something Gary had said at his state-of-the-NHL news conference a few days earlier, on May 28. He said, "The franchise situation is actually stable. We are not now dealing with any owner giving back keys to any team." I didn't feel that was correct. I felt there were a number of owners turning back the keys, and I wanted to go through it with him and get him to admit there were problems. I wanted him to deal with the fact that the players, with their millions in escrow payments, were having to fund these trouble spots, and yet they had no say in how the business was run.

I prepared by talking to three key sources: Bob Goodenow, Rod Fort (he and I had spoken a million times, done a one-hour TV special and met for dinner in Ann Arbor) and Richard Rodier, who now works for the NHLPA, but at one time was Jim Balsillie's lawyer. Balsillie, having tried to buy the Pittsburgh Penguins and Nashville Predators, had made an offer to buy the Phoenix Coyotes and move them to southern Ontario. The majority owner of the franchise, Jerry Moyes, accepted Balsillie's offer and put the team into bankruptcy. The NHL responded by announcing that Moyes had been stripped of the authority to make decisions about the team. Rodier fought Bettman in bankruptcy court over the matter, so he had an understanding of the situation in Phoenix.

I also knew that Hurricanes owner Peter Karmanos wanted to sell half of the Hurricanes and according to *Forbes* magazine the value of that franchise was down 9 per cent from the year previously.

The entire empire of Dallas Stars owner Tom Hicks was in financial turmoil. It was rumoured that Bill Gallacher from Calgary was one of those waiting to pick up the team at a bargain price. Meanwhile, the major shareholder in the St. Louis Blues since 2006, a private equity firm called TowerBrook Capital, was talking about selling—in keeping with its plan to exit the investment after roughly five years. That meant that Dave Checketts, the managing partner despite owning only about 20 per cent of the team, was going to need to find a new investor. In March 2011, Checketts revealed that he'd raised capital in hopes of buying TowerBrook's share of the Blues, but the two sides couldn't agree on a price, so the franchise was for sale.

With all these teams in play, it didn't appear as if the franchise situation was stable. So, during game three, Bettman and I had a ring-ding-a-dong dandy (an Ed Whalen expression) on-air debate, on Gary's fifty-eighth birthday. He was badly sunburned from sitting in the sun without sunblock during his daughter's graduation ceremony at Cornell University, his alma mater. I started by singing "Happy Birthday" to him.

The interview began with me trying to establish the sale price of the Tampa Bay Lightning. The new owner, hedge fund manager Jeff Vinik, who also owned a minority stake in the Boston Red Sox, had agreed to a deal worth a total of $80 million to $120 million in cash and assumed debt.

Gary said the league didn't usually publicize what franchises sell for, but he said the Lightning went for "far more than was reported" and that the previous owners, Oren Koules and Len Barrie, who had bought the franchise in 2008 for $200 million, "sold and they actually got money back."

He started that "Ron, Ron, Ron" thing again when the subject of Dallas and Bill Gallacher came up. I asked whether the players' escrow money had been subsidizing the team. He denied both allegations, but confirmed that Gallacher was hoping to buy the team over the summer. (As of the summer of 2011, the Stars had yet to be sold.)

We talked about St. Louis and Carolina, and he said, "We've had a great season, hockey has been terrific, these playoffs are great, we're watching a wonderful game and you just want to tick off franchise after franchise? What inside of you compels you to want to go in that direction?"

I said I wasn't trying to ruin the night, but that the same players who were giving us the great show were leaving money on the table, via the escrow, in case the league's revenue projections fell short and player compensation exceeded 57 per cent of hockey-related revenues.

At the end of the interview, there was a sense that I'd struck a nerve but hadn't got any real answers.

After the show, Grapes and I sat in the hotel room with our garbage can full of beer, talking and pouring them back. He knew the CBC was after me all the time to ratchet it down and not disrupt their partnership with the league. And he knew that Bettman wanted desperately for me to say that the new NHL, with its tight standings, was wonderful, instead of questioning the salary cap and the new rules.

Grapes said, "You know, Ron, it's not fair. You are throwing snowballs for the players. Let the NHLPA step up for themselves."

I told Grapes that if I'd been interviewing Goodenow, I'd be throwing snowballs for Bettman, and that it was my job to bring in the other point of view. I agreed with Thomas Paine, a founding father of the United States, who was always after the monarchy and said that somebody has to speak on behalf of the oppressed.

After a few more, Grapes said, "I bet you if you phoned any player in the league and asked him to come on and confront Bettman, he'd say, 'No way.'"

I said, "I'm not going to do that, because that would put players in an untenable position."

Grapes mimicked me. "I'm not doing that, that would put players in a un-tent-able position." Then he pointed to his beer. "Is this you talking or is it *this* talking?" And we both laughed.

At the time of the Bettman interview, Vancouver fans were still mad at me because in January that year, I had questions about one of their top scorers, Alex Burrows. Jerred Smithson of the Nashville Predators had a five-minute boarding penalty and a game misconduct for a hit on Burrows on December 8, 2009. Smithson went in with his shoulder, but Burrows ducked, absorbed the hit with his head while going into the boards, and came out of it with a little blood on his lip. Because there was an injury on the play, the referee, Stéphane Auger, assessed a five-minute penalty. But when the league reviewed the tape, they rescinded the game misconduct because they felt Burrows had embellished the injury. I was curious about the league's decision.

On January 16, Vancouver was set to play Nashville again. Burrows and referee Auger had words before the game. I had no trouble believing Burrows' claim to the media that Auger had talked to him about the embellished hit and how it made Auger look bad. But after the game, Burrows made two claims: he said that in their pre-game chat Auger told him that he would "get [Burrows] tonight." I felt that was ridiculous. But there was an interference penalty on a faceoff that Auger called in the third period that was so bad, it was certainly circumstantial evidence. In addition, Auger was shown winking after the call. I believed it was a call of revenge. And the wink, well, that was vintage Auger. However, I didn't believe Auger would have tipped Burrows about his plan. Then Burrows complained of not being allowed to skate around during the TV timeout. Now, I don't know which referee—Auger or Dennis LaRue—put a halt to that, but I do know Burrows had a history. In the 2009 Stanley Cup playoffs, he used the TV timeouts to chirp at Chicago's goaltender, Nikolai Khabibulin, which was a bush-league move. Guys just don't do that. In fact, the league's VP of hockey operations, Colin Campbell, had had Burrows on a watch list for some time. (The league had kept these "watch lists" since 2006–07, but there was no paper trail.)

One mea culpa. At this point, I showed the Burrows-embellished Smithson hit and pointed out how Burrows had tried to draw a penalty, but I was cruel in my depiction of how Burrows was acting. I indicated that, from a referee's perspective, Burrows was thinking, "Has the ref given a major penalty yet? No? I'll stay down." I was going off on him as if I were in a referees' locker room, and it was the wrong thing to do.

I do, however, think it's fair that I showed a compilation of Burrows' previous transgressions to make my next point, which was that none of them had resulted in a suspension: a 2008 spear on Pierre-Marc Bouchard of the Minnesota Wild; charging J.P. Dumont of the Nashville Predators; chirping at Aaron Downey of Detroit in a 2009 pre-game warmup; punching Zack Stortini of the Oilers from the bench; and taunting Khabibulin.

Burrows had clearly made his bed. But it raised the question that, if he continued to be let off because he didn't have a previous record, how would he ever get a record? That was the gist of the segment. And in the 2011 Stanley Cup playoffs, when Burrows bit Patrice Bergeron on the finger, it helped me rest my case. Luckily, he didn't have a history.

Not everyone was happy with my examination of the subject. I received some letters from B.C. One guy had been very friendly at a speaking event that I'd done a few months earlier. So friendly, in fact, that he asked me to sign his name tag. After the feature on Burrows ran, he FedExed the name tag back to me and told me to stick it where the sun don't shine.

Naturally, I assumed he was talking about Vancouver.

In the wake of the Burrows/Auger/Ron "affair," Canucks management flew to Toronto and met with my boss, Scott Moore, the executive director of CBC Sports, to address the issue of fair and balanced reporting. I got my knuckles rapped. I was told I'd injured our brands—my brand and the CBC's brand.

That was a new one. I said, "Oh, I have a brand injury. What's the healing on that?"

And now, the day after the Bettman interview, Scott flew into Philly to meet with me. Scott's background was with TSN and Sportsnet, where he was good at bringing business to the table. Rights agreements were his forte. On Scott's first day at the CBC, he called a meeting and informed the staff we had to become better partners with our corporate sponsors and the sports leagues. The CBC had been a good journalistic entity, but Scott made it clear he did not think we were supportive enough.

In the old days, the CBC didn't worry as much about being a good corporate partner. In every news organization, there are always questions about whether to sacrifice content in the name of business and how seriously you should take your responsibilities as a journalist. Ed Whalen was a good influence in helping me find that balance, in the sense that he hosted *Stampede Wrestling,* which was pure showbiz. Grapes has been a good influence, too. They are similar. Ed understood he was only going to live so long, so what the hell? Make a few extra bucks on the side and give people a few laughs. I sense that outlook in Grapes, too. You have to have a bit of fun at some point. I was a lot more like that twenty years ago. But now, things are more serious. We are talking about career-ending hits. I feel I have to speak up for the players to provide balance. I can't let that part slip—I don't know why. Now I find myself being the one guy constantly hitting on the NHL.

Scott and I met at the hotel. He said, "Look, Ron, I have three problems with the interview. Number one, the subject matter was very confusing to most of our viewers. Nobody would have understood what you were talking about, so I consider it a bad interview in that regard. Number two, after you went through the teams and Gary asked you, 'Why would you bring these things up?' you said, 'Well, for the players who are paying escrow.' Well, Ron, if you want to work for the players' association, why don't you get a job with *them?* Number

20. During the 1993 Western Conference final between Toronto and Los Angeles. This is the show immediately after Don's infamous "pimp" episode. We were on a probation of sorts.

21. Grapes never likes to look shorter than me. I bet the guy who took the photo heard about it afterward!

22. Grapes would like this shot better—he looks tall, powerful, handsome and rich!

23. Our patented Detroit City octopus opening, from 1998. That's a fifty-pounder.

24. At the Nagano Winter Olympic Games in 1998. I'm asking Don what he thought of Jean-Luc Brassard. Bad idea!

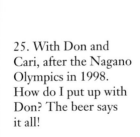

25. With Don and Cari, after the Nagano Olympics in 1998. How do I put up with Don? The beer says it all!

26. (Left to right): Floor director David Sealy, producer Joel Darling, me, Don and publicist Christian Hasse. Just before going to air, Don wants to know the birthplace of a player, so I am searching on the computer. Putting kids "on the map" is our favourite deal.

27. This is my favourite publicity photo. Don and I are at Glen Eden ski hill, an hour northwest of Toronto, promoting Hockey Day in Canada in Whitehorse. Don sleighs me.

28. With Don at the 2011 Heritage Classic between the Canadiens and Flames at McMahon Stadium, Calgary. One of us did not get the "what to wear" memo.

29. At the Air Canada Centre in 2002, for my first game after the contract ordeal. This night was a chance for me to thank the fans.

30. With Cari and Sherali Najak, the producer who inspired me the most.

31. With a replica of the Stanley Cup in 1995. I am glad it is a copy—unless you win it, you don't get to touch the real deal.

32. In the 1990s, Mr. Hockey, Gordie Howe, was on hand to perform the ceremonial puck drop at a game I refereed in the old Colonial Hockey League.

33. Reffing a pre-season NHL game between Buffalo and Pittsburgh. That's an interference signal. I also called a chintzy trip on John LeClair that still haunts me a little.

34. In my Aussie swagman crushable hat in Sydney in 2000, wondering if it's the rat's ass.

35. With Lanny McDonald at a roast in his honour in 2010.
I'd travel anywhere to give Lanny a hand. He was always there
for me in the beginning.

36. Houseboating in the Shuswaps in 2002 with (from left to
right) Jerry Murphy, Marty Vellner and Terry Krushelnicki.
Four high school pals doing our version of *Degrassi*.

37. At sea off the British Virgin Islands in 2007, driving a fifty-three-foot Beneteau we named *Nanuk*. This is day one of a vacation, spent travelling to a spot called "The Bitter End."

38. With Marianne Limpert and producer Chris Irwin. Marianne's silver medal–winning swim in the 200-metre individual medley at the 1996 Olympics in Atlanta remains the single greatest moment I've witnessed live.

three, if you continue to badger our partners this way, we are all going to be out of a job in four years."

The CBC's competitor, Rogers, was looking at buying the Leafs, which meant the CBC might lose the rights to NHL hockey in four years. Scott seemed to be saying that if we were more supportive of the NHL, they would ignore the money and renew our contract. "When we get back and the play-offs are over, we will redo your contract and you will sign an addendum that will put you in the same position as some of our big-name news people. There is no shame in this." He was demanding balanced reporting—no opinion, no editorial. I felt I was being asked to give up the ability to think for myself in exchange for a salary. It was ridiculous. It's hockey. We all have opinions.

I said, "Wow, this is serious. I'm going to call a lawyer and I'll get back to you." I was so mad I was vibrating. And I was so wound up, it took me twenty minutes to consider whether I even knew any lawyers that could represent me.

I called Newport Sports, who had acted for me in negotiations, and learned that it's Contract Law 101 that no one can demand you change the terms of a signed contract. I got some good advice on how to handle the situation. So I called Scott and I said, "Look, I'm willing to discuss the interview, and I'm willing to talk about our approach, but if you're asking me to let you unilaterally change the terms of our existing contract, the answer is no. If that's a problem, then you can go to human resources or call Newport Sports."

At that point, Scott didn't continue arguing, which allowed me to save face. I respected that because I knew what he was up against. I'm not an easy guy to direct. Bosses will tell other bosses, "When you're going to deal with Ron, be sure you are well prepared. Have every angle covered because he'll have a million questions. He'll fight you on everything you try to tell him to do."

It's part of the human contradiction. I say that criticism doesn't bother me because I learned that, as a referee, you cannot expect not to get yelled at, and in the host's chair on *HNIC* I get drilled in the press because it comes with the territory. But I have this bad habit at work—as soon as somebody tries to dial me in, it hits me hard.

Imagine what it's like to try to deal with a guy like me. A guy who cannot stand the thought of being prideful and yet is so full of pride it hurts.

23

IN THE CROSSHAIRS

Before the CBC hired John Shannon back, NBC hired him to produce the 1993 All-Star Game at the Montreal Forum. A couple of weeks before the broadcast in February, they still didn't have a rinkside reporter. John suggested me. John Davidson was the colour man and Marv Albert was the host and play-by-play guy. At the very end of the broadcast, with forty seconds to go, we had to get an interview with the MVP of the game, Mike Gartner, who had scored four goals and an assist.

Through my earpiece, John ordered, "Ron, jump over the boards and get the goddamn interview and say good night." So I got the interview and said good night and made it to time. Marv wrote me a very polite, complimentary letter afterward, which I appreciated.

In June 1997, Shannon had been hired back after an eleven-year absence. He was hard to replace. He had big talent, and his work had merit. I always enjoyed him, and of course he'd given me my start—I owed him a lot. But John was too rough around the edges for the CBC. He, like Don, was old school. They came from a world where you said what was on your mind. They didn't have to hide behind words.

John could get hot, and when he did, he would tear a strip off a person. Unfortunately, a director from outside the sports department was working with us one night in June during the playoffs, and he objected to the way John handled him during a tense situation. The director complained, and Alan Clark, who was executive director of CBC Sports, suspended John—sent him home for two weeks. I felt very bad about that. John was really dedicated. There are a million producers who are very well organized and can turn out a good cookie-cutter show. John had the quicks to make a live show flow. Unfortunately, part of his quickness included his temper.

Grapes and I get into it during playoffs, too. By the end of the eight weeks of playoff hockey, we are still the best of friends, but we are also very close to being the worst of enemies because we are tired. It comes from working in the crosshairs for a little too long.

I've been mad at him many times without being too, too hot. In game three of the 2002 final, near the fifteen-minute mark of the third overtime period, Igor Larionov scored the winning goal to put Detroit up 2–1 in the series. The next day, a day off, we were sitting in the stands, watching practice. Pierre McGuire from TSN came over and started to talk about Larionov's goal. He asked me, "What happened on that goal, anyway?"

I said, "I don't know."

Pierre started to talk about how it looked as if Carolina

goalie Arturs Irbe thought that Larionov might pass across to Mathieu Dandenault and that's why he went down, or something like that.

After Pierre left, Grapes said, "Don't tell them that you don't know! You never say we don't know what's going on. Geez, you give him the chance to tell us what he thinks happened on the goal. All those guys, they just love that."

I said, "What are you, nuts? They don't care. I don't care and they don't care. Pierre was just making small talk."

So the next morning, Grapes and I met up at 9:30 a.m. to go to the morning buffet, and he was still on about it. "Don't give those other guys the satisfaction of saying you didn't know, you and me. We're supposed to know, we're *Hockey Night in Canada*. You shouldn't be talking to them anyways."

We sat at the table, going back and forth, arguing about whether it was right or wrong to tell Pierre McGuire that I didn't know what happened on the goal. Finally, we stood up and headed to the buffet, and it was closed. We'd argued all the way through to 11 a.m.

Later, I went back and looked at that play, and I discovered that Luc Robitaille had actually grabbed a Hurricane sweater at the far end of the ice, which prevented the player from getting back and covering, so Larionov was left open to score the goal.

As we got set for the final game of the series, I heard that a pro-CBC story was going to run on *Hockey Night in Canada*, and I talked to our producer, Paul Graham, about it. He said that head office had asked him to assign Scott Russell to do a voice-over feature about how unfair it was that Réseau des

Sports (RDS, the French-language version of TSN, which was owned by CTV) had outbid the CBC for the rights to Montreal Canadiens' broadcasts. The CBC's angle was that it should be the network's inherent right, as the Canadian distributor and the nations' public broadcaster, to have the rights, because they are a part of francophone history.

I said, "What are you talking about? RDS outbid them. That is their prerogative. It's the Habs' right to get the money. This is crazy. What are we? Communists? Whose idea is this?"

Paul said, "This is directly from CBC president Robert Rabinovitch."

I said, "When we run this in the second intermission, keep me out of it. I'm not introducing it. I'm not tagging it." I thought it was ridiculous to run such a slanted feature in the middle of the Stanley Cup final.

Grapes came into the studio while I was in the middle of this tirade. He could see me getting more and more worked up. Finally, he said, "Hey, take it easy. You're wearing down. Save a little for Coach's Corner."

My contract had been renewed in 1998 with no hassle whatsoever, but I knew the talks were going to go sideways when my contract came up again later in 2002. I was fed up. The CBC was constantly getting involved in editorial content. If I were going to stay on, I would need to negotiate for respect. So I hired an agent.

Don Meehan is the most powerful and influential hockey

agent in the country. He's a former wide receiver for McGill, where he got his law degree. He moved to Toronto in 1975, and in 1981 started up Newport Sports Management. His first big client was Pat LaFontaine, the hottest junior prospect in the country in 1983. Pat, who played centre for the Verdun Juniors in the Quebec Major Junior Hockey League, had 234 points that year and took home the Jean Béliveau Trophy, beating Mario Lemieux, whose points totalled 184 that year with the Laval Voisins. Meehan convinced LaFontaine that he was prepared to work harder on his behalf than anybody else. Today, Meehan represents 150 players in the National Hockey League.

A bunch of us from work would sometimes go to a bar in Toronto called the Madison Avenue Pub, which started out as this little pub in the basement of a house in the early 1980s. Today, it's a happening place with bars on several floors.

Meehan lived near the Madison, so I'd see him there and got to know him a bit. And when he'd go to the Leafs games, he'd sometimes join us afterward. These were the years when we broadcast live from the rink. Now, we broadcast our host segments from the CBC building downtown.

In 2001, Meehan invited me and 119 others to a celebration of his fiftieth birthday in Ireland and Scotland. He chartered an aircraft and flew us all over there to play golf at St. Andrews and in County Cork. St. Andrews Links is made up of seven golf courses. The most historic and best known is the Old Course, which has been around since the fifteenth century and is where they play the British Open every few years. It's often called the home of golf. The course is also known for its double greens and the Road Hole bunker at the seventeenth hole, which is so deep you need a forklift to get out of it. Another neat thing about the course is you can play it forwards or backwards.

We also golfed in Ireland at Tralee, Ballybunion and Old Head. The golf courses in Ireland have such lush greenery that even the bushes look like velvet. Arnold Palmer designed Tralee. When he saw it completed, he said, "I may have designed the first nine, but surely God designed the back nine." You can see the Atlantic from every hole. It was an unbelievable golf excursion.

One of my favourite memories is of the first night, with Bob Gainey, who won five Stanley Cups with the Montreal Canadiens, Bob Clarke, the famous captain of the Philadelphia Flyers in the 1970s and '80s and later GM and executive vice-president of the team, and longtime broadcaster and NHL coach Harry Neale, sharing beers and stories at a pub at St. Andrews called Jiggers. We started drinking at noon and went until three in the morning. Gainey and Clarke had selected Canada's men's hockey team for the 1998 Winter Olympics in Nagano, Japan, so they had lots of stories about that. But there were 120 of us on that trip, so there were hockey stories galore.

Bobby Clarke never watered his horse. He sat there drinking pints for thirteen hours and didn't go once. We were all in awe of his huge bladder. The guy was a camel. Dominique, our bartender, said, "I've never seen anything like that. We're going to put a plaque on that stool. The stool Bobby Clarke sat on and never once used the shunky. From now on, it will be his."

We moved from St. Andrews over to Killarney Park Hotel. What a place! My room had a fireplace and a great view, but I spent most my time in the bar. It was late into the night, around 4 a.m. A few of us were still sitting around trading war stories when Cliff Fletcher walked in and ordered a tequila. The next day, you would never have guessed. He was in his mid-sixties, but he was made of granite.

I remember Bob Gainey walking with me back to my room. Bob's an incredible human being. I got to the door and I said, "Aw, Bob, I forgot my sweater."

And he said, "Ron, there are plenty of sweaters in this world."

I said, "Bob, you don't understand. Cari gave me that sweater, and if I don't return home in that sweater, I might as well just stay here." So back we went to the bar to retrieve it.

I hung with a lot of the western guys while I was there, including Lyle Odelein, the Columbus defenceman from Quill Lake, Saskatchewan, and Kings winger Kelly Buchberger. I liked Chris Dingman, who played left wing for the Hurricanes but was traded to Tampa that year. He ended up helping Tampa win a Cup. He was a fun guy, born and raised in Edmonton. Spending time with those guys was a real highlight of the trip.

Meehan paid for the golf fees, hotels, flights, the whole package for everyone. You have to figure that 120 guys eating and drinking at the most exclusive golf courses in the world was a big ticket. I felt like a freeloader. The only request Meehan made was that Harry Neale and I emcee his big birthday bash in Killarney, Ireland. That was it. I thought, "I can pay him back by having him negotiate my next contract, and I'll give him a commission or pay him a set fee."

There was an article in *Toronto Life* in May 2008 by Gare Joyce that said Meehan's company "represents more NHL players than any other two agencies combined, enough to fill the rosters of six teams. It has 17 full-time employees and offices in the US, Russia, Sweden, Finland and the Czech Republic . . . Meehan won't discuss salaries, but even if his players make the league average, all told, they're earning upwards of $300 million a season (a number that increases substantially when you factor in endorsements)." With that kind of operation behind him, I'm not sure Don Meehan was counting on my negotiation to feed his family.

In any case, all hell broke loose.

24

CONTRACT 2002

Don Meehan had to negotiate some big contracts that summer, including deals for José Théodore, who'd won the Hart Trophy, and Jarome Iginla, the runner-up. Meehan told me he figured my "marginal revenue product"—salary—should be $900,000. I was making $475,000. I laughed and said, "You're dreaming.'" I'd known Meehan's work for years through all the research I'd done on players. I liked that one of his clients, Michael Peca, had sat out a whole year to get what he felt he was worth. It reminded me of my mom walking off the job on principle. I admired that kind of spine. I was willing to do that, too. I was even willing to switch jobs, but only after things became adversarial.

On September 25, 2002, Meehan met Nancy Lee, the executive director of CBC Sports, at a little Italian restaurant close to the CBC building to negotiate my deal. What they arrived at wasn't anywhere near Meehan's projected entry point, but I was happy with it. Nancy had to kick it upstairs to Harold Redekopp, the executive vice-president, for final approval, and we would be done.

The next day, Nancy came back, saying Redekopp had approved most of the terms, but not the money. She offered $80,000 less than what she had been willing to commit to over dinner. When Meehan called to tell me this, I was in Ottawa hosting an hour-long special called *When the Circus Is in Town*, a behind-the-scenes look at *Hockey Night in Canada*, part of the CBC's fiftieth-anniversary celebration. When I heard the news, I thought, "Well, why did she negotiate in the first place if she didn't have the power to finalize the deal?"

Meehan and Lee were back and forth in the press. In a Canadian Press article, Lee said "there was a gap in the expectations," and Meehan said "the difference was marginal."

Meehan sat down with Redekopp. Meehan said that Harold told him, "We really don't need Ron because Ron has eighteen producers telling him what to say." When Meehan told me that, I said to myself, "Bullshit." I felt Redekopp had no clue about how people felt about the show or what went on in the studio. I shouldn't have been so defensive, but I was upset with that remark. The money was not what drove me. But I had worked for the CBC for seventeen years, and I thought I was being treated with disrespect. The CBC had the audacity to run stories favourable to the CBC, and yet it worried about what we said on air, and then accused me of being a talking head?

Michael Jordan's agent, David Falk, tells a great little story in his book *The Bald Truth* about a contract negotiation with the Bulls. Jordan told Falk, "If I ever hear you negotiating the deal before I hear [Chicago Bulls owner Jerry Reinsdorf's] number,

I'll fire you." He wanted to know what Reinsdorf thought of him. The money the Bulls offered him would reflect that. I felt the same way about what the CBC thought I was worth.

I had volunteered to emcee a charity golf tournament that week in Calgary for Dale Henwood, who was president of the Canadian Sport Centre, which provides support for high-performance athletes so they can succeed in international competition. Based in Calgary, it's one of the top Olympic training environments in the world. I liked getting out to the west as often as I could, because Mom and Dad still lived there. Cari came with me. On September 30, 2002, we were at my folks' when Don Meehan called me in the mid-morning. I thought, "Great, here's the call firming things up." I never in my wildest dreams thought there were going to be any further issues.

Harold had offered only a 3-per-cent raise.

I said, "Now what?"

Meehan said, "Are you ready to walk away?"

I said, "Yes."

Meehan was amazing. He said, "Good. Don't fear the unknown when you're doing the right thing."

"Good," I said. "We're done, then. Great."

Cari, who was beside me, thought I meant the deal was complete. She smiled and gave my arm a squeeze.

I hung up the phone and said, "CBC decided not to sign the contract."

Cari said, "Oh, really?"

I said, "Yeah. We're done."

Cari looked at me and said, "We'll be fine." And then we both got up and walked quietly up the stairs to tell my folks.

25

AN INDEPENDENT CAT

Dad was like most pro hockey players' parents. He looked stricken. He said, "God, Ronnie. You're making almost half a million dollars on hockey and you had to ask for more?"

"It's not about the money," I said, then repeated Meehan's mantra: "Don't fear the unknown when you're doing the right thing."

Mom was full of her usual spit. She understood how I felt.

The next three days were like being in some sort of movie. The CBC announced that we had parted ways. The local CBC station picked up the press release first and contacted me. I drove over to the studio and did an interview for CBC News-world, which felt kind of funny, but I thought it was some sort of conciliatory gesture that the network was allowing me on the air. I may have been delusional, but that's how I took it. I was asked if I was upset, and I said, "No, it's totally their pre-rogative to pay the host what they think the host should make. I'm just saying for what I am selling, they are not buying." But I was not talking about money. I was talking about what the CBC thought I was worth to them. It was very cordial, and I was totally comfortable.

I headed over to the Glencoe Golf and Country Club to

emcee the charity tournament. Reports were flooding the airwaves. Being out west was nice, because I was away from the centre of it all. I was glad to be among old friends. Bruce Dowbiggin, a *Calgary Herald* reporter I know, came up to me to find out what was going on.

I told him the truth. "I have a firm belief in what my role on the show is worth, and I have decided to stick with that. It was a litmus test of respect, but you know how it is in our vocation. There are a million people who'd love to have your job, and it's easy to say how grateful you ought to be—just take what they offer. But that's intimidation, and I couldn't look you or Mike Peca or Bob Goodenow in the eye if I didn't stand up for what I knew was right."

Bruce wrote in the *Herald*, "I know it's funny to say about a guy who is paid that way, but I don't know a man who is less motivated by money than Ron. He's a really different, independent cat."

That evening, I stood at the microphone at the charity tournament. "If you haven't heard, I just walked away from my job at *Hockey Night in Canada*. Anybody looking to buy a car?"

I honestly didn't know much about what was reported, because I totally ignored the coverage. Until I started this book, I had never looked at any of the clippings or emails from the time. Cari's sister, Cindi, was fantastic during that stretch. She kept Cari up to date. But I didn't pay one bit of attention to it.

CBC insiders said some nice things. Harry Neale said, "We're like any team, and in my opinion, we just lost our best player. MacLean and Cherry had a heck of an act going. People liked them and watched them, even though they didn't agree with a single thing they said."

Some guys were calling for my head, like John Doyle at the *Globe and Mail*. His television column was titled "Sidekicks Are Easier to Replace." He started out, "Don Cherry is the clown prince. Foils like Ron MacLean are a dime a dozen." He felt the "best bet for CBC" would be "a female sidekick for Mr. Cherry . . . Viewers would undoubtedly tune in to see sparks fly and watch Mr. Cherry try to get chummy with a female sports reporter."

That was interesting, because anyone who knows Don knows he is a complete gentleman around women. There is no way he would ever yell at a woman. One time he did remark on female sports reporters by saying, "Now, I have to say to you ladies that you can't have it both ways. If you want to be treated like men, then when you do get treated like men, you can't whine. If you can't stand the heat, then get out of the dressing room." To which I responded, " I would blush at this discussion, but luckily I'm wearing a pancake foundation— with white eye shadow."

Everybody had the money wrong. The Vancouver *Province* had me asking for a million dollars. Most papers had the CBC and me $200,000 apart. It wasn't until October 2 that *Toronto Star* reporters Chris Zelkovich and Michael Clarkson reported that we were $25,000 a year apart for a four-year deal, which was about right.

Grapes tried to help behind the scenes. He told the CBC brass to be cool, because he knew I would probably be quick to get my back up if they went overboard. And he told me,

"Don't put a gun to their head. Now that you have gone, be gracious so that you're not getting them to the point where they're looking so bad that they'll never make a deal."

Brian Burke called me and said the same thing. "Give them a chance to save face. Be careful what you say about them. If the tide turns, you have to give them an out." I felt that way anyway. I told everyone who interviewed me that there were no hard feelings. Brian offered, "Let me know if there is anything I can do."

Tie Domi called, too. He said, "Ron, Curtis Joseph took a stand, and now he is in Detroit. I think if he had it to do over, he'd still be wearing a Leafs jersey." It was Tie's way of saying, "You'll be sorry if you go to another network. Stay where you belong."

I did interviews on radio stations all over the place, and there were lots of callers phoning in, saying, "You could be back doing the weather in Red Deer next week." And I'd answer, "You don't understand. I'd be happy doing the weather in Red Deer."

It was all a bit of a blur. I told myself it was a neat phase of my life. "Now maybe I'll get a teaching certificate, or start working in broadcasting somewhere else."

October 1, 2002, was day two of being jobless. Martin O'Malley reported on the CBC News Viewpoint website that when he started to write his column that morning, "emails protesting the dropping of MacLean were coming in at the rate of four or five a minute. At this point, they're coming in at 19 a minute. This is the biggest email reaction to anything that has appeared on CBC News Online, bigger than

Trudeau's funeral, or Gzowski's death, or the wars in Kosovo and Afghanistan."

According to the *Toronto Star*, the whole affair "sparked more heated language around Parliament . . . Bloc Québécois Leader Gilles Duceppe had nothing good to say about Cherry . . . He called Cherry's salary a waste of taxpayers' money." I imagine Don loved that one.

Then CTV offered me a job. Ivan Fecan, the president of Bell Globemedia, which owned the network, had been director of television programming at the CBC from 1987 to 1994. He developed some of the CBC's best programs, including *Degrassi High*, *Road to Avonlea*, *The Kids in the Hall*, *Royal Canadian Air Farce* and *This Hour Has 22 Minutes*. In 1994, CTV hired him as group vice-president of Baton Broadcasting.

Meehan told me Ivan and Rick Brace, who had just been appointed president of the CTV Television Network on October 2, would meet with me in Calgary to seal the deal. I figured Ivan would take anybody if it meant sticking it to the CBC. He'd have hired Rick Mercer to sweep floors and then televised it just to bug them. I certainly wasn't dismissing the offer, but I'd had a few calls from Joel Darling, among others at the CBC, who told me the door had not been slammed shut, so I didn't think it was right to play the CBC and CTV off against each other. There were other offers, too. Glen Sather, the president and general manager of the New York Rangers, talked to Meehan about a job for me at the Madison Square Garden Network.

On October 2, the *Toronto Sun* ran a story calling the situation "The MacLean Madness." There was an Internet petition with 8,000 signatures, and the *Sun* had printed another petition that you could mail in. Robert Remington of the *National Post* reported, "Angry fans flooded the CBC with 10,000 emails and paraded in front of the network's headquarters in Toronto with bullhorns to protest the deposing of Mr. MacLean after contract talks broke down."

Cari and I received thousands of emails, great notes from people all over, and so did *HNIC*. Some were profane, several were angry, but most were funny. "Don't let him go, you guys are MORANS!" "The mouth doesn't function properly without the brain." "No Ron and I'm gone." Most people talked about how *HNIC* was part of their Canadian heritage and the CBC had no right to mess with it.

Not in a million years did I think there would be such an outpouring of support. I finally reached Meehan and told him, "I couldn't get through to you. My phone would not stop ringing!" Meehan told me people were demonstrating in front of CBC headquarters in Toronto. His office was deluged. He said, "We are avalanched with interest! I imagine CBC is getting the message that people liked what you and Don Cherry were doing."

Meehan laughed when he told me he had a call from his older sister, a retired housewife in Cambridge, Ontario. He said, "She watches *Hockey Night in Canada* every Saturday night. She's a hockey fan, but has never called me in relation to any of the negotiations of the players that I'm involved with. She told me, 'I want to make one thing clear with you. I look forward to watching Ron every Saturday night. You've got to do something to rectify this situation. I'm counting on you.'"

"Ron," he said, "I think the key point to consider is that there are forces at play. I mean, this thing has moved the throne speech off the front page. From my perspective, according to the reaction of the Canadian public, *Hockey Night in Canada* is an institution on Saturday nights, and people don't want CBC fooling around with it. It's a tradition."

Meehan told me Nancy Lee had asked to meet again. He said, "We have them where we want them. They're reacting to public pressure. I've never seen anything like it! We can throw the book at them."

I replied, "Well, that's not really what this was all about. I know that you positioned yourself well and you negotiated brilliantly. You know leverage better than anybody, but that wouldn't be the right thing to do."

We got into a bit of a wrestling match, with him trying to convince me to take advantage of what had happened. He said, "Ron, this has worked out perfectly for us. You took a huge risk. The country has responded the way they have, and this is going to be beneficial for you now."

I said, "No, Donnie, really. Go with the 6 per cent we negotiated with Nancy. It's fine." It was the principle all along. "If I go up $25,000 per year, I'll be happy." It was never about the money. It was about the respect. I realize I was pretty defensive. I was in a constant, almost painful quest for respect from the people I worked with. The remark about me having eighteen producers telling me what to say burned deep.

Cari and I took Mom and Dad for dinner at Catch, a new eatery in downtown Calgary. I joked that I'd better order fish because I needed brain food. During dinner, I got a call from

Bruce Elliot, who was president of Labatt and later was president of Second Cup until 2008. Labatt was the primary sponsor of *Hockey Night in Canada*. John Heinzl of the *Globe and Mail* had reported that the brewer had an estimated $5 million invested in *HNIC*, and its biggest worry was that fans would abandon its beer to protest my absence. Bruce said, "Because we have people picketing around our plant in Moncton, I'm going to let CBC know that their problem has become our problem." He said Labatt was working on a six-point resolution that it would deliver to the CBC so that the matter could be resolved. I replied, "Thanks for all your help, Bruce, but I think it's going to get resolved in the morning."

Meehan told me later that, irrespective of my wishes, he made it very clear to the CBC who had the leverage. When he arrived at their meeting, Nancy made no indication that they were back at the table because the network had miscalculated the public's wishes. Meehan said he was smiling when he asked, "So why *did* you ask to meet?"

She replied that the CBC had reflected and thought it was in the best interests of both parties—why disturb a relationship that has been so successful? They felt that maybe, with a little more effort, we could come up with something that would be suitable for both sides. Meehan loved it. Later, he told me, "It doesn't get any better than that."

On October 4, I spoke to William Houston at the *Globe and Mail*. I said I felt "a great overwhelming sense of appreciation for the viewers. It was typically Canadian. Everybody went to bat for me. What can I ever say to thank them?"

In the end, what mattered most was the way the people

reacted. I wanted the CBC to understand that it was wrong to come in and tell us what to say and do on our broadcast as if they knew better than we what was in our best interest. I was happy that the corporation finally understood that Grapes and I had a relationship with the show. The viewers put the CBC in their place.

When we did the first Coach's Corner a couple of weeks later, on Thanksgiving weekend, Grapes began with, "So what's new? Anything happen over the summer?" I answered, "Quiet. Quiet on that front." I was going to say, "I had it planned all along to sit down with a big turkey." But when it came time, I wasn't feeling it. I thought, "Screw it. Just thank people and get over yourself." So that's what I did.

Don Meehan never asked for a fee. I'd broach the subject of an invoice and he'd say, "We'll worry about that later." Finally, he said, "Ron, we're friends, forget it." Meehan is a wine collector, so I went down to our wine fridge and pulled a bottle of Mouton-Rothschild 1993, a rare French first growth. I also got him flowers. Fresh flowers every month for a year.

26

FRENCH IMMERSION

In the summer of 2003, I told a joke that was misinterpreted and that surfaced in the *Globe and Mail*.

On July 18, Don and I had driven out to the Charles W. Stockey Centre for the Performing Arts in Parry Sound, Ontario, on the shores of Georgian Bay. The event marked the opening of the new interactive museum, the Bobby Orr Hall of Fame, located in the building. Bobby's trophies were on display—the Canada Cup, the Hart, the Lester B. Pearson, the Art Ross, the Norris, the Conn Smythe and the Calder— and that day they also had the Stanley Cup on display. It was an unbelievable celebration, with at least three thousand people there. They were listening to a steel drum band, watching Aboriginal dancing, kids were getting their faces painted, and all kinds of food was laid out. It was a giant carnival.

At 1 p.m. I welcomed the crowd, and then Michael Burgess sang the Canadian national anthem in English and in French. I took the microphone again and mentioned that Grapes was in the crowd and would be speaking shortly. Don and I rarely spoke at the same occasions, kind of like Batman and Robin— they shine best when they are in the cave or fighting crime. I liked to tease Grapes, and so I thanked Michael Burgess for his beautiful rendition of the anthem, adding, "I know Don loves our anthem, but I am not sure he's thrilled about the middle part," meaning the French verse. "Remember, Don has nothing against French immersion. He figures we just don't hold them under long enough." I'd been telling that joke since 1996. Peter Mansbridge was always after me—"Ron, you can't say that!" But Don's joke was not about the French. It's just that he sees Quebec standing up for itself and making political gains the way he wishes Ontario would.

Several politicians got up to say a few words. Andy Mitchell, the secretary of state for rural development and for the federal economic development initiative for Northern Ontario, went on a little longer than most, and when he stepped down, I said, "Bobby, I wish your career had lasted as long as that speech." The crowd laughed. Everybody was in a good mood.

Finally, it was time for Grapes to come up. In 1974, when Don was just a rookie NHL coach with the Boston Bruins, the team had just received a new shipment of twenty-four hockey sticks. You can tell by the way Don dresses and by his big, ostentatious Lincolns that he is a bit of a neat freak. Everything has to be just so. He went into the dressing room, and he was surprised by this incredible mess of little wood chunks and sawdust everywhere. Someone had cut one-sixteenth off the top of each and every hockey stick. Don was really upset, and he started yelling, "Who's the kook cutting the tops off the hockey sticks?"

The team trainer was John "Frosty" Forristall, whose claim to fame under coach Harry Sinden was being the first to paint a stitch on Gerry Cheevers' goalie mask. Forristall looked at

Don and said, "Bobby Orr did it, Don." And Don said, "Well, in that case, what an interesting thing to do!"

I introduced Grapes. "Don has always been a big motivator. He told me about how, when he was a child, his father used to walk five miles to school with him every day. And of course, he had to—they were in the same class."

Grapes made his way to the stage, and the first thing he did was look up at the darkening sky and say, "Hmmm, the clouds are coming in—looks like a storm. Don't worry about it. Bobby can stop them." He turned to Bobby and smiled. "Bobby, hold the clouds back, will ya?" It was funny, and we all laughed. Grapes topped it off with an old but very good story he always tells about his first year in Boston, when Phil Esposito scored 61 goals and had 127 points.

Phil was the king of garbage goals. God help the goalie who let out a rebound when Phil was in the slot. In fact, the great hockey historian Stan Fischler called him the highest-paid garbage collector in the United States.

The next season, 1975–76, Phil was on a roll again. He had 16 points in 12 games. Phil loved playing with Bobby. They were magic together. But Phil didn't fly through the air like Bobby did, so he felt he didn't get the same credit. One day, Phil came to Don and said, "Grapes, it's always Bobby Orr this and Bobby Orr that. Once in a while, how about moving Bobby out of the way for me?"

A little while later, the team was on the road in Vancouver. Harry Sinden called Don and told him he had traded Phil to New York. Harry knew it would be tough news for Phil. He told Don, "Go get Bobby and take him with you when you tell

Esposito." So Bobby and Don knocked on Phil's hotel room door, and Phil answered. He was wearing a pair of fancy silk pyjamas. Don and Bobby exchanged looks. Don sat down, and Bobby went over to look out the window. Espo looked at Don and said, "Grapes, if you tell me I've been traded to the Rangers, I'm gonna jump out the window!" Grapes yelled, "Bobby, get away from that window!"

The crowd loved Don's story, and then Bobby spoke. It was all very funny and moving and altogether a wonderful event because everybody had a great time. We had a ball that day. Everybody was killing themselves laughing. I felt good.

Unbeknownst to me, the occasion was telecast live on CBC Newsworld, and Bill Houston from the *Globe and Mail* happened to be watching. He called Cari, and she called me while I was driving home. Houston wrote that I was "in hot water." He also accused me of being a potty mouth. He said I had "been criticized in the past for using off-colour jokes on the air." Houston's column went on to say, "Jacques Demers, a Stanley Cup–winning coach who now works in broadcasting in Quebec and has appeared several times on *Hockey Night*, said he was offended. 'I wasn't there, but I don't like what he said. I don't know what's the problem. I'm a French-Canadian, and I don't know why he's saying it.'" When Don questioned Jacques about it later, Jacques said, "Well, Don, I have to live here," which I thought summed it up nicely.

Houston's columns continued. The next week, he intimated I was a racist and quoted Mario Brisebois, a writer for *Le Journal de Montréal*, who compared the French immersion comment to someone saying "an ethnic group was all right depending on how long they had been hanging from a tree."

I've always been quite concerned about Don's and my beer-hall sensibility. Years earlier, I was speaking at a high school hockey tournament in Ontario, and a little kid came up to me and said, "Mr. MacLean, would you sign an autograph for my brother?" And the guidance counsellor who was showing me around asked him, "Did you want an autograph from Mr. MacLean too?" And the kid said, "No, no. Grapes is the man. Grapes is right—get rid of the foreigners." My world is filled with books on ethics, and I spend a lot of time thinking about the ethical aspects of what we do on Coach's Corner.

One person I've emailed from time to time is Anne Wortham, associate professor of sociology at Illinois State University. Anne wrote a piece called "Black Victimhood: A 'Paradoxical Sequel' to Civil Rights." What stands out in that article for me is how she discerns between a real victim and a perceived victim. She says that to be a real victim, you have to be injured either by being deprived of your dignity or your ability to work or by a similar transgression. Anne's paper said that people use victimhood to sashay politically. It does a great job of explaining how many people "cling to their group's history of previous injustice and in a current dispute or dilemma use that history to silence people who disagree with them and shut off debate." The stance of victimhood is a technique that can be used as an advantage.

In the case of the French immersion joke, there was no injury. No one was being marginalized or being denied opportunity. Anne's words resonated with me in regard to what Houston was writing.

My joke was studied and discussed to death. The CBC distanced themselves from it and me. They said I was at the event because Bobby had asked me, and it had nothing to do with the network. Cari was furious. She stepped up and told the papers to back off. She asked everyone else to lighten up. It was just a joke, for Pete's sake.

In 2004, there was a move afoot from certain corners of the organization to get rid of Grapes. A *Philadelphia Inquirer* article by Tim Panaccio quoted an unnamed source as saying, "There is a small but strong contingent of senior CBC staffers who 'want desperately' to jettison Cherry." It was no secret that, politically, Don wasn't their cup of tea. These men and women of letters were led by Harold Redekopp, the executive vice-president of CBC Television in charge of English-language television programming. He'd come from radio. Don's rough exterior turned Redekopp off. Harold was about to retire, and he took aim at CBC Television's number one son.

Don told me Harold Redekopp had said to him, "It will be my legacy to get rid of you." He would leave his mark by dumping Don Cherry. Some guys would have replied, "Screw you! After all I've done for you." But Don wouldn't take the bait. He would not show his cards. He was too wily.

Meanwhile, a lot of things happened that didn't forward Grapes's case. In January 2004, Grapes got into scalding water for insulting French guys and Europeans.

Grapes had a code that said you could wear a visor, but if you did you couldn't run around playing a physical game. He said that Ulf Samuelsson and Peter Forsberg, who both wore visors, ran around being reckless because the visors made them feel safe. He also noted that they were both born in Sweden. One time, when accused of calling Swedish hockey players chicken, Grapes said, "I have never called a Swede a chicken, because I have nothing against chickens."

When we launched into Coach's Corner on January 24, we reviewed a fight between Calgary's Jarome Iginla and Jordin Tootoo of the Nashville Predators. Don said, "You know what I think of Tootoo. I like him, but here is Iginla, a fifty-goal scorer fighting Tootoo, a six-goal scorer—Iginla's the most valuable player in the league last year, I think, and he breaks his hand? The career is over. That's the instigator rule. A teammate can't step in. The instigator rule—the worst in the world!"

Then we got into visors, and Grapes mentioned Tie Domi's ten-year-old son, Max, who played with Don's grandson, Del. "Max, he's tougher than Tie. He's Tie with hands! Tie never wore a mask. If he did, Max would have come in—'What are you doing, Dad? Turning into a suck?' You know, it's so politically correct. You can't win saying they shouldn't put on visors. I listen to the writers, I watch the TV guys, I hear the guy on the radio. They say, 'Bless your little hearts.' They are so worried about the guys having their visors on, what skin is it off their nose?"

Don was rolling now. He started firing his index finger at

the camera. "I said with helmets twenty years ago, we're going to have more head injuries. We're going to have more cuts—I predicted. And that's it!"

We looked at video of a few more guys getting roughed up, and Don started in on visors again. "And take a look at most of them—you check it—most of them have got visors on that do it. There's no respect at all. And I remember, I played when the helmets were just coming in, and I remember a guy named Bobby Barlow [with the Rochester Americans in 1967–68]. He played ten years, he put on the helmet and I couldn't believe it, he came to me and he said, 'I've been hit in the head more, crashed more, since I put the helmet on.'"

I tried to interject, but he swept me aside. "'Bless your little hearts,' all you sportswriters—you don't understand. It will be made mandatory, so you can go to bed at night and write 'those stupid hockey players.' But I'm going to tell you something—most of the guys that wear them are European or French guys."

I knew right away what Don said was not good. I also knew I had to stop him from airing further thoughts on French and European players. I searched for something to say to neutralize the situation. This was not going to be an easy fix.

I tried rephrasing his point. "Take a look at Tootoo and Iginla. You might have been right at one point because of the way it was implemented in European hockey first, but now everybody—40 per cent of the NHL's wearing a mask."

Don hammered home his original point. "Absolutely, and most of the guys—the tough guys like Tie Domi—cannot wear them. They will make it mandatory. There is no doubt about it. And it's a sad thing. We've gone from helmets to— well, it's a sad thing . . ."

Fearing he was headed back for trouble again, I tried to interrupt, but he started jabbing me in the lapel, shouting over me.

"I predicted! Did I not predict?"

"Yes!" I agreed, and sat on the edge of my seat, ready to jump in while he finished his point.

"Concussions and cuts! And they're there. The proof is in the pudding. The do-gooders, the whiners and the ones on TV and the writers who don't understand, you've won again!"

I said, "All right. Well, I'll ask you, what should they do with major penalties?"

Don shouted, "Give him a major penalty! A guy cuts a guy, give him a major. Never mind this four minutes. Get him out of the game!"

I said, "All right. All in favour of visors say 'aye.' I feel so much better that you're going to let us have it. On the Coach's Corner on *Hockey Night in Canada* on CBC. We can all sleep tonight."

But not everyone did.

The phones lit up, and Harold Redekopp sprang into action. He issued a statement saying that Grapes "unacceptably stepped beyond [his] role by expressing an inappropriate and reprehensible personal opinion."

All this wasn't making what Don had said any easier to ignore. It caught the attention of the Official Languages Commissioner, Dyane Adam. She announced she was going to launch a formal investigation into what Don had said in case he had breached the Official Languages Act.

Redekopp released a statement. "CBC Television categorically rejects and denounces the personal opinions Mr. Cherry expressed during the segment." Redekopp and CBC president Robert Rabinovitch put Coach's Corner on a seven-second delay, which meant the guys in the production truck had a chance to hear what we said seven seconds before it went over the air. If they didn't like it, they could cut it out.

Don's job was in serious jeopardy. His contract was up at the end of the year, and I was worried the visor remark might be the excuse they'd use not to renew it. Then Nancy Lee decided not to assign Don to the World Cup of Hockey that August. They hired Brian Burke instead.

There was tension all around. I remember going into the Air Canada Lounge in Montreal. The women working at the counter were hot at Grapes. They asked me, "How can you work with that horse's ass?"

I took up Don's cause with our bosses. I wrote a letter to Nancy and said, "Do you think that Don pointing out that Peter Forsberg and Joe Sakic and Luc Robitaille and Jarome Iginla and all these guys are wearing visors is in any way hurting their careers? Does that make them victims? Are they going to be paid less in their next contract because Don Cherry has said this?" In my mind, French and European players might have been annoyed by what Grapes said, but their careers were not impacted. I felt it was like Anne Wortham's idea of a completely false sense of victimhood. The only people I heard complaining were reporters, a couple of politicians and Dr.

Emile Therien, president of the Canada Safety Council. He was a driving force behind the requirement that junior and minor hockey players wear visors. Interestingly, his son Chris played for the Philadelphia Flyers, and Don always thought it was a little bit of poetic justice that Chris played without any face protection.

The *Globe and Mail* ran an article by Gayle MacDonald at the end of April with the headline "The Puck Stops Here for Grapes." It started out with a quote. "'The love-hate relationship between the CBC and Don Cherry is so strained that the two sides are preparing to sever their 23-year relationship at the end of the Stanley Cup playoffs,' said a long-time friend of Mr. Cherry, who asked not to be named. 'Harold [Redekopp, executive vice-president of CBC TV] and Bob [Rabinovitch, CBC president] have the biggest issues with Don,' said the source. 'And the ironic thing is those two guys are leaving the company' . . . Mr. Cherry says he hopes he and Mr. MacLean don't part ways. 'Although I sometimes don't understand him, and I don't like his left-wing thinking and he's a referee . . . I still have fun with him doing Coach's Corner, and I can't imagine being on television without him. Oh God, I've never said that before. He's going to think I'm going nuts.'"

On Monday, June 7, we covered game seven of the Stanley Cup final between the Calgary Flames and Tampa Bay Lightning. At the end of the game, in which the Lightning won the Cup, Don and I sat down for our traditional beer. He was unusually quiet. I could tell he was concerned about not coming back. He was thinking he might have just done his last Coach's Corner.

That was the final straw. I got hold of Ivan Fecan—I was ready to move. I had three years remaining on my contract, but there was a ninety-day termination clause available to either side, and I was ready to use it.

Ivan and CTV president Rick Brace arranged to meet me at the Toronto Club on Wellington Street, Canada's oldest private club, founded in 1835. There are only three hundred members. You have to be invited to join, and five to ten members have to vouch for you. The red-brick clubhouse is built in the Renaissance Revival style, which has an austere, Victorian look, with small square windows on the upper floor. I was ushered in the front door, and the smell of old polished oak and cigars filled my nose. I spotted Ivan immediately. He had the most beautiful hair—a long, white mane, just like Emmylou Harris. The meeting was very hush-hush. The maître d' was to meet me and bring me to a side room. I tried not to make it appear too obvious that it was my first time there. The food was delicious (I had trout). We ate and worked out the big move. I don't remember if we talked about money.

Later that day, I sat down with Grapes and ran the conversation by him. He didn't want us to move to TSN either, but he realized we might have to. Grapes thought he was toast at the CBC.

I called Don Meehan to ask him his thoughts about what had developed. He said two things. First, he reminded me about our contract negotiation two years earlier. He said, "Let me understand where you're going here, because this was important to you and this is what you gave up then. You gave up the opportunity for much more money then. Why the turnaround now? Why would this option be viable now?" Then he said that *Hockey Night in Canada* was an institution, and he asked what made me happy. "Do you like what you do, how you support the game of hockey? And what about all of the charitable endeavours you are involved in? Your profile is what helps them." Of course, none of that mattered, because I was acting out of spite. Then he said, "Any show outside of *Hockey Night in Canada* would be a notch below."

I told him I would think about what he'd said.

I needed a break, so I played a game of beer-league hockey and had a couple with my buddies. Chasing the puck is good that way. I went to bed feeling antsy. Meehan's advice stuck with me. I tossed and turned and finally got up and went to my computer. I emailed Rick Brace at 3 a.m. and said, "Rick, I feel badly, but I just can't do it."

Meehan had known Brace a long time. He followed up with an email, being gracious and thankful for their interest, but letting them know that, at that time, I was going to stay where I was.

I'm not sure whether the CBC got a whiff of what had happened, but getting rid of Don was suddenly taken off the table. And life returned to normal.

27

I WALK THE LINE

Grapes and I are like Frick and Frack. We argue just as much on the plane, in the car or at the hotel after the game as we do on the air, but not always with the same energy. It sounds a lot meaner when you only have a couple of minutes to get your point across. The fact that we don't always agree helps us get along, in a funny way. He sees things as black and white, and has incredible standards and expectations for himself and everyone else. My opinions lie more in the grey areas in between, and I've always said, "Never have expectations. Expectations will kill you." This is my own take on accepting people and things that are outside our control. I always had a sense that the Golden Rule was wrong. That's just bartering. I think you should do unto others what is right, and expect nothing in return.

Nevertheless, Don and I are similar men. I hate to call us cynics. "Skeptics" would be a better word. I think that has been part of the magic of our relationship.

I considered calling this book *Hockey Knights* because, although I know it's audacious, I see similarities between Don and me and the two guys from one of the greatest books ever written, *The Ingenious Gentleman Don Quixote of La Mancha*.

Don Quixote was a knight, and his buddy, Sancho Panza, was his squire. Cervantes wrote about their friendship and their exploits. They set out to perform daring feats in the name of honour, bravery and chivalry to garner the admiration of the masses, and that invited one disaster after another. It's funny because Don and I can be delusional about our "enemies." And when we've targeted society's actions and ideals surrounding war, or issues in Quebec or the treatment of First Nations people, we've ended up with conflicting, troublesome and at times hilarious results. And when Quixote and Panza's adventures were complete or the show was over, they entered into a dialogue about it.

Don and I have built a life around conversation over beers at night. We throw several subjects on the table and then, through discussion, decide whether each would be good for *Hockey Night*. In May 2011, Bob Nicholson ripped into star players in the NHL who did not show up for the International Ice Hockey Federation World Championship in Slovakia. Dan Barnes of Postmedia News quoted Nicholson as saying, "I think there is a certain time that players should be here. I'm not going to identify those players, but those players know who they are" and "You know what, Hockey Canada and Canada have been pretty good to those players through the under-18s, the juniors and Olympic Games. I thought they would have thought about that before refusing to come this year. The bottom line is, it comes down to the player. Every player has their own reasons, some of them are very good for personal reasons, some are a little lame."

Don thought he had a point. But I put a bug in Don's ear. Because the event is Hockey Canada and the IIHF's baby,

Nicholson has a vested interest. I said I thought it was typical of Canadian hockey to try to curry favour with IIHF president René Fasel rather than sticking up for Canadian players.

First of all, why was there no thought that each player he slammed had just played ninety games, plus a round of the playoffs? Each guy is beat up and battered and desperate for a break. He hasn't seen his family in weeks. Most were members of the World Junior team that generated many millions of dollars for Hockey Canada. And how much of that money gets streamed back to the players? I would love to know what the cut of that is.

I also find it disingenuous of the NHL to complain about Olympic participation. The NHL always goes on about how it is offering up two billion dollars' worth of inventory, the products of their own resources, to make the Olympic Games, when really it's minor hockey that develops these NHL stars. Minor hockey bears the cost of developing the next Sidney Crosby, and yet the NHL has the audacity to say, "We should get special treatment because these are our guys." Well, they weren't your guys until they turned eighteen. What does the NHL do to support minor hockey, the program that makes these guys? Very little.

Hashing out the whole issue over Nicholson's remarks is typical of how the seeds are sown on what we discuss on *HNIC*. That particular conversation hasn't yet come up on the show—in fact, it may never come up. But a crack that I make weeks, months, maybe even years ago will be brought back verbatim if I offer a cue. It's amazing how Don locks away these discussions and just pounces on them every time the bait is thrown.

Not once, but maybe two thousand times, Don has said to

me, "Perception is reality, Ron." When I picked up Grapes at his Mississauga home for the very first time, there was a huge rawhide bone in the front entrance. Don said, "Ron, with you gone so much, you should buy a big bone like this one and leave it inside the front door. The burglar comes, sees that bone and thinks, "Good grief, if that's the size of the bone, imagine the dog!"

Don and I have had a lot of discussions on the issue of moving franchises back to Canada. One night, I pointed out some problems with having a team back in Winnipeg. Don thought I was crazy and told me he thought the franchise would be a roaring success. He told me I should just shut up and quit whining about it. I agreed he was right for the moment, because the U.S. economy is in desperate shape. "But," I said, "Don, Don, it's Winnipeg. There is a chance that if the dollar fluctuates and goes back to 65 cents U.S., the franchise will be in huge trouble. You wouldn't be a journalist worth your salt if you didn't point that out. And what kind of journalist would you be if you didn't report that for us at the CBC, the increase of Canadian teams from six out of thirty to seven out of thirty translates to higher ratings for *Hockey Night in Canada?*" Mind you, that financial windfall is tempered by the fact that we can't possibly program all the Canadian teams on one channel at the same time, so we have more competition from other channels. My point with Grapes is that a journalist has to look at all the angles. It's not whining, it's just being realistic about the concerns.

During the finals, Don and I had quite an argument in the car about tipping. Ken, our limo driver in Vancouver, is quite the card—really good company. Don wanted to take care of paying him, so he handed Ken his plastic and said, "Here, take my credit card and add twenty bucks."

When Grapes played, hockey players were notoriously tight with a buck. And when Grapes would go out to the bar, he had rules. You don't go drinking if you don't pay your way. If Don saw somebody sneaking away without putting in his twenty bucks, he'd call him out. He'd stand up and say, "Hey! You're not leaving. I didn't see you put in a twenty." And a big fight would ensue. So he thought he was doing well with the tip, and thirty years ago he'd be right. I said quietly, "Grapes, you can't just add twenty bucks to whatever it is—it could be a $400 bill." He said, "No, no, for *each trip* I want him to add $20." I said, "I know, Don, but if the game goes into triple overtime and Ken is sitting outside in the limo waiting for us, that's not enough." Grapes was getting hotter and hotter as we talked about it. He felt I was being ridiculous and that he was being perfectly fair. But the next morning, he came to breakfast and said, "All right, all right, forget it. You take care of the limo."

The night of the last game of the Stanley Cup final, Don gave himself a self-talk. "Don't take the bait if Ron spouts off one of his stupid left-wing, liberal philosophies. Just don't bite. We've had a great run here, let's not go out fighting like we always do." He came up to the room for beers with a resolve to behave. He admits that he tends to get quite miserable toward the end of the season. We are both tired, and I think he has withdrawal symptoms. I'd ordered up two Whistler lagers to toast the completion of our twenty-fifth year on Coach's Corner together. When there is cause for celebration, I like to order "cocktail" beers.

After four or five pops, he got into a bit of a lather about our opening. He took me to task for the music that was chosen for the show that night. He especially hated "One" by U2, which ran under the closing montage. He felt it was girly—a bunch of guys who sound like teenage girls, singing about how sad life is. And then he mentioned a commercial that Telus was running. It features two gorgeous birds, cockatoos or parakeets. The music under it is AC/DC's "Thunderstruck"—a great rock and roll riff. The commercial is magnificent. The birds land with their wings spread like capes on superheroes. And the song adds rock and roll and energy. But Don disagreed. "You and your friggin' artsy fartsy thing!" He banged his head against the wall with each word for emphasis.

Don gets really wound up about the music. Years ago, during the 1993 final between Montreal and Los Angeles, I chose the music for the opening of the fifth and final game: "The Lion Sleeps Tonight" by the Tokens. After the game, he gave it to me in spades. I tried to explain that I'd chosen that song because the Canadiens are called the Lions of Winter, and in the song the lion is somewhere in the jungle. You can just imagine me trying to tell this story. We started in on the beers and he took a swig. "Oh, I got it. Now give me this again? The trees. The lion in the trees has been sleeping. Is that it? And now you're telling me 'o-weem-o-way.' What the hell is o-weem-o-way? And how does it fit in to the Stanley Cup final?" I tried to explain, but he carried on, refusing to let it go until we were laughing so hard that we were spitting beer.

Harold Bloom, in his book *Where Shall Wisdom Be Found?*, says that Don Quixote and Sancho Panza figure out the truth through conversations. Bloom says people have great trouble breaking out of the "prison of themselves." But in Cervantes' book, Quixote and Panza really hear one another, and they can change. Drinking beers in hotel rooms with Grapes after a game has provided some of my most illuminating moments.

Quixote and Panza, like Grapes and me, have a pattern of arguing and then reconciling, and we never fail one another in love, loyalty or mutual respect.

Sometimes the lively hotel-room banter spills over to the show, and the results can be messy. I don't know why, but I feed on trouble. It's my meat. On March 8, 2007, Chris Simon, a tough left winger with a scoring touch who was in his fourteenth NHL season, was playing a home game with the Islanders against the Rangers. In the middle of the third period, he was checked by Ryan Hollweg, who was trying to make a name for himself as an enforcer. Hollweg had twenty-one fights with the Hartford Wolf Pack of the American Hockey League in 2004–05, the year before he made it to the Rangers. And in 2006–07, his first full season with the Rangers, he ended up getting into thirteen scraps altogether. Simon had just five fights that same year, and spent 75 minutes in the penalty box to Hollweg's 131.

Hollweg came at Simon from behind, knocking him face first into the boards. There was no whistle on the play, so Simon took matters into his own hands when Hollweg skated by, catching him on the chest under the chin with his stick.

Simon received a twenty-five-game suspension, which is huge. It covered the rest of the season and five games of 2007–08. Just two games after the suspension ended, Jarkko Ruutu was chirping at Simon's teammate Tim Jackman. Simon skated up from behind, pulled Ruutu down and stomped on his leg with his skate. Ruutu is a pest who deserves some trouble, but maybe not that.

When Simon stomped Ruutu, there was a big stink about it. Ken Campbell of *The Hockey News* said, "What Simon did Saturday night should finally get him expelled from the NHL for good. And if the league doesn't have the gumption to do it, then the New York Islanders should."

I emailed Matt Brown, who is a teacher at the Edge School in Calgary. He's also an expert in both sports psychology and physiology. I'd read a novel Matt had written called *Shift*, about a rising hockey star who almost loses his career when he loses his values. Matt is a confidant when I want to talk about the psychology of athletics.

I asked Matt for his opinion on repeat offenders. He raised the point that First Nations children (Simon's dad is Ojibwa) often feel that they don't get a fair shake in life. Therefore, Simon might not have thought that the first suspension was legit. He may have felt he had been racially profiled.

On Coach's Corner on December 23, 2007, five days after Simon's second suspension, for his attack on Ruutu (he got thirty games), Grapes defended Simon. Dressed in a big, shiny, red jacket with a huge tie featuring Santa in an opalescent beard, Grapes began, "Now listen, kids. We love Santa. We have to say it. I have to say it. We love Santa. Everybody loves Santa. But remember December the twenty-fifth . . . baby Jesus' birthday. We must keep that in mind. We love Santa, but it's baby Jesus' birthday. I had to get that in. We love Santa, but let's not be silly."

I wished everyone a Merry Christmas, and then we went to video of Chris Neil of Ottawa getting two minutes for shoving Jarkko Ruutu's brother Tuomo. Grapes hated the way the Ruutu brothers chirped at other players, and thought they deserved to be taught a lesson. "Watch him laugh—look, look, look, look. Wouldn't you like to go up and smack that guy? I gotta be careful. When Simon got in trouble, a lot of people said a few things, and I said a few things, but those guys asked for it and they got it."

Grapes cautioned the "kids out there" not to stomp other players with their skates. "You never do anything like that. Never, ever do anything like that. But you can understand it somehow."

Then he chastised the league for being too tough on Simon. "And by the way, I have to say something. Those last two incidents that he's done, he's got fifty-five games. You know how many games his victims missed playing?" Grapes made a big zero with his index finger and thumb. "None. I'm not making an excuse for it—none—I just thought you'd like to know that. Now, I have said many, many times—how many times have I said, going back thirty years, I try to talk to people—you know, I see these media guys and stuff like that and jack-of-all-trades . . . I try to tell people that if Chris wanted to hurt him, he could have hurt him bad. The same thing with . . . Hollweg, was it?"

I nodded, "Right."

"Hollweg, when you try to say that if he wanted to hurt him, he could've, and the hockey people—I know it sounds terrible, but he let up and he hit him on the chest. Now, this could've been avoided, all this stuff could've been avoided, this last one here, if they had listened to me thirty years ago. Why they have the benches on the same side is beyond me."

I held up my finger. "Before we continue, can I just say the thing that I wanted to say to add to that? 'Cause people say, 'How in the world can Colin Campbell and the league give him just thirty games when he got twenty-five and the message didn't sink in?' And I have a theory on that too." And I brought up the idea Matt Brown and I had discussed. "You'll have to ask Chris Simon if this is how he feels, but a lot of First Nations kids go to bed at night and wake up in the morning feeling they won't get a fair shake in life, and he may not have thought that twenty-five—"

Don groaned.

I pointed at him, "Just what you said about Ryan Hollweg! He may have thought [the suspension] was ridiculous."

Don held up his hand. He had a list of things to talk about and wanted to get on with it. "Well—"

But I was a little hot and pressed my point. "He may have thought . . . that's why . . . just 'cause he got twenty-five doesn't mean . . ." I could see a smile playing on Don's lips. He thought I was just spouting "liberal crap."

"No, I'm serious!"

Still in a relatively good mood, he shrugged. "All right."

I had a full head of steam. "You have to ask Chris, but . . . thirty is good, the league has shown that obviously you can't cross that line, but until Chris accepts that he's getting a fair shake, the message won't sink in. That's a little defence of him, too, to go along with what you're saying." I paused and ceded to Don. "Benches on the same side . . ." But it was too late. I had tugged on his cape.

"What are you saying, that uh . . . Natives have an inferiority complex? That when something happens to them—"

At this point, I realized it wasn't a reasoned discussion. I thought, "This is not working. It's gone off the rails." I said, "I'm saying, why wouldn't they? Why wouldn't some kids feel like they haven't been given a fair shake in life? Ask Davis Inlet." In the 1950s, the Canadian government forced a number of Innu off their traplines and relocated them to Davis Inlet, an isolated spot on the coast of Labrador that lacked even running water.

"Fair shake in life!" Don shouted. "Go out and get your own fair shake in life and work for it!"

I closed my eyes and hung my head, thinking, "How do I pull out of this?"

I held up my hand. "Don . . . that's—"

"Don't give me that stuff. It's like when Ted Nolan didn't get the job . . ."

My eyes rolled heavenward. Nolan, who is Ojibwa, grew up on a reserve near Sault Ste. Marie, Ontario. He had eleven brothers and sisters and learned to play hockey on frozen ponds. He made it to the NHL with the Pittsburgh Penguins in 1985, until a back injury ended his career. He wound up coaching with the Buffalo Sabres, but repeatedly clashed with his general manager, John Muckler, and was fired after two years, even though he took the Sabres to the Cup final in 1999. They both denied rumours that Ted was undisciplined off the ice and that Muckler was a racist.

Don defended Muckler. "[They said when] Ted Nolan didn't get the job, it was racism. It wasn't racism! Him and Muckler got at it, and that's why he got fired!"

When Nolan was fired, there was a tremendous backlash. Two hundred people showed up outside the Marine Midland

Arena in Buffalo, chanting his name. The rally was organized by the New York chapter of the American Indian Movement. Jean Knox, whose husband, Seymour Knox III, had founded the Sabres, was part of it. After that, no one would touch Nolan.

I said, "Well, since you bring that up, if you were an NHL club and you saw all the reaction when Ted was fired in Buffalo, wouldn't you be a little leery of hiring him a second time?"

Don said, "Well, yeah . . ."

I said, "So he is in a case where prejudice—"

Don shook his head, "Wasn't racism though, it was because—"

I said, "Yes, it is."

Don said, "No, it isn't! It was between him and the GM, that's why he didn't get it. It wasn't racism at all and . . ." Still angry, but wisely realizing we were stomping into dangerous territory, he held his hand up in front of my face. "Let's never get into that again." He gritted his teeth and, angry about losing the time to talk about everything he had planned, he said, "I've lost the whole thing."

I bumbled around. I held my hands up, trying to calm the storm. "That's good. That's good."

He said, "No, it isn't! Well, we might as well just sit here, then. How much time do we have left?"

I said, "No, we got a couple minutes for sure, or three . . ."

"A couple minutes? A couple minutes?" Petulantly, he leaned back and waved his hand dismissively. "Well, let's go to the troops [the final feature]."

"No, we've got more time than that," I cajoled. "It's Christmas. Let's get back into the Christmas spirit."

"No, no, no, I had nine thousand things I wanted to talk about."

I tried to be reassuring. "Well, we've got lots of time—"

He threw a bah-humbug wave toward the camera. "We'll talk about them next week."

With three minutes of dead air looming, I said, "No, no, come on. We can do it! We've got to do it."

"Do what?"

I started to count off on my fingers all the things he wanted to talk about. "Well, listen, we'll make a little truce here. The benches on the same side is one thing you recommended . . ."

He threw his hands in the air. "No! You ruined the whole thing. The whole thing is—"

I was worried that I'd just sent him to the gallows. I continued to try to dig us out. "The other thing you said is, puck over the glass, and sure enough, it showed up . . . foot in the crease, it showed up . . . touch icing, the players have all said it . . . instigator rule . . ." He looked at me stone-faced. I wasn't getting anywhere. I said, "So why don't we show Sid the Kid?"

He wasn't buying it. He narrowed his eyes at me. "You wanna show him? Show him, then. Go ahead."

"Sure!" And as we went to video of Sidney Crosby, I continued my attempt to placate him. "We'll do this instead of the benches on the same side, but you were right—"

"Yes, yes, I guess so," he said sarcastically.

"Sid would be pleased to make Coach's Corner."

"Oh, I guess he would. Yeah, sure." Then he said, "I gotta show him, because I show Lecavalier and I show the rest of the guys. So I gotta show him."

"It's good."

"Keeps 'em all happy." He imitated players whining at him, "Oh, Don . . . Donnn . . ."

In the video, Crosby deked Bruins defenceman Andrew Ference and scored. Meanwhile, Don continued spouting off on everything that was bugging him. Referring to Ference, he said, "Look at Dr. Suzuki there, that left winger . . ." I'd done an interview with Andrew the previous week, and he had brought up the issue of greenhouse-gas emissions and talked about how the teams were donating money to offset whatever carbon emissions their flights created.

Grapes considered Ference to be in lockstep with the environmentalist David Suzuki and was disgusted by it.

" . . . that 'Sky Is Falling' Suzuki . . ."

"Ahhh," I sighed.

Still stewing, Grapes said, "That was sickening last week, by the way."

"What? What is going on with you here?"

"That junk! That's not . . . What is this stuff going on here?" We were back on camera now, and Don continued to vent. "We're *Hockey Night in Canada* and we're talking about saving the world and all that stuff. Let's talk hockey."

I tried to keep it light. "Well, that's the whole idea behind December the twenty-fifth!"

"Let's talk about some *good* guys."

I said, "Okay!"

"Let's talk about the troops." We went to stills of the troops in Afghanistan, having Christmas dinner. "Now let's show the troops here. We're gathered around turkeys and having a good time. Look what these guys are gathered around." Don wanted the second slide, which showed the troops hunkered down, surrounded by their munitions, but it was late coming up. Impatient, he shouted, "Show the next one! Look what these guys are gathered around. Ammo! They're the guys over there. God love you. We want you to come back. That's the Van Doos. *Bonne chance*—is that what you say? Anyhow, they're good guys, God love ya, come back, and all the troops overseas, but especially those guys. I'm out!"

In our debriefing, Grapes said, "You know, Ron, you live in the land of Billiken."

"What?"

"Billiken," he repeated. "That's the god of the things as they ought to be."

And a few days later, he gave me a statue of the elflike creature. He'd found it in Kingston in 1952. According to legend, it brings good luck if you find it, and even more if you steal it.

There was a media backlash against my land-of-Billiken outlook on Chris Simon. *Toronto Star* TV critic Chris Zelkovich jumped on me for what an irresponsible tack I had taken—what a silly question I had raised. Tom Benjamin, a blogger I respected, wrote, "Ron's way off base with this notion."

And do you know who else was on Don's side? Phil Lafontaine, national chief of the Assembly of First Nations. Somehow, I got to be the bad guy for bringing up this ridiculous notion that First Nations kids feel victimized. It was just like the debate I had in Grade 12, when the class took my opponent's side. I thought, "I either articulated this very poorly or came across as too arrogant. I guess I'll never learn."

28

A FAIRY-TALE ENDING

My first Olympic assignment was in 1988 in Seoul, South Korea. The schedule was a killer. From 9 a.m. to 5 p.m., I did play-by-play of field hockey in Seongnam. It was assumed that, because I knew ice hockey, I would know field hockey. The players carry sticks, but that's where the resemblance ends. Then, from 9 p.m. to 1 a.m., I took over the host's desk. After my shift, I would re-tape the openings, because they would be aired on a tape-delayed basis to different parts of Canada. And so I would get out of there at two in the morning, get back to the hotel at maybe 2:30, get up four hours later and work another eighteen-hour day—and repeat, for sixteen days in a row. But I was twenty-eight years old—no sweat.

Just ahead of the field hockey games, I'd get to the stadium, and I'd have to do my business. They had Asian toilets, which are no fun. Each is a porcelain bowl, set flush with the floor, with grooves for your feet. You assume a crouching position as if you are downhill skiing. It's basically a hole in the ground.

In all, I spent a month in South Korea, because there were two weeks of preparation leading up to the Games, and then the Games themselves. On day fifteen of the competition, a few days before it was time to go home, South Korea qualified for the gold medal match in women's field hockey. Seong-nam Stadium was packed. I got there as usual and went into the bathroom. I hit the first stall—it was occupied. Second stall? Occupied. There were sixteen stalls. I went all the way down to the end, opened the last one, and discovered a North American toilet. It turned out there were eight Asian toilets and eight North American toilets. For an entire month, I had painfully stretched my hamstrings using a Korean toilet, and now, on the second-to-last day of the Olympic Games, I discovered the real deal.

Ben Johnson was busted for using the steroid stanozolol after running the 100 metres in a world record 9.79 seconds and winning the gold medal, all of which was later erased from the record books. But what do I remember about the 1988 Olympics? Those damn toilets.

My next Olympic experience was in Albertville, France, in 1992. One morning, we were supposed to cover cross-country skiing, but it was postponed because of inclement weather. So we prepared to go to our second event, in the town of Pralognan-la-Vanoise—women's curling. Curling was a demonstration sport at these Games. Canada was to play on sheet number two. But there was a problem with the ice-making equipment at the venue. Only the outside sheets, numbers one and four, were usable, so Canada's game was postponed.

We were six hours ahead of the Eastern time zone. It was 3 p.m. in France, which made it 9 a.m. in most of Ontario and Quebec. I signed on and said that, unfortunately, the women's match that was supposed to be broadcast was not being played because they were "having trouble between the sheets, like so many of you last night." I got a call from Alan Clark and Doug Sellars, admonishing me for my juvenile humour. "You're thirty-two years old. Surely you have a little more maturity than that."

It was a tough Olympics for Canada—the first week was a bust. Figure skater Kurt Browning, the three-time world champion, was expected to be one of our heroes, but he had a bad experience. He'd injured his back. I watched him skate onto the ice for the short program, and his face was ashen. Within ten seconds, he went Bambi while attempting his combination jump. I was in the kiss-and-cry area—so called because it's where the skaters wait with parents and coaches to receive their marks. I sat there thinking, "Good God, what do I ask him when he comes over?" Tracy Wilson, the former Canadian bronze-medal ice dancer, was working for CBS. She was right beside me with Katarina Witt and Verne Lundquist. I said to Tracy, "Any recommendation on what I say to kid-glove the interview when he comes off the ice? Because I know he'll be devastated."

She said, "Well, Ron, his choreography was spot-on. He clearly designed a program that would appeal to a French audience, and they embraced it fully. You can compliment him on the choreography and then just say, 'But obviously, the combination jump at the beginning was a problem.'" Tracy had given me a point of entry. She was right, and I was your host-with-the-most, an expert, although I had never seen a live figure skating performance in my life. But even I could see that Kurt was the only one who moved exactly to the notes. Every little motion was in sync with the music. I knew he was special, even if he had a horrible result that day.

In men's hockey, Canada was playing in the quarter-final

against Germany, and that should have been be a gimme. We should have blown them away and moved on. But we were tied 3–3 after regulation. And nothing was decided in the ten-minute overtime, so the game went to a shootout.

I was watching from down at one end of the arena in Méribel. Sitting to my right was Marcel Aubut, who at the time was the president and CEO of the Quebec Nordiques. Next to him was Rangers president Glen Sather. They were trying to figure out who Canada's coach, Dave King, was going to select as the five shooters.

Jim Peplinski, the former Calgary Flame, was upstairs in the booth, working as a colour man. He was with Don Wittman, who was calling the game. In my earpiece, I heard Peplinski say they'd been given Dave King's list of shooters before the game: Joé Juneau; Dave Archibald; Wally Schreiber, a good penalty killer; Jason Woolley, a defenceman, which was unusual; and Eric Lindros. I nudged Aubut and handed him the list. He said, "Are those your picks, Ron?"

I said, "No, these are the actual picks. Dave King gave us the list before the game." Aubut looked at me with an instant smile. He elbowed Sather, who hadn't heard our conversation, and said, "Do you want to wager on the five guys? We can bet the tab for dinner tonight."

Sather took the bet. The shootout started. By the time Wally Schreiber, the third shooter and an unlikely pick, came out, Sather was kind of mad. He couldn't believe that Aubut had got it right. And then the fourth guy, Woolley, hit the ice, and Sather was very upset. He slammed his list down and yelled, "Cockroach!"

Here I was at the Olympic Games, with Canada's medal hopes going down the drain. I knew I should be totally invested in watching the shootout, but I couldn't take my eyes off the interaction between these two guys.

The teams went through their five shooters and the game was still tied. And then Eric Lindros scored, while Sean Burke stopped Germany's Peter Draisaitl. Canada won the semifinal against the Czechs and lost in the final to the "Unified Team," also known as the CIS (Commonwealth of Independent States), which by either name was the former Soviet Union.

I got up on the morning of February 15, 1992, and turned on the TV. Everything was in French because we didn't have the CBC feed in our hotel rooms. The seventeenth skier was on the course, and across the bottom of the screen her name was posted—Kerrin Lee-Gartner of Canada—and her time to beat. But I don't speak French, so I couldn't understand what the announcers were saying.

There were several bottles of a fizzy orange drink called Orangina stacked in the cool air outside on the windowsill, and I was grabbing one when I said to Cari, "You know what? I think Kerrin Lee-Gartner is leading the downhill!"

The race ended, and I phoned around and confirmed that Kerrin had indeed won the gold. She was the first Canadian downhill racer to ever win an Olympic gold medal. There was total jubilation all over the country. Later, in the studio, where I sat with the crew waiting for her to arrive, all of us were falling in love with this rosy-cheeked, sandy-haired athlete and her Cinderella story.

It started when Kerrin was very young. Several uncanny

things happened. She grew up in Nancy Greene's hometown of Rossland, British Columbia. Nancy was Canada's top ski racer in the 1960s. She paved the way for future generations in the sport. Everyone called her Nancy Greenski, and in a 1999 Canadian Press survey she was voted Canada's female athlete of the twentieth century.

When Kerrin was small, she was up on a hill near her home, wearing a snowmobile outfit and leather boots, sliding along on wooden skis, holding two long poles taller than she was. The local newspaper snapped a photo, and the next day it ran with the caption, "Is this the next Nancy in the making?"

In a small town, people know and care for each other. Kerrin knew Nancy's parents. She would go for tea with Nancy's mom, Helen, and her father, Bob. She'd knock on their door and they'd let her go into Nancy's room to play dress-up with Nancy's medals.

Kerrin's future husband, Max Gartner, had played pro soccer in Austria and Germany. He then started working for the Canadian junior ski team, where he met Kerrin. They married in 1985. Kerrin and Max were an outdoorsy, wholesome couple, likeable and understated.

Max worried about Kerrin. First, she was in the most dangerous sport in the world for women. And second, he knew that Kerrin was convinced she was going to win the Olympic gold medal in the ladies' downhill in 1988. When it didn't happen, Kerrin was devastated. Max, who was her coach, thought, "Oh my God, she really thinks that winning gold is her destiny." When 1992 came around and Kerrin had another chance, he was so anxious for her, he could barely hold it together.

Canadians woke up hearing that an unknown had just won gold in the downhill. Kerrin had tried to speak with her folks by cellphone at the finish line, and they did connect for about twenty seconds, but she couldn't hear them. Between the flower ceremony, the urine test, the media conference and the lead-up to the medal ceremony, Kerrin and Max were whisked thirty minutes by car over to our studio, where I was hosting the morning portion of the Olympics.

They rushed in, happy and excited, but very low-key. I think they were in a state of shock. We went live immediately. We talked for about five minutes, reviewing the race, and then I pointed to my ear. I said, "I'm having a really tough time doing the interview. There's a constant distraction in my earpiece. I don't know . . . Terry, Jane, can you hear? Ron MacLean?"

We heard Kerrin's dad, Terry, respond. "Yes, I can."

Kerrin's eyes widened and she slapped her leg. "No way!"

Terry and Jane congratulated their daughter, and then Terry said, "Kerrin, you may have done the skiing, but I think you and Max won this race. I'm so, so proud of both of you."

Kerrin took Max's hand. "Oh, thank you. We're pretty proud at the moment too."

I said, "Well, you should be. Canada has a hero. Thank you so much for joining us in Tsawwassen, and I know you'll be at the Canadians. Keep up the good work. You've obviously done well for Kerrin to be the great gal and skier that she is."

Jane said, "We couldn't be more proud of her. Love you, Kerrin."

Kerrin replied, "I love you too."

We were ready to sign off when Terry said, "I need to throw this in there, Ron. I think that guy sitting beside her, looking so great on my TV right now, has an awful lot to do with how things turned out today." Kerrin took Max's hand and gave him a thousand-megawatt smile. Max looked down at his lap, trying to hold it together.

We said goodbye to Terry and Jane, and then I asked Max about them. "How did you become part of this clan?"

"I'm very proud to be part of the clan," Max started out. "I think the Lee family is an unbelievable family, and they stick together really nice, and . . ." His resolve gave way and he began to cry. Kerrin reached for him.

I told him, "You know what? I sat down with my wife, Cari, and we were reading the bio about how you two got along together so well and had these great times together."

Max was sobbing, and now Kerrin was near tears. My eyes were a little wet as well. Trying to release some tension, I leaned forward, slapping the desk and chuckling. "Now I'm going to make *you* cry, Kerrin! I've done it to Max and I'm going to make you cry!"

I admitted I got choked up over their fairy-tale ending, too. "But in this community you really need each other, and you put your life on the line every time you go down the hill."

Kerrin was wiping her eyes, and with tears threatening, her voice broke. "Yeah, we obviously stick together through thick and thin . . . Max is here supporting me, and obviously he's been a nervous wreck all day. It will be good to have a few moments where we can just settle down and actually believe that this has happened."

I said, "There can't be two better people alive as ambassadors, both for skiing and a life in sport. You richly deserve this moment, and the great news is that you get to share it the rest of your lives with all of us. Thanks. It was emotional for all of us."

Kerrin says that, to this day, people still come up to her and talk about the day Max cried on TV.

29

YOU'RE TELLING ME THAT'S A GUY?

Beginning with the CBC's coverage of the 1996 Olympics in Atlanta, I covered the daytime shift and Brian Williams hosted in prime time.

Behind the scenes, the Olympics are a mishmash of commentators flying by the seat of their research. At the 2008 Olympics in Beijing, for example, Bruce Rainnie, another former radio guy (from CJLS in Yarmouth, Nova Scotia), was scheduled to cover rowing in the first week, then canoeing and kayaking, but he suffered from kidney stones and had to back out. Trevor Pilling, our executive producer, decided we had to have a key commentator at that venue. He pulled Scott Oake from track and field and swimming and gave him a crash course on rowing. Canada was expected to do well in these events, and they did, winning gold, silver and two bronze. Scott had only thirty-six hours to prepare, while Elliotte Friedman scrambled to replace him in track and field and swimming. Whoever the network sends has to have an overall good knowledge of sports because that's how it goes at the Olympics.

I have many great memories of my years covering the Olympics. One of my favourites was the incredible accomplishment of Donovan Bailey in 1996, when he won a gold medal in the

100 metres in Atlanta. Donovan was an incredible athlete. For three years—1995, '96 and '97—he was the Gretzky of sprinting. He ran faster than any man alive. His top-end speed was close to 43 kilometres per hour. He was superhuman, indestructible, until he popped his Achilles heel in a pickup basketball game, and that was the end of his career. But in 1996, it was a joy to watch him sprint.

Another highlight for me was when Leah Pells, a Canadian 1,500-metre runner, performed really well in Atlanta. She just barely qualified through heats, and then she ran a terrific semifinal and ended up fourth in the final. To be the fourth-fastest 1,500-metre runner in the world is amazing.

The biggest thrill of the '96 Games was the silver-medal swim by Fredericton's Marianne Limpert. I had been impressed with her at the Commonwealth Games in Victoria in 1994. She and I were both from small towns, and she was an only child too. I felt an affinity. I secretly hoped she would win. She ended up in the 200-metre individual medley, but got nipped at the finish by a woman named Michelle Smith of Ireland, who was over in lane number one. Marianne didn't know that Michelle was coming on. She thought she had won the race.

Watching Marianne during that race is as close as I've ever come to being overcome with emotion while covering a sporting event. Normally, I'm very detached, thinking ahead about what to say in the upcoming interview. But not that day. It was truly electric to see her swim the final 50 metres, knowing she might win the thing. It was incredible.

It was a thrill to watch, and so was the 4 x 200m freestyle relay. One of Marianne's colleagues on the team was a woman named Shannon Shakespeare. I interviewed both of them live after they finished fifth in the event. I said to Shannon, "I noticed that you guys had a little huddle before the race, and I wondered what it was you talked about. What kinds of things were said?" Shannon said, "Well, Marianne was saying Ron's ass is looking pretty good today." I opened my mouth, but nothing came out. For once, I had no snappy reply.

Ireland's Michelle Smith was subsequently proven to have cheated over a drug test. In 1998, she received a four-year suspension after an out-of-competition drug sample was found to have been spiked with alcohol, of all things. She denied there was proof she had been responsible, but to no avail. She continued to deny that she had used performance-enhancing drugs, which the use of alcohol in a sample could mask. Her coach and husband, Erik de Bruin, was a former Dutch shot putter and discus thrower. He was suspended from the 1996 Olympics after having tested positive in 1993 for excessive levels of the male sex hormone testosterone. Banned from swimming when she was twenty-eight, Michelle went back to school in Ireland and in 2005 she graduated with a law degree.

In 1998, I headed over to Nagano, Japan, for the Winter Games. Grapes and Cari flew over a few days after me. When Grapes is not covering hockey, he is like a fish out of water. The Olympics are a prime example—they are not his thing. He worked the Olympic Games only because the NHLers were there.

Don and Cari flew first class on Japan Airlines. Cari was carrying bags and souvenirs made by Roots. Canada's figure skating champion Elvis Stojko was heralded as a potential gold medal winner that year, so his picture was on the front of all the Roots bags.

Cari got all settled in and was dropping off to sleep when Don nudged her. He was holding up one of the Roots bags. "Who is this woman?" he asked.

Cari said, "What are you talking about?"

Don pointed at the bag and said, "This woman on the bag. Who is it?"

Cari said, "That's not a woman, Don, that's Elvis Stojko."

Don's eyes went wide and he said, "You're telling me that's a guy?"

Leading up to Japan, I'd been keeping an eye on Brian Stemmle. I knew his sister, Karen, a member of the national alpine skiing team. I'd run into Karen and another team member, Lisa Savijarvi, at Brad Richards' charity golf event in Prince Edward Island. They were a fun couple of girls. Meeting them prompted me to take an interest in Brian's career.

Brian had suffered a horrific crash during an alpine ski race in 1986 at the Hahnenkamm, a legendary course in Kitzbühel, Austria. He broke apart at the seams. It hurts to even say this, but he split his perineum—that's the line between your testicles and your anus. It was a horrible, horrible accident.

Remarkably, he made it all the way back to ski in the Olym-

39. With Brad Richards at the Sportsman's Club in Charlottetown, Prince Edward Island, in 2005. Brad and his family and friends have become good friends of mine.

40. Practising a new interview technique—the headlock!—on NHL commissioner Gary Bettman.

41. With Stuartt, our thirteen-pound miniature schnauzer, in 1993. It looks like she's thinking $e = mc^2$.

42. Our Schattentier standard schnauzer, Lewis. He was chosen because he appreciates my puns.

43. Our local lifestyle magazine, *West of the City*, profiled me and my beer-league hockey team, the Coyotes, in 2002. I still lace 'em up twice a week.

44. My parents, Ron Sr. and Lila. This was the last professional photo taken of them together, and it's my dad's favourite.

45. Mom at Christmas 2007—her last. Asthma, diabetes, high blood pressure, kidney cancer, macular degeneration and pancreatic cancer—what do you give someone who's received all that with a smile?

46. Cari and Dad, arm in arm at Dad's condo in Oakville in 2010. Dad's thirty-two years in the military explains the remarkable way he has soldiered on since Mom's passing in 2008.

47. With Cari and Dad on Canada Day, 2010. I co-hosted the show on Parliament Hill, with the Queen and Prince Philip in attendance. It was a privilege to show gratitude for being Canadian.

48. With my dad, Ron Sr., at a father–son Christmas luncheon.

49. Official photo as an honorary colonel of 1 Air Movements Squadron, based out of Winnipeg. This role gave me a chance to work with the bravest of the brave and to honour my folks, who were both with the air force.

50. On the set of *Battle of the Blades*, in a state of "glide" to be alive.

51. With Kurt Browning after he presented me with a Gemini Award for Best Sportscaster. Kurt is always hyper-aware of what is going on around him, and so full of life, he cannot stay still.

52. Getting some vitamin H (Heineken) in the British Virgin Islands.

53. Reading *Don Quixote* at Runaway Hill in the Bahamas.

54. With Cari at a corporate speech she booked for me in Toronto in 2011.

55. Cari and me, sitting on our sailboat's lifeline. In truth, she is my lifeline.

56. With Bruins goaltender Tim Thomas, on the ice in Vancouver after winning the 2011 Stanley Cup. He's putting in a good word about Vancouver's Roberto Luongo. That is the true spirit of sport.

57. At the 2011 Calgary Stampede. Whenever I'm onstage at the rodeo, in front of 22,000 fans, I "cowboy up."

pics again. That's just amazing to me. And he damn near won the downhill. He had the top time until he caught an edge near the bottom. It took him outside one of the flags, and he stopped. He stood, looking back uphill and at the sky behind him, which was blue as blue could be. As I watched, I thought, "Wow, what an image." I didn't mind that he didn't win. His recovery and determination were what made him a hero.

When the Games were over, we stayed at a friend of Cari's named Shoichi, who lived in Neyagawa, Japan, Oakville's sister city. I got up one morning and was surprised by a bath they had poured for me. It was filled with rose petals and bath salts and smelled really good. I got in, splashed around, unplugged the drain, and that was that. But when I emerged from the bathroom, the family seemed panic-stricken. The bath had been meant for everybody. Water was such a precious and expensive commodity that I was supposed to shower first and then step into the tub for a soak. They explained in their broken English that I had been invited to go first because I was the guest of honour.

Sydney in 2000 nearly broke me. I was forty years old, and I found the nine-hour hosting job very difficult. Each evening, I would host live from 6 p.m. until 3 a.m., but that wasn't the hard part. CBC Radio had asked us to do a one-to-two-minute show each day. I recorded it at 4 p.m., and that really, really messed me up. It sounds silly, but I spent a lot of time working on it, which prevented me from having a nap. I'd get off the air at 3 a.m., arrive back at my hotel at about 4 a.m. and listen to the revellers outside my window. Sydney was alive at that hour, just crawling with people. It was cool, but loud. I'd set my alarm for six hours later and drop dead asleep, then get up at 11 a.m. and prepare for the show. Thank God we had computers and VHS machines. If I was covering swimming that day, I'd cue up the national swimming championships. It helped in two ways: it gave me stories and results and helped me pronounce names correctly.

I'd work all day, and then shower and go over to do that damn radio bit. The mental strain of having to think about it was irritating, too. I wanted to look ahead and focus on hosting each night, but the radio bit was forcing me to look back and put together a story based on the previous day. I was struggling with having to look ahead and back at the same time.

Toward the end, I had to talk myself into hanging on. "Five days to go. Just get through it!"

I had learned how to better deal with the anxiety that still surfaced once in a while. Five years earlier, in 1995, I'd been backstage at the NHL Awards when I heard the words I've heard maybe a million times, "Here's your host, Ron MacLean." My mind started to weigh the consequences of a bad performance, and immediately I became too self-aware. It ignited a terrible anxiety attack within me. I learned to deal with it through a story I'd heard, a story about the brilliant figure skating pair (and real-life couple) Sergei Grinkov and Ekaterina Gordeeva. At the 1994 Olympics, just ahead of their second Olympic gold medal, their choreographer, Marina Zueva, said to them, "Don't worry about the judges. They are just happy for a day out of the office."

So, on the night of the NHL Awards, I told myself, "Get out of yourself and think about the other folks. The people sitting at the dinner tables. If you were in their shoes, what would you want? A laugh and an interesting thought. Somebody not to bore me or to preach at me."

In Sydney, we learned that the CBC's crew was a little too bare-bones. That Olympics nearly killed everybody who went over from the network, and it made us realize we couldn't have people stretched that thinly again. It was tough, because a couple of times I was close to incapacitating exhaustion. I was not having fun.

Before the Games began in 2000, we did a preview show. *Crocodile Dundee*'s Paul Hogan is Australian, of course. In an interview, he said something that has become one of my favourite lines: "You don't go back to someone's house because you like the furniture." It's a profound statement that stuck with me, so I wanted to incorporate that into my on-camera introduction. I thought it would be a good idea to say it while wearing a Crocodile Dundee hat, which looks like a Tilley hat made out of leather. I found one at a hat store and tried it on. I looked in the mirror, and the saleslady said, "Is it the rat's ass?"

I turned it over in my head. "Rat's ass? That's funny, in Canada we say 'cat's ass.'" I looked in the mirror again and decided it *was* the rat's ass. I smiled at the compliment and, feeling fairly Crocodile Dundee-ish, I paid for it and wore it out onto the street. I was about halfway down the block before it dawned on me that, with an Australian accent, "rat's ass" means "right size."

Don, Cari and I were together again at the Salt Lake City Olympics in 2002. Unlike Sydney, those Games were a joy to do. I would anchor in the afternoon and then host a hockey game while Brian Williams did the evening shift. On the nights when there was no hockey, we would go back to the hotel room—except, instead of me and Don with the bucket of ice and the clicker, it was me and Don and Cari. Don has a code of behaviour around women. He's very gentlemanly, never swears, minds his manners and all that. About eight days into the Games, Don pulled me aside and said, "When's Cari going home? Can't you get rid of her?"

Of course, Cari wasn't going anywhere, so we'd sit in front of the TV, watching all the events. Don, the big, tough guy that he is, absolutely cringes while watching figure skating. Especially pairs. Every time the skaters attempt a jump, he turns away from the screen. There are two things he can't look at—pigs on their way to slaughter and figure skaters doing their jumps.

Grapes has an expression about hurting something helpless. "To make someone suffer is to pick the wings off a fly, and then watch it spin and spin aimlessly." He knows figure skaters are under immense pressure and may fail, and he doesn't want to see that moment. He has hated pork trucks since the movie *Babe* came out in 1995. You know what they say about the British— they love animals, it's mankind they can't stand. Grapes has got a deep-seated love of dogs.

I do the driving when we go on location. And if I spot a pork truck ahead on the road, I'll look at my watch and say,

"Geez, I'm hungry. Are you peckish? I'm starting to get a little peckish." And he'll say, "Yeah, I wouldn't mind stopping for something to eat." I'll start talking about bacon and eggs and sausages and build the story up before we pull alongside the pork truck. When he sees the pigs, with their snouts pressed up against the holes in the crates, he'll look at me and go, "Awww, geez, Ron, why'd you have to say all that?"

We were watching the figure skating at the Salt Lake Olympics, and something happened that was one of the greatest things I've seen in my life. During the pairs competition, just before the long program, Jamie Salé, who was going to have to do side-by-side triple-toe loops thirty seconds into the routine, was warming up. Jamie's routine was that, just before the announcer gave the one-minute warning, she would do one good double. Her partner, David Pelletier, was down at the far end of the arena. Their Russian archrivals, Anton Sikharulidze and Elena Berezhnaya, were at the other end of the ice. Jamie started her steps and saw the Russians' pattern. She thought they were setting up for a lift and moved her pattern to one side to avoid them. But rather than go diagonal, they were doing an "S" pattern and preparing for a throw. Jamie's back was to them as they came flying around the corner at full speed. Berezhnaya was out front, arms extended behind her, looking like a figurehead on the bow of a ship. Anton was holding her hands. Jamie spun around in time to collide with Anton in the middle of the rink. His leg hit her hard in the sternum. Down they went, Salé and Sikharulidze.

Anton managed to push Elena out of danger. She spun away unharmed, and he wasn't hurt, either. His legs are as thick as hundred-year-old oak trees, and he has guns like Georges Laraque, but Salé is tiny. The first thing Anton did was skate over to Jamie. They were both in shock. He said, "Are you okay? Are you okay?" She understood it was a totally honest mistake and no one was to blame, but she couldn't answer because she had been badly winded. He graciously leaned over and helped her up. He basically dusted her off, and the program got underway.

That night, both couples skated beautifully, with the Russian pair winning gold. The crowd was stunned. Jamie and David had skated the performance of their lives, and everyone watching thought they had won. It turned out they *should have* won. An investigation revealed a scoring scandal. It was alleged that the French judge, Marie-Reine Le Gougne, had agreed to vote for the Russians, no matter how the skating unfolded, in a trade for raising the scores of some French skaters in the ice dance competition. The IOC got involved, and six days later, Jamie and David's silver medals were elevated to gold.

It's funny how, as a society, we've gone from having saints and royalty as our heroes to choosing entertainment and sports stars as the people we look up to. Before the Industrial Revolution, most people were serfs, uneducated and too busy working to worry about creating their own moral compasses. Religious people were virtuous, and kings and queens inherited divinity. But the Industrial Revolution came along, and people had more time because of the way work got done. So they started to participate in sports.

Instead of Marie Antoinette, athletes became heroes. When Otto von Bismarck defeated France in the Franco-Prussian War, French aristocrat Pierre de Coubertin made it his mission to make France "more battle hardened and ready" through sports. Coubertin organized the first modern Olympics, in Athens in 1896.

Since that time, the Games have been hijacked by nationalism, money, drugs and politics. That's why I'm so big on the honour part of it rather than the winning part of it. Sports are now motivated by dollars. Competitive balance is all about keeping the fans happy. But in that moment between the Canadians and the Russians, with that spirit of cooperation, where Anton and Jamie took care of each other, it surpassed all of the politics involved. They looked out for each other, and the rest took care of itself.

At the 2004 Olympics in Athens, Greece, everyone was sure that Canada's world champion hurdler, Perdita Felicien, was going to win gold. Sadly, her leg caught on the first hurdle and she stumbled and lost the race. It was a shock to everybody. She tried to leave by the nearest exit after her race, and the security guard ordered her over to another one. He said, "No, you're an athlete. You have to go where the runners go off." He indicated the mix zone, which was a gauntlet of cameras and interviewers, essentially like the red carpet outside an awards show. I will never forget how she handled the guy. Her whole world had just caved in, and she was gracious to him. That was my favourite moment in Greece. I'm sure Socrates would have approved.

We were in Torino, Italy, in 2006. The Canadian men's

hockey team was wiped out in the quarter-finals, 2–0, by Russia. It was a huge disappointment, and the CBC wanted to interview Wayne Gretzky. He insisted that I do it. I guess he felt I had a sympathetic ear or a soft touch. The Olympics had begun with allegations that Wayne's wife, Janet, was involved in a betting scandal. Ultimately, it turned out she had not broken the law. But it seemed to cast a real pall over the team because Gretzky couldn't be himself. He had to be guarded. There was a curtain drawn around him, and I think that hurt the guys.

Later that night, we all ended up at a restaurant called Camillo's. There was Wayne and Kevin Lowe, Wayne's dad, Wally, and a whole group of Hockey Canada members. Wayne said that they desperately missed Scott Niedermayer. On the advice of his doctors, Niedermayer had withdrawn from the team in order to undergo arthroscopic surgery on his knee. One of the team's Achilles heels was that they couldn't seem to adjust to the wide ice. International ice is 200 feet by 100, as opposed to the 200-by-85 NHL surface, and Niedermayer was good on big ice. He was a key loss for the team. They played well, but just didn't score. Brad Richards led the team in scoring with two goals and two assists.

The next Olympics, in 2008 in Beijing, would lead me on a different path, beyond sport.

30

MOM'S KINDRED

Mom was terrified of pancreatic cancer because her father had died of it. When she was diagnosed with stomach cancer in the fall of 2006, she didn't want to hear any of the details. The oncologist had real trouble pinpointing where it had spread. For a year and a half, we danced around the fact that it had metastasized into her pancreas and was killing her.

Her first bout of cancer came three years after Rose Cherry died. Mom and Dad had flown down to our place for Christmas in 2000. The second evening they were there, we were sitting in our living room, visiting and making plans for the next day. Suddenly, Mom said, "Ronnie, I need to tell you something."

My skin felt prickly. She was smiling, but her eyes looked worried. And then she told me she was going in for exploratory surgery in the new year because she'd had an ultrasound and it showed something unusual on her kidney. She said, "Dr. Wilkins says there is a nodule there, but he is only going to take maybe a quarter of my kidney."

My take on life continues to be that we are all dying. It's coming to us all, so we need to deal with it. My first thoughts were, "Okay, what can we do next? What do Mom and Dad need? Obviously, I have to get out to Calgary to be on hand for Mom's operation."

I was with her and Dad when she woke up in her room at the Rockyview Hospital in southwest Calgary. Dr. Wilkins came in—he was terrific—and said to Mom, "We removed the entire kidney, but the cancer was encapsulated, which means we don't think any bad cells have escaped. So you won't need any further treatment." He made it seem like no big deal, like changing a car battery.

Mom was downright cheerful. She thanked the doctor and asked if she'd be able to go home that day or the next. I thought, "What a tough nut she is."

That was the last of it until we dealt with a new diagnosis six years later.

By February 2008, the cancer was beyond treatment, and she was advised to stop chemotherapy. Her symptoms started to really bother her by May, so she was given drugs to alleviate her pain. She didn't want to go back to the hospital. She wanted to be home.

In the spring of 2008, Irish writer Nuala O'Faolain gave a remarkable interview to Marian Finucane on Ireland's national broadcaster, RTE Radio One. Six weeks earlier, Nuala had been diagnosed with inoperable lung, brain and liver cancer. She said, "I think there's a wonderful rule of life that means that we do not consider our own mortality . . . The two things that keep me from the worst of self-pity are that everyone's done it . . . The second thing that really matters to me is that in my time . . . billions of people have died horribly, in Auschwitz, in Darfur, dying of starvation or dying from multiple rapes in the

Congo, dying in some horrible way like that. I think, 'Look how comfortably I am dying. I have friends and family, I am in this wonderful country, I have money, there is nothing much wrong with me except I'm dying.'"

The impressive thing, I think, is that these words were not drafted or constructed for posterity. She was a great writer. Five of her books were on the *New York Times* bestseller list, and yet this spontaneous exchange was her masterpiece—brutally frank, beautifully balanced. Mom was Nuala's kindred. It was how Mom felt about death, and it was Mom's gift to cut to the chase that way.

I was scheduled to go to Beijing to be the prime-time host of the 2008 Olympics. Brian Williams had jumped ship in 2006 and joined TSN. I was next in line at the CBC to host the Games. Prime-time hosting involves a lot of juggling.

Naturally, I was worried. Mom was sick, but still living at home. She was hanging in, doing as well as could be expected. I sat down with Mom and Dad. They insisted I go to Beijing. Mom said, "Don't change your plans to suit us, Ronnie, you have your own life to live."

Mom and Dad had moved to Oakville in 2004. We found a really nice, spacious condo for them with a large balcony and a view of Lake Ontario. I dropped by the night before I left, to say goodbye. We laughed like we always did when Dad told his favourite Don Cherry story for the fiftieth time. It revolved around a surprise visit Don and I had made to them in 1988.

Mom and Dad had been getting ready to move to Calgary from Red Deer. Mom was at the dining room table, wrapping glasses in newspaper and stuffing them into boxes, and Dad was down in the basement.

Every time Dad told this story, Mom would start to laugh and, enjoying her reaction, Dad always hammed it up a little. "The doorbell rings. Lila goes to the door and I hear this screech! Don Cherry was standing at the door, and Ron standing behind him. And I came galloping upstairs to see what was going on. Why was Lila screaming? And here, of course, is Don Cherry. They had decided that because they were driving they would detour into Red Deer and have a brief visit with us. And here I am, in an old pair of jeans with the knees out, and a T-shirt with the sleeves all ripped."

Mom interrupted. "I don't know what I was wearing, but it wasn't something I wanted to be seen in."

Dad continued, "Don sat there, nice as you please, sang 'The Old Orange Flute,' that famous Irishman's song." (Don got a kick out of singing that one in a Catholic home.)

"He had a beer, of course," Mom said.

Dad said, "He stayed a half an hour or so."

"Forty-five minutes."

"And then he took off," Dad said. "He was a very likeable guy, although you wouldn't think it to watch him sometimes on Coach's Corner. Ronnie, you and Don don't do the things now that you used to do years ago, like the cotton batting in your ears, and Don with crazy hats."

I said, "The cotton batting was an April Fool's prank and happened just one time, Dad."

Dad said, "Don wears those different jackets, though, and people love that. You and Don are birds of a feather, I think.

Ronnie, you get respect because you shoot from the shoulder."

"Ronnie likes to keep the fire smouldering," said Mom.

"Look whose talking!" I responded, and we all laughed.

I had a flight to catch, so I got up and moved over to Mom. She struggled out of her recliner. They had matching velvet, rose-coloured recliners. Mom's was the one on the right. Getting up on her own was a big thing for her. She was so proud. She fought her way to a good, firm, erect stance, and I put my arm around her. She felt so little and bony. She squeezed my hand and looked into my eyes. "Be a good boy, Ronnie."

We weren't an openly affectionate family, but my voice was soft when I said, "I love you, Mom. I'll see you soon."

And that was it. Cari and I left for Beijing the next day, July 31, 2008.

Nine days later, Mom was in the hospital. Just before the live telecast of the Beijing opening ceremonies, she'd been rushing around, getting ready to watch me do my first prime-time hosting gig, and she fell and broke her hip. Our friends Pat and Linda Festing-Smith called to let us know she'd had surgery and all was well.

For the next few days, the reports were all positive. She was out of bed and walking around. The doctors were concerned about long-term mobility issues, but the cancer was under control and she was on the mend.

A few days later, we started getting reports of a turn. Mom was not eating and had started to get a little foggy. We tried in vain to talk to her on the phone, but it was extremely difficult because of the time difference and my schedule. Every time we called, she was asleep.

Finally, the doctor pulled Dad aside and said, "Mr. MacLean, your wife will not be going home with you." Dad was shocked. He said, "You mean it's fatal?" And the doctor replied, "Yes, her system has crashed. She hasn't got a hope. Don't do anything to agitate her. Leave her alone, keep her lips moistened, but no food, she doesn't need it now." But Dad was in denial.

We called the doctors and asked for a timeline. They said it could be weeks, but it could be days. Cari decided to go home to see for herself what was going on. She left on August 18 and landed on the afternoon of August 20. The closing ceremonies were to take place on the twenty-fourth.

Cari went straight from the airport to the hospital. Dad, Cari's folks and Pat and Linda were all there. She stayed until 9:30 p.m. and took Dad away to give him a break. Cari was home for an hour when the phone rang. The hospital told Cari "something has happened," and they needed to return to the hospital right away. So they knew.

Cari knew I was set to go on the air, but she was worried I'd hear about Mom over the wire. So she sent an email to my BlackBerry. "I am so sorry—your mom is gone. Your dad and I are at the hospital. Call me when you can. Xx, Bug."

The CBC was in the middle of a beach volleyball game, so I had about half an hour. "What do I do next?" I wondered. "Okay, I've got to get back to Dad and Cari. But first, I've got to let our director, Sherali Najak, know, and then I've got to sign off the show." There was a lot to be done.

I made some notes and then took the anchor chair. "Back to diving in just a moment. I don't want to jar you with this news, but my mom, who is eighty-two years old, succumbed to pancreatic cancer. Mom's condition has been tough for about a year now, but she broke her hip on the eve of the Olympic opening ceremonies, and if you know anything about cancer, once that trauma was added to the weight of her circumstance—it was a very difficult last fourteen days.

"I just want to quickly thank all the staff at the Oakville-Trafalgar Medical Centre. Some of the doctors weren't even the attending physicians. Tom Stanton, you, a great athlete, came by every day. Patrick Festing-Smith, a great sailor, a great helmsman, he was by every day. My dad is eighty-six, tougher than most of the athletes I got to enjoy. What a run it was.

"You guys were incredible in the rowing you did, the weight-lifting you did back home. So, thanks to you. My wife, Cari, got home in time. The news just broke about two hours ago. Grapes would always say, 'I'll be fine, don't worry about me.' I'm probably in that bubble of denial that you get in when you're involved in television. But the truth of the matter is, I gave her all I had all my life, so there is no harm in not having been there for the final moments. But I've got to get home now, it goes without saying, to help out.

"Ian Hanomansing is here, and the Lord works in mysterious ways. Scott Russell, this really is his baby, so the ship is on its way. She's got a comfortable lead and nobody better to steer her. Scott will come in and do the prime-time show through to the end.

"When we come back, more of the diving. Enjoy the Games. The 29th Olympiad, when CBC Television continues, in a moment."

I didn't break down, but my voice caught a little when I mentioned Grapes. When Rose had died, and I was on camera telling our viewers that Don had a situation at home, I knew that Don felt I shouldn't bother saying anything because no one would care. At the time, I used the words, "Don would want you to know, 'Don't worry about me. I'll be fine.'"

I knew, of course, that he was wrong. People did care about him, and when I repeated those words in relation to me and Mom's death, it kind of rocked me.

The CBC sent a car for me, and it took me directly to the airport. Air Canada and Delta met me in Chicago and Toronto and escorted me through, because the connecting flights were tightly timed. I thought I might sleep on the plane rides, but it didn't work that way. My mind rebelled. I swallowed a few lumps when I thought about Dad. He and Mom were in their fiftieth year of marriage. She didn't quite make it to their anniversary.

Dad decided to have a private viewing. He knew I would be arriving home in Canada on Friday. He told the funeral director, "I want to wait until Saturday to give Ron a chance to have a nice sleep first."

While I was in transit, Cari and Dad went back to the house to get something for Mom to wear. We had given her a nice dress for Mother's Day, so that was the dress they chose. They both stared into the open closet, and Cari said, "What about shoes?"

Dad said, "Why would she need shoes?" And despite the solemnity of the task, they both started chuckling. It was just like Mom to provide one last laugh.

I saw Mom lying in her casket at the Oakview Funeral Home. I went over to give her a kiss, and that was good. I guess. I think I could've lived without it. I say that, not knowing what it's like not to see someone you've lost laid out in a casket. But it wasn't her in there, if you know what I mean.

We didn't have a funeral. We had a private burial, with Dad and Cari and me. Life is a short window, and we're all going to pass through it.

I hadn't been to church in years. I only went back when Mom died. It gave Dad and me something to do together. In childhood, before I became an altar boy, I fidgeted through the entire Mass, which seemed like fifteen hours. I was bored out of my tree. Then, when I took my training and helped serve Mass, I loved it. I was part of the action. As I mentioned earlier, I loved to sing when I was young. I had a great voice that disappeared with puberty. One time, while I was serving Mass in Halifax, the visiting bishop was looking for me to bring the wine for the blessing, but I didn't notice because I was carried away with the hymns and stood there singing and singing.

I did enjoy watching the priest organize the Mass—putting on his vestments or costume, trying to connect with the sermon, grabbing the audience. Last year, as Dad and I were leaving, Father Coughlan was at the back door saying goodbye, and I shook his hand and said, "Great show. Another great show."

31

JUSTICE, NOT VENGEANCE

One of the most heartbreaking stories I ever covered in hockey was the death of Dan Snyder. His story touches me deeply, partly because I realize that it was youthful recklessness that got him killed, and it could have happened to me or a hundred other guys I know. It only takes one wrong turn.

On September 29, 2003, Dany Heatley was driving home from a team function in his Ferrari 360 Modena. Snyder, his Atlanta Thrashers teammate, was in the passenger seat. Heatley was going between 55 and 82 miles per hour in a 35-mile-per-hour zone. He lost control and skidded into a brick pillar and an iron fence. Dan fell into a coma and died six days later. Heatley, who had a badly injured knee, has always said that he can't remember anything from that night. He pleaded guilty to second-degree vehicular homicide, driving too fast for conditions, failure to maintain a lane and speeding. He was sentenced to three years' probation and ordered to give 150 speeches on the dangers of speeding and to pay $25,000 to Fulton County for the cost of investigating the crash.

Grapes and I attended Dan's funeral in Elmira, Ontario. It was so crowded, we stood on the lawn listening to the service over the loudspeaker. Dan Snyder's folks, Graham and

LuAnn, carried themselves with dignity. Later, they stepped up in court and advocated for Heatley. Fulton County District Attorney Paul Howard wanted to put Heatley in jail to make him pay for what he had done. Graham felt the DA's motives could be somewhat political.

Howard had worked on another prominent sports case. In 2000, Baltimore Ravens linebacker Ray Lewis was charged in connection with a stabbing outside a nightclub in Atlanta, right after the Super Bowl. Two people were killed. Lewis was arrested and then released on a million-dollar bond. The charges against Lewis were eventually dropped, and the outcome cost Howard political points, so he was meticulous in his approach to the Heatley case. But the Snyders didn't believe that sending Heatley to jail would be helpful for him or for them. Graham's only request of Heatley was that if he ever remembered what happened, and why he was driving so fast, he would call Graham and tell him. Heatley has yet to make that call. But he put his life back together. He was traded to Ottawa in 2005, then a few years later asked for a trade to San Jose. In the summer of 2011, he was traded to Minnesota. I admire him greatly for gutting it out. I am sure it's been really hard to live that moment down. And I look at the Snyders' generosity toward Heatley as a shining example for humanity.

Each year for five years, I attended Brad Richards' golf event in Prince Edward Island and then scooted over to the Dan Snyder Memorial Golf Tournament. The Snyders used the proceeds to build a new rink in Elmira, and the rest went to a charity, 37 Rising Stars. The Snyders decided on restorative justice, not vengeance.

One year, I had about three hours' sleep over the four days in PEI and almost missed my flight. Thankfully, my buddies at the Summerside Police Department got me to the airport. I slept on the flight, drove to Oakville to get my clubs and change, drove to Mississauga to pick up auction items from Don Cherry for the Snyder event, then drove two hours to Elmira. We played the event, then I emceed the dinner. Between golf and dinner, I went to Tim Hortons to get a rescue coffee. I was so dog-tired that I recall thinking, "Please don't let an emergency arise today. I don't think I'd be able to handle it."

In John Manasso's book *A Season of Loss, a Lifetime of Forgiveness: The Dan Snyder and Dany Heatley Story*, he wrote about how I showed up at the Snyders' a week before Christmas 2003 to present to them with a Gemini Award (which is kind of like the Canadian Emmy Award) I'd picked up for Best Sports Broadcaster. I knew the visit to Elmira to give them the Gemini wouldn't bring Dan back, but Dan would have won many more trophies, and it was something I could give them. It was easy to find them—everyone in town knew their address. LuAnn was on the phone when I knocked at their door. They welcomed me in and we chatted awhile. Graham was clearly devastated. He missed his boy and the action at Dan's games. We talked music a bit. The Snyders love rock. Dan's brother, Jake, is a huge fan of the Tragically Hip and Pearl Jam. To this day, I keep Dan's photo on my Hockey Closet wall. Dan Snyder—number 37.

Hockey is such a brotherhood. That message was never delivered more poignantly than on February 5, when we talked to Ottawa Senators assistant coach Luke Richardson, his wife, Stephanie, and their daughter Morgan. They were honouring Luke and Stephanie's daughter Daron, whose battle with mental illness ended in suicide. It had happened just five months earlier.

February 8 would have been Daron's fifteenth birthday. On that date, throughout Ottawa's schools and hockey rinks, Daron's class and teammates, friends and supporters wore purple, Daron's favourite colour, to promote awareness of the Richardsons' new foundation and initiative Do It for Daron. The idea is to encourage talk about the subject, get rid of the stigma and find solutions.

On the second day after Daron succumbed to her illness, Luke came home and Stephanie said, "You better brace yourself." The family room was jammed with NHL players, both active and alumni.

Paul Coffey had "his chair." Billy Ranford was literally moving in. Garry Galley was designing arrangements as though practising a breakout. One-time Peterborough Petes defence partner Mike Dagenais took over the phones.

For a long time after Daron died, Luke wouldn't answer the phone right away, just because he knew there were times he could not speak. He'd play back the message and feel the hug. One frantic afternoon, while running around, he looked at the call display and saw an area code he knew but a number he didn't recognize. He was going to let the phone take the message, but then for some odd reason he picked up.

This was the first call he'd taken from anyone outside of Stephanie, Morgan or extended family. The call came from a man who had meant the world to him. A guy who had been his first defence partner when Luke broke into the NHL with Toronto. A guy who took him under his wing. The same guy who got behind the wheel of a car when his friend Keith Magnuson was in no shape to drive, even though he'd had a few too many himself. It was a poor decision, and it resulted in Magnuson's death.

The call came from prison. It was Rob Ramage.

32

METROSEXUALS

I know Grapes is going to read this and say, "Of course you mentioned Brad Richards. He's your boyfriend." One of our producers, Kathy Broderick, keeps telling us, "Guys, you can't call Brad Ron's boyfriend. It doesn't sound good." Well, I do know Brad, and I like him. I also think he's a helluva hockey player. He won the Conn Smythe and Lady Byng trophies, as well as a Stanley Cup, with Tampa Bay in 2004. A 2008 trade sent him to the Dallas Stars, where he was an offensive force. He became a highly sought-after free agent in the summer of 2011 and signed a big contract with the Rangers. He's a cool guy. To me, he's hockey's answer to Steve McQueen.

But the great story about Brad is how we met. In 2005, during the lockout, CBC Sports producer Mike Dodson and I worked on *Movie Night in Canada*. Every Saturday night, the CBC ran three movies back to back. We'd go to a small place in Canada, some hockey place like the Red Deer Arena, and do on-the-street interviews with the kids, then throw to the movie. I would say things like, "Here's Dustin, who plays for the Foothills Junior Pee Wees, and you love movies?"

"Yes."

"What's your favourite movie?"

"*Big Daddy*, with Adam Sandler."

"This is Warren from the Prince George Cougars. What's your favourite movie, Warren?"

"*The Waterboy*, starring Adam Sandler."

"Great. And you are?"

"Jeffrey."

"Jeffrey, from the Niagara Junior Purple Eagles. What's your favourite movie?"

"*Happy Gilmore*, starring . . ."

"Adam Sandler. I know." We'd tape these goofy things and go all across the country doing it.

In March 2005, I was in Charlottetown to do a shoot at the University of Prince Edward Island, and we invited two NHLers who lived on the island to join us on *Movie Night*. They were Grant Marshall and Brad Richards, who both played for Stanley Cup champions. Grant played for New Jersey, Brad played for Tampa Bay. They were to do a quick thirty-to-ninety-second interview. When we were done, Brad asked me, "Where are you going tonight, Ron?"

I said, "I'm going to the Merchantman Pub across from the Delta Hotel."

"That closes at 11. After you get out of there, you might want to meet us at the St. James' Gate."

It sounded good, and so Mike Dodson and I walked into this bistro, and there were these good-looking metrosexuals, all dressed in black. The bartender, Brody, drew in the girls. He is to the St James' what Grapes is to Coach's Corner. Brody's most attractive quality is that he's unaware of his good looks. Then there was Brad Richards, decked out in Hugo Boss, looking as if he'd stepped off the cover of *GQ*. His buddy Trevor Birt, a police constable in Summerside, was there too. Trevor turned out to be quiet but deep, the Clint Eastwood of the group. Cory Doucette, the owner of the bar, was Humphrey Bogart sitting in Rick's Café.

They looked like they'd been dropped in from a scene in New York. I thought, "Nothing about this fits with what I imagined PEI would be." I was sure we'd be walking into a peanut-shells-on-the-floor, lumberjack-shirt, round-Arborite-tables place.

The St. James' Gate was a snazzy spot, but it was dead. There wasn't a soul in there at 10 o'clock except us. But by midnight, it was like Cirque du Soleil. The bar was packed. That's a very Maritime thing. They drink at home, and then they come out to party. It turned out to be a really fun evening. We shut the place down at about 3 a.m.

The next day, I was scheduled to go to the Queen Elizabeth Hospital for a visit with the spinal cord injury patients. I was honorary chair of the Canadian Paraplegic Association. Bob Egan, Blue Rodeo's steel guitar player, was involved with the association too. He is a fascinating guy. I had met him at the farm of Jim Cuddy, the lead singer of Blue Rodeo, who hosts an annual Labour Day party near Alliston. Everybody pitches tents and overnights it. The event starts out with games, like swimming and softball and horseshoes. Then there is a night-time barbecue. Later, the musicians pull out their guitars around the firepit. A couple of years ago, I qualified for a very exclusive club called the Firewalkers. Membership requires that you accidentally fall into the pit.

After the night at the St. James' Gate with Brad and the boys, I was feeling a little groggy. Brad caught up with me at the hospital visit. He invited me out to the Sportsman's, another bar he liked. When Brad and I sit and talk, I usually drink too much and he doesn't. The Sportsman's was owned by a guy named Gary Kennedy. Gary's father, Forbes, played for Boston, Detroit, Edmonton, the Leafs and Philly. He was a real scrappy, gritty guy. He played for Dick Irvin Sr., but he's most famous for playing for the Leafs in the 1969 game where Pat Quinn elbowed Bobby Orr and knocked him out. There were millions of fights in those days, and Forbes Kennedy from PEI was right in the middle of a bunch of them.

The Sportsman's is adorned with hockey memorabilia. I just loved it. It was my kind of bar, like The Vat in Red Deer. Just think of your favourite dark, dirty, dusty, dank bar—that's what I like. Gary was great. They got him out of bed and he came down and met me. We all hit it off.

I found out that Brad's buddy Trevor goes by the nickname House Cat, because he comes over to your house and never leaves. House Cat is a real thoughtful guy. He sent me a book by Jeanette Walls called *The Glass Castle*, knowing I would like it. It's about a drifter who is homeless and raising three kids. Each Christmas, the drifter would take his kids out and show them the night sky, then ask them to pick a star. That would be their gift. It's a hell of a story.

I hate to say it, because it is kind of embarrassing to talk about these deep conversations when you are stone-cold sober, but when House Cat and I go for one, we talk about love versus respect and which is more important. I always side with love and he argues for respect. Most guys do. But over the years we have come to conclude they are one and the same. Gary's brother, Mike Kennedy, and Trevor and I have become a tight circle of friends.

That same night, Gary made us a drink called a Scary Gary that's not on the menu. It's his own concoction of nine different liqueurs—it's tropical and milky and tastes sort of coconutty. Galliano is the predominant flavour, and there's Bailey's in it too. Unfortunately, it smells exactly like the soap at the Delta Hotel. I found that out the next morning while in the shower. I unwrapped a bar and it took me right back to my second Scary Gary. I haven't had one since.

In the summer of 2010, Brad was in Oakville for a visit with his Dallas Stars teammate James Neal. I'm pretty good friends with James as well. There was a little partying, and by the end of the night, everybody came back to our house. Cari and I live on the edge of some woods. So I threw some logs in the firepit, and Neal was pulling branches off trees to feed it. We started barbecuing steaks around 4 a.m. It was a fun night, just bedlam.

The next morning, Brad, James and I squeezed into my little Mustang and drove up to Georgetown, Ontario, for a visit with Brad's cousin Dave. Around 2 p.m. I was chasing Dave's son, Nolan, a cute little guy, around the pool, pretending to be a barracuda. Brad threw Nolan into the pool and I dove in to grab his toes, but I didn't judge the depth properly and my forehead hit the grate at the bottom. I surfaced, and because it was a scalp cut, the blood was just pouring down my face. I said, "I hit my head." And Brad, who has a really dry sense of humour, said, "Yeah, Ron, I think you might need two stitches."

I grabbed a towel and went into the house to look in the mirror, and it looked like somebody had taken an axe and driven it into my head. It had swollen up immediately, and there was a crater the size of a Premium cracker. I thought, "That's it. My career is over for sure." We packed ice on it and headed for the emergency room. The doctor did an unbelievable job of stitching me up. The scar is barely discernable. He did an especially remarkable job for a small town like Georgetown.

Later on, I drove back up to the hospital and gave that doctor one of my Gemini Awards. I thought it would make a good gift because the statue has two faces: one represents a person in front of the camera, and the other, a person behind the camera. The doctor was playing the role behind the camera, fixing the face in front. First, I waited a week to see if he'd done a good job.

I give my Geminis out to people I admire, including Dany Heatley's parents, Graham and LuAnn Snyder and Grapes. Donny Meehan's got two, because I'd forgotten I'd given him the first one. I shipped one to the Chilliwack Bruins to give to cousins Casey Guliker and Derek Baars. Derek was born blind. The boys were regulars at Chilliwack Chiefs games, a Tier II Junior A team that played in Chilliwack before the Bruins of the Western Hockey League came to town. They'd sit in the stands and Casey would spend the entire game doing a private play-by-play for Derek. Dad has the one I won in 2008, after Mom died, and Todd Swanson, my best friend from Red Deer, has one.

I gave away my ninth Gemini, from the 2007 ceremony in Regina, to J.P. Ellson. He's the guy who brought the Rolling Stones to Saskatchewan, for the first time ever, in the fall of 2006. In 2007, he brought the Geminis, the Juno Awards, the Canadian Country Music Awards and the Western Canadian Music Awards to the province.

He happened to be at the Geminis that night. Cari was with me. She was raving about what he had done for Saskatchewan's music scene. So when I won the Gemini, I just handed it to him on the spot.

The only Gemini I have at the house is the original, from '92. They are nice to have, but I always feel kind of undeserving.

In 2000, I was asked to be the Calgary Stampede parade marshal. I'd been on parade floats before and never understood why. Once, in Red Deer, I saw Brian Sutter in the crowd and I thought, "What the heck am I doing on the float when a guy like that is in the crowd?" Former Stampede marshals include Bing Crosby, Wilf Carter, Bob Hope, Pierre Elliott Trudeau and Rick Hansen.

I was riding along at the Stampede, feeling a little like an imposter. Everybody was hollering, "Where's Don? Where's your buddy?" And Stampede president Rob Matthews kept telling me about the actor Sam Elliott, who'd been parade marshal in 1998. He said, "Ron, you wouldn't believe it! Women were coming out of the crowd like crazy. They were swooning and bringing him roses. It was nonstop!"

I looked into the crowd. There were definitely no women holding out roses. Suddenly, out of the blue, a football colleague from high school named Colin Sheedy, who had gone on to play for the Calgary Dinos, made his way through, holding a tray loaded down with Styrofoam cups filled with Bailey's and coffee. Sam Elliott attracted the girls, but I had booze and good buddies.

Considering all the players I have met over the years, I don't hang out with many of them. But every once in a while I make friends with one of them. I was hired for events in Buffalo. Sabres consultant Joe Crozier and I would interview guests on the JumboTron during intermissions. It was a lot of fun. Grapes came along with me on November 7, 1997. When I mentioned that the Sabres were really getting their game together, he said, "Well, of course they're getting their game together. Hasek's stopping pucks finally. He was horseshit in the first months." There was a big backlash because Grapes was on the JumboTron at the time, so all the kids heard it. The Associated Press interviewed a kids' coach who was in the crowd who said Don "overstepped his boundaries," and the story gained wider coverage.

The *Buffalo News* reported that Don refused to apologize, saying, "I have no regrets. I never apologize. I didn't think it was that big of a deal." He told the *News*' reporter, the late Jim Kelley, "We have murder, rapes and killings in Buffalo and the headlines jump all over me because I said 'horseshit'?" Don called the Associated Press reporter a jerk and said, "They don't write that I stayed behind in Buffalo, signing autographs. They don't write that earlier in the day I was at Toronto's Sunnybrook Hospital, visiting sick kids." Personally, I thought the whole thing was just silly.

We used to go to a restaurant in Buffalo called Mother's. I would chat with Danny Gare, Brad May, Rob Ray—whoever was there. One time, I met Darryl Shannon, a big defenceman for the Sabres. Darryl's a nice guy, quiet and really bright. We sat up until the wee hours of the morning, drinking wine and talking. Finally, as he got up to leave, he said, "One thing you should know—I'm pretty well connected with the Compuware Group, Peter Karmanos's family, because I played for the Windsor Spitfires. If you're looking for a good investment, I recommend Compuware." I chuckled at that, because money is a foreign language to me.

The next day, I phoned to thank him for the good conversation, but he wasn't there, so I left a message. "By the way, I took your advice and invested in Tupperware." I knew that when he heard it, his heart would stop for a minute as he second-guessed himself. "Did I say Tupperware? Or did MacLean just screw up because he was drinking?"

One time, my high school friend Marty Vellner asked me if I would be interested in investing in a grapefruit farm in Argentina. I know—it sounds like a joke, right? But Marty's friend seemed to be well educated on the whole agricultural industry. He said Coca-Cola was running short of the grapefruits they needed to produce Fanta. Apparently, you start with lemon trees and eventually graft them into becoming grapefruit trees. I'm still a little unclear as to why.

I handed Marty $35,000 to invest in land and trees. Cari kind of rolled her eyes, but she was okay with it. There were immediate cash calls. The weather system in the Pacific, El Niño, was wreaking havoc with winter in North America. They said it caused a drought in South America that wiped out our lemon trees. When the second $5,000 cash call came within six months, I opted out. We all discovered that we didn't even own this land that we'd "bought." Marty can always outlast the cash calls, and then he becomes the tycoon. He and his family are very business-savvy. I smile every time Marty gets to talking finance. It's captivating, but where I'm concerned, it goes in one ear and out the other.

I have just invested $50,000 with a group that's converting basalt, the rock that is used in all the cobblestone streets in Europe, into fibreglass. My golfing buddies suggested it. It sounds quite interesting.

33

THE GOODY

In March of 2009, when I was first approached to host *Battle of the Blades*, the CBC Television show that turns hockey players into figure skaters, I thought it would be a colossal disaster. My boss, Scott Moore, asked me to meet with John Brunton and Kevin Albrecht from Insight Productions. We had lunch while they pitched the idea. I thought it was goofy, and as I listened, I thought, "Brutal! It can't work."

The only thing I latched onto was that four-time world figure skating champion Kurt Browning would be the other cohost. I'd never seen anything Kurt had been associated with that wasn't good. I told the guys at Insight, "If Kurt's in, I'm in." I knew the CBC was banking on this idea.

We got ready for the first show at a boot camp in a small arena in downtown Toronto. It was an unbelievable bluff, because even though the CBC were high on it, they weren't totally sold. We were basically winging it. It's astounding how it came together.

Kurt and I skated and worried while we prepared for the show. Just before the first episode, we found out that Kurt's pants no longer fit. The preparation was so intense that each of us had dropped fifteen pounds.

I prepared by renting an hour of ice in Oakville, twice a week for four weeks, that summer. The toe picks that are a feature of figure skates were tricky, because I was used to hockey skates. There are six picks on the front of a figure skate. The big one at the front is used to plant your foot to do a jump. I had those shaved off, which helped, but I still had trouble the first year. I sort of crawled around the ice. But in year two I did a waltz jump and a poor man's arabesque, or spiral.

Back in 2006–07, I had done a series of hockey tips called "Think Hockey." Two of these segments aired every Saturday night as part of *Hockey Night Canada*, one during the pregame show and the other between the first and second games of the doubleheader. We shot sixty-five tips, involving pros and coaches. Now, while figure skating, I practised something I had learned while doing the "Think Hockey" segments, and when Ron Davidson from Ottawa saw that I was good on my outside edge, he gave me a piece of advice that Sidney Crosby uses tremendously well. He advised me to power up with the outside edge of my right skate instead of using my left skate to push off. He also taught me to cross under. Crossunders are an integral part of how figure skaters power up, especially when they go backwards. You cannot do crossovers with picks, because you'll trip.

The venue for season one of *Battle of the Blades* was Maple Leaf Gardens, which of course had been retired several years before, when the Leafs moved to the Air Canada Centre. Before each show, Kurt and I sat and waited in two recliners, since there were no dressing rooms. I sat on the left and Kurt had the chair on the right, but he barely sat in it. Kurt's a ball of energy. HarperCollins publisher Iris Tupholme told me that when she first joined HarperCollins in 1992, Kurt was ready to write his book *Kurt: Forcing the Edge*. She met with him at his hotel. While they talked, he jumped up and down on the bed and caught so much air she was worried he was going to fly through the picture window.

When Kurt gets ready for *Blades*, he is constantly on the move—jumping, stretching and dancing. There is always music playing in his head. We'll be talking about what we are going to do on the show, and he'll be doing the zombie from Michael Jackson's "Thriller" routine. Kurt is forty-five years old, but he's hilarious. It's like hanging with a hyperactive ten-year-old.

For the opening of our first show, we planned to start at the Zamboni entrance, skate to centre ice and stop. We would do an arms-out razzmatazz surfer-dude move, with our knees facing each other, and then we'd tear down to the camera at the far end of the arena to do our opening. But the key was that we had to stop at the right moment, look at each other and do that move to the beat of a Bryan Adams song.

When we tried it, I couldn't hear the beat. There was just too much else to focus on. Thankfully, Kurt would count in, "Five, six, seven, eight," just to help me through it. The first show was good, and Kurt explained to me that in the figure skating world, all skaters identify a move they call a "goody" after a great performance, and they replicate this goody before the next skate. In our case, it became our surfer-dude stop. From then on, five to ten minutes before each show, Kurt and I would find a quiet moment backstage and do our goody. It was supposed to bring us good luck. It seemed to work. We got through the fourteen shows, the ratings were great and we were renewed.

As soon as Kurt finished the first season of *Battle of the Blades*, he headed for Lake Placid, New York, to join the cast of the touring show *Stars on Ice*. He's been a key player in that show for about twenty years now. In the 1990s, he was a headliner along with Katarina Witt, the two-time Olympic gold medallist from Germany. Katarina came in as a judge on *Battle of the Blades* as a favour to Kurt.

After every *Stars on Ice* performance, Kurt and Katarina would get dragged away to do photo spreads or interviews. The other skaters would wait around for them to finish up so that they could get on the tour bus and head to the next city. But the cast began to get a little resentful and bored of all the waiting around, so one of the guys said, "Kurt Browning is treating us like mushrooms here on *Stars on Ice*." He was referring to the old expression that mushrooms are like secrets—they grow when they are kept in the dark and are fed . . . manure. This particular cast member thought it would be funny to take off his clothes and do a naked headstand against the wall. His idea was that, when a man is naked and stands upside down, his package looks like a mushroom. So whenever they waited for Kurt and Katarina to finish interviewing, a couple of the guys would hang out naked and upside down in the dressing room. The girls heard about it, and they started doing the same thing in the women's dressing room. Everyone got a big laugh out of it and it helped while the time away.

In December 1998, when Katarina Witt did a photo spread

for *Playboy* magazine, she insisted—as an homage to her colleagues—on including a photo taken upside down against a tree. And that was her little goody, as the figure skaters call it.

During the final show of season two, I caught a glimpse of the judges, Olympic bronze medallist and Canadian Olympic Hall of Famer Toller Cranston and British Olympic gold medallist and four-time world champion Christopher Dean. They were really focused on the ice while they were judging. Here I'd thought the show was going to be a dud. On this occasion, I looked at these icons of the figure skating industry, on the edge of their seats, and thought, "Wow, was I wrong again!"

34

TAKE ME TO THE RIVER

In June 2010, we were in Philly, covering the Stanley Cup final between the Flyers and the Chicago Blackhawks at the Wachovia Center (now the Wells Fargo Center). On Wednesday, June 2, Philly beat Chicago 4–3 in overtime. The next game was on Friday, so I had Thursday off. It was the day after my interview with Gary Bettman on club ownership.

It was a really funny day. Don was shooting the twenty-second edition of his *Rock'em Sock'em* videos. I just went along to keep him company—what else was there to do? We went down to the old Spectrum, where the Flyers had played until the end of the 1995–96 season. I met Dave "The Hammer" Schultz, who was there to tape an item for the video, and then I just watched them shoot. The building was boiling hot. There was no air conditioning, and Don was wearing a yellow-and-black checkerboard jacket. He looked like a jester. It was so hot, it was ridiculous. I was dressed in a suit and had to take off my coat, but Don has a tremendous power of mind over matter. I was in a lather just sitting there with my feet up. Looking at Don, I thought, "How in the world is he not perspiring?" But he wasn't. They shot until noon, and then we went back to our hotel, the Hyatt Regency at Penn's Landing.

At about 1:30, we sat down in the restaurant, which over-looks the Delaware River. There were doors leading to an outdoor patio, and there were only two people sitting out there—a couple in their early forties. The man was wearing this white Ralph Lauren polo shirt with an indigo horse and rider embroidered on it. As I sat down, I glimpsed the logo and it reminded me that I had a horse race—the Queen's Plate, Canada's oldest thoroughbred stakes race—to host for the CBC on July 4. The hand of anxiety gave my heart a little squeeze when I realized I hadn't started prepping for it. As soon as the playoffs were over, I would have to get my head into horse racing.

Don was digging into his Philadelphia cheesesteak sandwich and washing it down with a beer. In a feeble attempt to eat healthy, I had the stir-fry with a Diet Pepsi. Don was telling a story about Dave Bolland, a centre for the Chicago Blackhawks. I'd heard it about twelve times already, so I was kind of on auto-pilot. Grapes was going on about how he loved Bolland and how he'd enjoyed watching him play for the London Knights. And he told me how he'd seen London coach Dale Hunter at the game the night before and had talked to him about Bolland and the Knights. He was describing Bolland's scrappy play and run-ning over Bolland's stats. "Listen to this, willya—2005–06, 140 points and 104 penalty minutes." And he started in about how Bolland got under Joe Thornton's skin in the San Jose Sharks series. "Bolland stuck to Joe and used his stick and—"

Suddenly, this woman ran up onto the patio. She looked panic-stricken, and in a thick French accent she began yelling, "Help! Help! Someone is in the river!"

My first thought was, "What's the big deal? Someone is swimming in the river." She hadn't said, "Someone is *drowning* in the river." But then I recognized her as the woman who had been sitting on the patio, and it dawned on me that her husband, the guy in the Ralph Lauren shirt, wasn't with her.

I started to connect the dots. "Oh, maybe her husband is in the river." Then I wondered, "How the hell did that happen?"

Anyway, I knew from the amount of boating I had done that you can't easily pull a person out of the water. It's a difficult thing to do. I spotted two stanchions connected by a green velvet rope that the hotel used as a divider between the bar and the restaurant. I unclipped the rope and ran down the patio. There was a boardwalk across from a pier underneath, but it was about a thirty-foot drop from where I was standing. I had to find a way to get there. I jumped over a fence off to the side and was able to work my way down some planters and steps to the big cement pier.

I noticed the polo shirt lying on the ground. Again, my mind turned to the Queen's Plate. "Damn, I gotta get ready for that race."

I spotted the French woman's husband in the river. He was swimming toward shore, dragging someone behind him. They were near a little wooden pad that looked like a forklift pallet or a skid, the size of a mandarin orange crate.

Below me, there was a two-by-twelve piece of wood that ran along maybe a foot off the waterline. I decided I could stand on that. It was about eight feet down. I bent and held the top of the pier, then used one foot to find the kind of grip you would use when rock climbing. Finally, my full body was hanging, and I let go from about two feet up and landed on a narrow wooden platform that edged the wall.

I stood, one foot in front of the other, on the platform and watched the rescuer bring this guy over to the raft. As they got close, I could see that the guy who had been drowning was African-American and had packing tape wound around his throat. He also had a yellow rope circling his shoulders and legs. I thought, "It looks like someone tried to kill this guy." I had a quick look around, wondering if someone was watching us.

The rescuer plopped the potential victim onto the small raft, and wearing only clingy wet underwear, he jumped up onto the platform and hustled off. He'd done the heavy lifting. Now it was my turn.

I held out my hand, and the potential drowning victim took it with his free hand, but I was unable to pull him out because he was fully clothed. He was extremely grateful to be saved, and kept saying, "Thank you, man, thank you," over and over again. This reinforced my attempted-murder theory.

I had to let him back down half into the water and half onto the little raft. He managed to free his other hand, and that allowed him to wiggle out of the rope and remove his coat. It looked like army surplus, but it was grey more than tan. He also removed the tape around his neck. He was wearing jeans, shoes and a T-shirt. I would guess he was thirty years old, and quite strong and fit. Two other men joined us and were standing on the pier above me. I handed him one end of the green velvet rope and helped pass the other end up to the new people on the pier. Then I grabbed his right hand again, and the three of us were able to pull him up out of the water onto the platform, and from there onto the pier.

Paramedics and police arrived, and a crowd gathered. He continued to say, "Thank you, thank you!" I wasn't sure whether his was a suicide attempt or he had been a victim of foul play, but before I headed back, I patted him on the back and said, "Better days ahead."

As I approached the hotel, I could see that Don watching the scene from the balcony. He called down, "Look, don't tell people I couldn't get there! Just tell 'em I was having a beer." I gave him the thumbs-up. Don was very fit for seventy-six, but there was no way he could have jumped the fence and climbed down to the platform. We finally sat down to finish lunch after this frenzy took place, and Don narrowed his eyes at me and sipped his beer.

I said, "What's wrong?"

He said, "You sure know how to put a damper on a great story."

35

THE STATE OF THE GAME

Different subjects in hockey catch fire at various times. Right now, it's concussions. I'd like to begin by saying there have been several positive tweaks to the game recently. The NHL has worked hard trying to get it right, but I think when we tried to retool the game in 2004–05, there were all these unintended consequences, and now we have to see whether they work or whether some of them should be scrapped.

The new interest in concussions reached its nadir with the January injury that forced Sidney Crosby to sit out the balance of the 2010–11 season. Then the whole issue was further brought into the light with the revelation that heavyweight enforcer Bob Probert, who died on July 5, 2010, had chronic traumatic encephalopathy, a degenerative brain disease. Bob donated his brain for medical research, and when they dissected it, they found small contusions that had begun to grow. These contusions meant he would almost certainly have faced brain issues in the future, issues that could've included headaches, depression, memory loss and dementia.

The league's history is full of tough guys who had health issues during and after their careers, often including addiction to painkillers and substance abuse.

The rationalization is that we are beginning to understand concussions today because we have better diagnostic tools, but that's silly. I was in Whitehorse in February 2011 for Hockey Day in Canada and spent time with some of the NHL alumni. A few of them told me that a lot of former players are messed up now. Nobody wants to talk about that. It's a big, dark secret.

Often, we blame the concussed victim. When Flyers defenceman Randy Jones checked Bruins centre Patrice Bergeron from behind in October 2007, Jones got a two-game suspension instead of a twenty-gamer because Bergeron had his back to the play. At the time, Bruins GM Peter Chiarelli objected, saying, "You can't mitigate the dangerousness of the Jones hit simply because Patrice was in a vulnerable position." His message, basically, was, "Would police decide not to charge an assailant just because the victim walked through a bad neighbourhood?"

Many superstars have had their bells rung in the past, especially in the days before helmets. Gordie Howe had a run-in with Ted Kennedy on March 28, 1950. Howe missed a hit, or maybe he was tripped, and crashed into the boards. He suffered a severe concussion, had a lacerated right eye, fractured his cheekbone and sustained a broken nose. In 1962, Jean Béliveau hit his head during a semifinal game with Chicago. He missed the rest of the playoffs and suffered headaches for two years. When Bobby Orr played for the Bruins in a playoff game on April 2, 1969, Leafs defenceman Pat Quinn rocked him with a vicious hit. Bobby Gould cold-cocked Mario Lemieux on March 30, 1987, and Scott Stevens crushed Eric Lindros in game seven of the Eastern Conference final in 2000.

In the Ontario Hockey Association, we went after a perpetrator guilty of punching a guy in the mask. It's easy to throw a punch at those big cages and think your opponent isn't going to be hurt. But with the impact, the brain can still crash around inside the skull. There may be no facial cuts, but there can be neck and brain trauma. Before facial protection, when the sticks came up a little bit, everybody was a little more wary. But try explaining why it's better to have stitches and teeth missing than scrambled grey matter, and people think you're crazy.

So, what are the options?

In 2010, the NHL's senior vice-president for public relations, Gary Meagher, gave a presentation to the general managers. He showed that the legal shoulder checks to the head that caused injury from 2007–08 through 2009–10 were split 50/50 between those that were lateral hits and those that were head-on, or what they call north-south hits. The GMs felt the victims should have been more aware in the north-south situations. I don't agree.

NHL players suffered about 100 concussions in 2011, with some of the best players in the game ending up on the shelf. On January 1, when the Penguins were playing the Washington Capitals in the annual Winter Classic, Capitals forward David Steckel blindsided Crosby, shouldering him in the head. Then, against Tampa Bay on January 5, the Lightning's Victor Hedman took Crosby into the boards headfirst. Whether Crosby suffered the concussion after Steckel's or Hedman's hit, the fact that the career of the greatest player in the game today was put in jeopardy has generated a lot of discussion.

Does it matter if the impact to the head was intentional or an accident? Should you be responsible for not messing up a guy's head with your body, the way you're supposed to be responsible for your stick?

The lack of awareness on the ice is another big factor in players getting hurt. There is a false sense of security now. In the old days, you were constantly being tapped and hooked. You used to have tip-offs from an opponent's stick that indicated you were in traffic. With the new crackdown on hooking, those signals are gone. Now, any contact between the stick and the body results in a penalty, so guys don't do it anymore and the skater flows freely. And since he can't use his stick on the puck carrier's body, the forechecker has to make a hit. I agree with Brian Burke's assertion that rather than plastering the defender, players should be allowed a limited amount of bear hugging or use of the free hand to guide him into boards.

By 2004 the hockey world was pretty much unanimous in the opinion that there was too much clutching and grabbing in hockey, which limited offence and stifled creativity. Rules were changed to promote scoring. Because nobody's allowed to lay a stick on an opponent and nobody's allowed to run interference, the players are flying at each other at unprecedented speed. And that has put hockey on a road to hell paved with good intentions. In my view, we have created a terrible element of risk.

Penguins GM Ray Shero responded to Sid's hit with the remark that we should govern head shots the way we punish players for high sticks, whether careless or intended. And that is what happened. In June 2011, the NHL's Competition Committee cleaned up Rule 48 at its Board of Governors meeting. A major penalty will be assessed in the case of "a lateral or blind-side hit to an opponent where the head is targeted and/or the principal point of contact." But will it work? To borrow from a statement by Prime Minister Stephen Harper when confronted by ethical issues, "You have to change hearts, not laws."

As a former referee, I prefer to change hearts. Rules tend not to grow the virtue in us. They curb crimes, so they serve a purpose, but in my view, new rules are not as effective as adjusting attitudes.

We now have two referees on the ice. One is always in the play down low—often in the way. It means another "moment of hesitation" for a defenceman who is already under pressure. If he shoots the puck over the glass, he's penalized for delay of game, so he struggles to settle the puck down, making himself vulnerable. To corral the puck, he often has to keep his body between it and forecheckers, with his eyes down on the puck, which means his back is pointed at the danger. Guys come crashing in pretty hard, and if the hit is high at all, the defenceman's neck and head have only one place to go—hard into the glass.

These changes in hockey are meant to increase entertainment for the fans. Let's give them shootouts . . . let's implement new rules to make the game faster. Speed is intoxicating. We see these guys going a hundred miles an hour and we think it's more exciting. But is it? Wouldn't a guy dipsy-doodling with great craft through a team be more exciting than a guy skating as fast as he can into the corner after chipping it in from the red line?

Perhaps we've taken away a bit of the playmaking because everything is happening at such a frenetic pace. It's impossible to be in control of the puck the way players once were. So often a game turns into a predictable Ping-Pong match where guys make the "easy play." Chipping it into the corner. Chipping it out on the glass. Back and forth.

A sport should evolve slowly. When you take a whole bunch of new rules and throw them at the wall, it changes the dynamic of the sport. And you set in motion the law of unintended consequences. One of which is concussions.

Maybe the biggest change in the NHL is the TV timeout. On October 17, 1991, I was covering an exhibition game at the Knickerbocker Arena in Albany, New York, between the Canadian and U.S. Olympic teams. CBS was also covering the game, and their director, Sandy Grossman, thought the idea of jamming eight 30-second commercials into each period was silly. So, that day we took four 70-second TV timeouts.

Not far away, in Pittsburgh, Scotty Bowman was salivating. He knew that if this format came to the NHL, Mario Lemieux could rest up enough during the timeouts to play an extra three or four minutes a night. The next year, the NHL adopted the new commercial format. It was soon modified to three 100-second timeouts.

I believe this change hurt the game. The stars are playing so much, they're bound to get hurt, and the third and fourth lines play so little, they spend nearly the entire game watching from the bench, frothing at the mouth for ice time. It turns these players into time bombs. After fifty-five minutes on the bench, they aim to prove themselves. Their fights are terrifying now. You've got guys who are as big as six foot eight and 270 pounds launching bare-fisted grenades at somebody's skull.

Years ago, to protect their star players, coaches started assigning bodyguards. Everyone was held accountable by the enforcers. Former Ottawa Senator Bill Huard dubbed them "hit men" or "gladiators." Now, that player has seen his role reduced.

When Bill McCreary Jr. caught Wayne Gretzky with an open-ice hit on January 3, 1981, Dave Semenko was placed on Gretzky's left wing. Gretzky stopped getting hit because Semenko would murder anyone who went after him. We've taken that out of the game in part because of the instigator penalty. But the disappearance of the enforcer is mostly a by-product of TV timeouts because they limit the enforcer's ice time. It's too tempting to have your top six forwards play the bulk of the time and use the timeouts as rest periods. Consequently, the fighter has become obsolete. The enforcer no longer plays the role that he used to. It worked during Probert's time, when the fighters played a huge role in protecting players like his star centre, Steve Yzerman. Today, who's around to prevent Crosby from getting smoked?

Twenty-three years of reffing convinces me that the "threat" of a fight keeps everyone more honest. It's interesting that, despite all these attempts to emphasize skill and scoring, hockey is still a rugged game. The Boston Bruins won the Stanley Cup with the toughest team in the NHL.

For eleven years, beginning in the mid-seventies, my *Hockey*

Night in Canada colleague Mike Milbury was a defenceman who could fight, but he was never really sold on fisticuffs. He's totally convinced that the only reason we have fighting is for the spectacle. It's a form of social policing.

The ice surface is too small. NHL rinks haven't changed in eighty years, but there's been an enormous change in the speed and size of the players. I like Finland's experiment with a 200-by-94-foot rink, 9 feet wider than a regulation North American surface but not quite as big as Olympic ice.

I also believe the elimination of the red line for two-line passes was a mistake. It created the breakaway passes people expected, but it also created a way to ice the puck without getting a whistle in your end, by having a forward just across the centre line touch it on its way past. Hardly an exciting hockey play, but one you'll see now maybe fifteen times a game. And that's far more often than you'll see a breakaway pass.

Most offence starts with a chip and chase, and once in the attacking zone the best option is to feed the point and have the defenceman shoot for a ricochet off either a forward stationed in the slot or one of the eight men clustered in front of the goalie. It's a lot like table hockey.

Without the red line, forecheckers come in at full speed. If a defenceman like Calgary's Mark Giordano or Chicago's Duncan Keith goes back to get the puck, he's taking his life in his hands. Remember that a puck can travel at least a hundred feet in one second. When the winger comes in that fast, he creams the defenceman.

In hockey at the moment, everything is about containment. Guys put their sticks in the passing lanes. It's not aggressive at all. In game two of the 1987 Canada Cup, Wayne Gretzky had five assists, and on each of those he created the magic by throwing a little stick, jabbing, hooking and taking the puck. He didn't sit back and wait for it. He didn't say, "Let's see . . . if I put my stick here, it'll hit it and then I can take off." Seeing guys do that today is not my cup of tea. It's a way more passive game now, and yet the guys are flying around faster than ever—and killing one another. The speed is there, but scoring is up only half a goal per game since the new rules came in.

Finally, the goal line is back to eleven feet from the endboards, versus thirteen feet at one time. Now the defenceman moves into an area the size of a phone booth behind the net, where visibility is extremely limited. The rule changes we've made recently are so stacked against that defenceman, it's nearly impossible to play the game as it was meant to be played.

I understand that players with far greater credentials than mine are working tirelessly to make the game find the right mix. But my fear is that we go for offence at the expense of safety. The appearance of speed may come at a price that is just too high. Again, to quote U.S. founding father Thomas Paine, "Be careful not to admire the plumage and ignore the dying bird."

36

SPORTS HAVE TO BE HONOURABLE

The city of Vancouver was Utopia for the sixteen days of the 2010 Vancouver Olympics. And there was a joyous feeling during nine weeks of the 2011 Stanley Cup playoffs. When I looked at the gatherings in the street of 100,000 or so, I thought, "Isn't it grand?" But I also had to ask myself why 100,000 people would stand together to watch a hockey game on TV. And the ratings were crazy. Eighty per cent of all Canadians watching TV on June 15, 2011, were watching game seven of the Stanley Cup final. It was just amazing.

But after partying for eight hours in the sun, that crowd in the street saw their beloved team trounced. This was a team that had held a 3–2 stranglehold on the title, a team celebrating its fortieth anniversary, a team that for nineteen of its first twenty-one years endured losing seasons, a team now poised to return the Cup to Canada. That win would send a message to the Eastern media, which too often ignored them. It was payback for all those years when the coverage slighted Vancouver's best—the Sedins, Roberto Luongo, Alex Burrows—and for insults like the time Brian Leetch beat Trevor Linden for the Calder Trophy. Suddenly, the bubble burst. And it ended in a riot. Sure, it was troublemakers who ignited the problem, but frustrated fans became cheap accomplices. They were easy to bait in the swirl of anger and alcohol.

We loved the Vancouver crowds at the Olympics, we loved them during the playoffs, and then, when they acted up one night, what? Our garbage doesn't stink?

I think the reason people got upset is that they are proud Canadians. I've never believed in proud Canadians. I believe in grateful Canadians. Most of us have no choice about where we were born and raised. We are blessed, we are lucky. It was neither a black mark for Vancouver nor for Canada. It was human fallibility, nothing more. This notion that we are somehow better than the rest, thanks to this lucky twist of fate, has to stop.

We in the media ratchet up the tension and hype, and then when people snap under the weight of it all, we're surprised. We are culpable. At the end of the Stanley Cup final, the CBC took out a full-page ad in *The Globe and Mail* with a picture of the Vancouver Canucks, saying, "Thanks for the ride." No mention of Boston, who won the Cup. So it turns out it wasn't Boston versus Vancouver, it was the United States versus Canada. But the players don't play in that world. When we wrap ourselves in the flag this way, it becomes an isolating shield. This is why Pierre de Coubertin, founder of the modern Olympics, frowned on medal standings. He thought there was no room for nationalism in sports.

Gary Bettman was booed mercilessly, and when he presented the Cup he had to duck water bottles and empty beer cups. Then the crowd broke out of booing Gary and started cheering Boston goaltender Tim Thomas as he stepped up to receive the Conn Smythe Trophy. Later, while interviewing him on the ice,

I asked him if it felt good to be cheered after all that booing. And instead of revelling in that moment, he said, "You know, Roberto Luongo, he's a great goaltender, and I have nothing against him." Luongo had opened a can of worms during the playoffs by saying he'd pumped Thomas's tires and complaining that it hadn't been reciprocated. And the fans jumped on Luongo for it. And here was Thomas, stopping right in the middle of celebrating to ease Luongo's pain. That is hockey. That's sports. Winning is so elusive. The minute you win, you just feel . . . relief. The real reaction is to think of the other side—"Those poor pricks. I've been there and I know how bad that feels."

I admired the Vancouver police, too. They were even-handed. They had almost everything back on track within three hours. There were a few broken windows and some looting, but no one died.

Facebook frontier justice came rifling through the next day. People were pleased to see the city getting into trouble. Twentieth-century writer and philosopher Elbert Hubbard said, "Anyone who idolizes you is going to hate you when he discovers that you are fallible. He never forgives. He has deceived himself, and he blames you for it." So many were condemning the city. I didn't want to see that from us, I wanted to see "us." Not "he went wrong" or "she went wrong," but "*we* went wrong."

I didn't witness any of the rioting that went on in the streets of Vancouver after the game. We rolled out of the Rogers Arena about 9 p.m., and because the police had tear-gassed everybody out of the core, it was eerily quiet. I sat in my hotel room on the twenty-third floor, looking at the sun setting over English Bay, and it was beautiful. The TV was next to the window, and I turned it on and watched images of the riot replayed.

I knew this would be huge news in the week to come, but time heals. I got thinking about how, just a week earlier in Detroit, Darren McCarty and Claude Lemieux co-hosted a fundraiser for the police in Michigan. There is quite a history involving the two of them. In the 1996 Western Conference final, Lemieux hit Detroit's Kris Draper from behind and into the boards at the Detroit bench. Draper was badly hurt, with a broken nose, a fractured cheekbone, a fractured upper jaw and thirty stitches on the inside of his mouth, and five of his teeth were pushed down and pressing into his throat. Lemieux received a two-game suspension.

The guy who rode with Draper in the ambulance was Darren McCarty. When they left the hospital, the doctor handed McCarty a pair of pliers. Draper's jaw was wired shut, so if he threw up there was a chance he would aspirate his own vomit and die. McCarty was to loosen the wire clips if Draper got nauseous or passed out. This ordeal created a real connection between McCarty and Draper. And so, on March 26, 1997, in a regular-season game between the Detroit Red Wings and the Colorado Avalanche, McCarty unleashed a year of pent-up fury on Lemieux. He absolutely rag-dolled him. Lemieux turtled, which was embarrassing for him and his team.

That fight was considered the tipping point for Detroit. They had long failed to live up to their potential and had blown chances to win the Stanley Cup in 1993, '94, '95 and '96. But what Darren McCarty did to Claude Lemieux that day brought the players together as a team. And they did go on to win the Cup that year.

All these years later, with all the shenanigans going on in the Boston–Vancouver series, when the police came to McCarty and asked him to appear at a fundraising event with Lemieux, there was forgiveness.

The first call McCarty made was to Draper, asking if he was okay with it. And the answer was yes.

As I sat on my bed and watched clips of the riots on one side and the warm, peaceful glow of the setting sun on the other, I thought about all the layers in the game, and decided that it comes down to virtue. McCarty and Lemieux. Sikharulidze and Salé. Tim Thomas. Sports have to be honourable.

I turned off the TV and sat there staring out the window for a long, long time.

37

WHERE SHALL WISDOM BE FOUND?

Some people get into trouble when they drink. I get into trouble when I read. In searching for answers, I read contemporary philosophers, financers, bloggers, novels, fairy tales, the classics, you name it. Lewis Lapham's book *Lights, Camera and Democracy* is my bible on how to approach what I do for a living. His essay "The Road to Babylon: Searching for Targets in Iraq" was the reason Don and I got into our infamous Coach's Corner debate over the Iraq war in March 2003. It's not as though I came up with the argument on my own. Most of the arguments I get into, I've stolen from some expert.

I have asked myself, "If you could change one thing about yourself, what would it be?" I decided I would get rid of gluttony. I've struggled with some of the seven deadlies, but especially that one.

One of the best essayists I've ever read is Joseph Epstein. I bought his *Envy: The Seven Deadly Sins* as my entrée into his writing. When I am asked what I would do if I could change one thing in the world, I say that I would eradicate envy. It's the biggest impediment to a happy life. Epstein's book was from part of a lecture series for the New York Public Library. It's brilliant—written with rapier-like wit, and no piety. Epstein says envy is the least fun of all the major sins. He tells a good joke about it. There's a genie who offers a wish to an Englishwoman, a Frenchman and a Russian farmer. The Englishwoman says that her friend has a charming cottage in the woods, and she would like one like it, but wants two more bedrooms, an extra bathroom and a brook on the property. The Frenchman says that his best friend has a beautiful blonde mistress, so he'd like one too, but he wants his to be a redhead who is more cultured and has longer legs. Finally, it's the Russian's turn. He says his neighbour has a wonderful cow that gives the richest milk that yields the heaviest cream and the purest butter. The Russian tells the genie, "I vant dat cow . . . dead."

There are days when I wonder, "What becomes of us?" I'm pretty pragmatic. Ed Whalen used to say, "They throw us in the ground, and that's that, Kid." I kind of agreed with him, yet I liked the idea put forth in the book *God's Debris: A Thought Experiment* by Scott Adams. He's the guy who created the Dilbert comic strip. The book is a parable. God blows himself up, and we're all pieces of God. It was one of the neatest ideas I've heard on the subject of life after death. I don't necessarily expect to see Mom when I die, but I hope I do.

To this day, I would love to dwell more on these kinds of things, but I haven't made time. If I could do more of anything, it would be to read more books. I remember the impact *The Catcher in the Rye* had on me. At the time, I thought Holden Caulfield was a lot like my mom. I'd sit in the back seat of the car and listen to her. She was a bit dark as she discussed, dissected and distilled a visit or a conversation. There was a real edge to her judgment. Not cruel—just full of details. Don's like that too.

I wonder if anyone has ever learned anything from something Don and I have said to each other. I hope so. If we have never given a viewer a teachable moment, that would be crushing to me. It's always my hope and intention to impart something of value. Our intentions are always good, but then we interrupt each other and talk in short sentences, with our thoughts flying off the wall in a million directions. There's no chance anybody outside of the two of us has a clue what we're talking about. It's good television, but it's pretty much like Wile E. Coyote and the Road Runner—total shtick. My great ambition to teach the world something becomes a complete gong show.

I have spent my professional life researching and getting ready for interviews. I take seriously the idea of hoping to give the listener something to take away. And it's very humbling to realize that, no matter how much I think I know or have learned, I can't quite trust myself to be right. I feel like I'm guessing at life. I'll set out to achieve something positive and I'll get absolutely nowhere—which is funny. It's how it should be. If you want to make God laugh, tell him your plans.

Who should we listen to? Jesus? Plato? Christopher Hitchens? We don't know. We're all guessing. I think it is fascinating that we go through our lives hoping that maybe the Pope or the Aga Khan has the key to unlock the secret and set us straight, or at least help us find peace. Looking for the answers, which has always been my drive in life, can be exhausting.

Although I mostly cover hockey with the CBC, I also cover other sports, including the Commonwealth Games. In 1998, we went to Kuala Lumpur, Malaysia, and did two hours of coverage every night. We had to link together all the sports that we were going to cover—track and field, gymnastics, swimming. My job was to provide intros and set-ups. When you do the same thing night after night, it can get very boring for the viewer, so we were always looking for an angle. Our producer, Terry Ludwick, suggested that writer Doug Toms and I go out each day with a camera and search for metaphors. One day, we had a shot of a train chugging across the landscape, much like you might see in an epic movie like *Out of Africa*, and I had an epiphany. The roots of it went back twelve years to 1986, when I watched the America's Cup sailing from Perth, Australia. I didn't know the first thing about sailing, but I got so absorbed in watching the boats on the beautiful waters of the Indian Ocean, I couldn't go to bed. The train shot resonated even more powerfully within me. When I am on camera in front of a hockey game, sometimes I feel I get in the way of the train that is moving behind me. I had to be careful not to get in the way in Malaysia. There was such a richness of culture—Chinese, Indian, Muslim—in a wonderful, exotic setting. Few words were required. It was a very helpless and beautiful feeling to be in a place like that. We had a young editor, Trevor Pilling, who put together a montage to the Tragically Hip song "Ahead by a Century." It was beautifully cut. Today Trevor is executive producer of HNIC. Talent will out.

Sherali Najak was with me there, too. He is one of the finest producers I've ever worked with. Sherali could respond to the demands of the technical and production staffs at 100 miles an hour, but he could also spot if an individual's blood sugar was low. His bedside manner was the greatest. Out of all the producers, he is the one that inspired me the most.

On show days when we're on the road, Sherali, our studio producer, Brian Spear, and I meet for breakfast at 9:00 a.m. Sherali brings a cool drink of perspective to all conversation. Brian is sharp and mischievous. He's about 6'5" in a lanky frame. We rip life apart and share a lot of laughs. Sherali says that Christians think all Muslims are alike. He explained that there are Protestants and Catholics and Presbyterians and Anglicans, and that the Muslim faith is the same way. There are various denominations of Islam.

One night, we were at a café in Malaysia and our audio ace, Howard Baggley, was singing a karaoke version of Bryan Adams' "The Summer of '69." Everyone was dancing, so I went over and asked a local girl to join me. She said no, and I came back to the table, deflated. Sherali laughed.

"Ron, don't take it to heart. She could not dance with you because she is Muslim and you are Christian. That just can't happen."

I love the guy. He has a warped sense of mischief, but a profound sense of love.

In the late nineties, Kelly Hrudey was hired as an analyst on *Hockey Night in Canada*. He would work alternate nights during the playoffs, between Don's appearances. Kelly is a charming guy and was garnering good feedback. His manner was a nice contrast to Don's rock'em, sock'em style. And so there was a big write-up about him in the *National Post*.

Don Cherry came in after this big article and talked about it on Coach's Corner. He said, "Well, I see Kelly got a great write-up in the paper today, and I have to admit, he's doing a good job. He's doing a real good job. I was watching him last night. You know, Ron, I'll have to say, he's a sharp dresser. And I couldn't believe that a guy who spent all that time down there in La La Land could actually be a good dresser. But I said to Rose, 'Rose, mark my words, there is going to remain one sharp-dressed guy in *Hockey Night in Canada*, and that'll remain me.' And I'm going to my closet, and folks, I promise you, I will have a few beauties for the third round of the play-offs. No doubt about it."

At that point, the producers put up a picture of Kelly in his Armani suit from the night before.

Don said, "There you go. You see what I mean? What a good-looking guy. He looks like Kurt Russell, doesn't he? The movie star." Then they showed another picture of Kelly in his Hugo Boss suit. Don said, "There's another beauty. Imagine, folks—I mean, don't get me wrong, but all that time down there in the sun in Hollywood, it could ruin a guy. I mean, not too many guys come out of Hollywood dressing well."

Then they showed a third picture of Kelly, an old one from the late eighties. He was wearing an oversized purple suit with silver flecks and broad shoulders. Don said, "Oh, Kelly, me boy, I knew . . . I knew Lotus Land would catch up with you eventually. See, that's the kind of thing I'm talking about, Ron. A lot of people out there in L.A., that's how they dress. Kelly, for your folks in Alberta, that's embarrassing. Not becoming at all."

And I looked at Grapes and said, "Clearly, Don, you were suffering premature jacket elation."

EPILOGUE

I'm not super-fit, but I'm in good enough shape. I go to the gym two or three times a week, where I do ninety minutes of weight training. I rotate through different exercises under the supervision of a trainer named Karen Finnell. And I play hockey—beer league, twice a week. I play for the Coyotes on Mondays and the Black and Whites Wednesdays. I've played with the same guys for years. We're tight.

Sometimes after games, we go for beers and I get on my high horse and start arguing about pride, talking about how it's wrong to be proud, that you have to be grateful instead. Angus Brimacombe, who is one of my buddies, says, "Always a cause, eh, Ron? Always a cause." I look forward to those beer-league games more than I do *Hockey Night in Canada*.

I'm a little bit careless, a little bit reckless. I go too far sometimes. I'll ski too fast, play hockey too hard, drink too much. I don't eat well. Okay, I eat very badly—a lot of cheeseburgers, chocolate and beer.

I never envision myself anywhere but where I am at the moment. That means I can't picture myself at sixty or seventy years of age. I'm glad to have made it to fifty. It's a crazy thing, but my mom once told me that she went to a fortune teller and the fortune teller told her, "You'll have a child, and he'll die young." That stuck with me. It was not something that I obsessed about, but I've given it a passing thought on my birthdays.

I remember sitting in front of the cake on my fortieth birthday, ready to blow out the candles, and thinking, "I won't see fifty." This was a fortune teller at a fair, for God's sake! Geez, Mom. Why would you tell me that? I think she did it because I refused to wear my bike helmet. She was a worrier, as all moms are. I have a team photo from when I was seven years old in Whitehorse. I'm the scrawny-looking kid, the only one wearing a mouthguard.

Now that I'm fifty, I have started to realize that I don't have many options left. I could open a coffee stand or a bed and breakfast. I always thought that when I was done in broadcasting, I'd set up a cool little bar on the beach in the Caribbean and call it The Wherewithal, after the Tragically Hip song that goes, "I've always loved that guy / And he's not on TV anymore . . . / He had the wherewithal." I'm not too sure Cari would go for that one.

Do I sound pretentious? Oh God, I hate pretense. I also hate the thought that anyone would put me on a pedestal because of my job. I am on TV, which means I do my job in front of millions, but it's still just a job. If you are going to judge me, do it on the basis of the way I treat people. I used to really get into it with my mom and dad. They never liked it when I got controversial, because, God forbid, I might lose my job. And, more than once, I've come close. I've always thought, "So what?"

When I refereed in the OHA, I had a supervisor by the name of Bob Morley who would always say to me, "Ron, you need to do something about the length of your sweater. You look like Fred Flintstone out there." Because I was on television too, I'd sign autographs in the lobby between periods. Sometimes the fans would get mad at a call and they'd fire the autographed papers onto the ice at me. A lot of humility comes with that job.

When Cari and I first arrived in Ontario in 1986, I was called in to ref a game between Brock University and Ryerson. The game was at St. Mike's Arena in Toronto. Brock was, hands down, the better team. The Badgers were coached successfully for a long time by Mike Pelino. In the third period, they were leading by five goals, but they could easily have led by fifty. There were about eight minutes to go when a Brock player crosschecked a Ryerson player at the blue line. The Ryerson Rams were embarrassed about the score. They were edgy and about to turn nasty. So I called over a couple of players from Brock. I was going to use my abundant charm to keep the peace.

I said, "Now look, fellas, chances are I will call something marginal against you guys here in the next few minutes. I want to do it just to keep this thing under control. It will put the Ryerson team on the power play and they'll be happy. It will stop them from worrying about revenge. Be forewarned, if I call something chintzy, it's just to sidetrack them."

A minute later, I called interference off a faceoff, and Brock went ballistic. They climbed all over me. The players were in my face, calling me every name in the book. I thought, "Well, that's interesting." It turned out the guy I called the penalty on was in the running for the award for the most sportsmanlike player in the league, so he couldn't afford the penalty minutes.

Here I'd been telling myself, "I am going to do something that is in their best interest." And they said, "Screw you." And not for the first time, nor the last, I walked away thinking, "Ron, you pompous ass."

In September 2006, I refereed the final two periods and overtime of the Buffalo Sabres' 4–3 pre-season win over the Pittsburgh Penguins. The other referee was Steve Walkom, who at the time was the NHL's director of officiating. We took over for Kevin Pollock and Chris Rooney, who refereed the first period.

After a few minutes, Walkom remarked, "It's too fast!" And I remember thinking that it wasn't fast at all. I'd been a solo referee for twenty-three years, and now I only had to worry about eighty feet. There was speed in the tight confines of the corners, but worrying about that was negligible because I was covering only half of the ice.

Pittsburgh veteran John LeClair amazed me. Daniel Briere, Sidney Crosby and Max Afinogenov didn't wow me the way LeClair did. I expected they would be as fast as they were. But he was just months away from being out of hockey, retiring because he supposedly couldn't keep up, and he was so fast! I called a chintzy penalty on him in the last minute. Later, I said to Craig MacTavish, "You know, John LeClair just blew my socks off with his speed coming down the wing!" And he said, "Yeah, Ron, but he has a bad back, so he might only be able to do that one in every ten games, and that's why he's going [retiring]."

I did find it was hard to stay out of the way, but beyond that, honestly, it was no different than refereeing a Junior C game. I don't mean a horrible insult to the NHL, and it is not conceit. I just mean that art is the same whether you're teaching at Harvard or teaching at Joseph Welsh Elementary in Red Deer. All the things I feel about broadcasting—let your guest be the star, look for those teachable moments—are the same in the art of refereeing. It didn't feel at all like it was a step up. Even though Steve Walkom and the cameras tried to tell me it was.

I try to catch all the games during the week. I'll have one game on the computer and one game on the TV, and I have to resist researching, because then I'll stop watching. And if I stop watching the game, I miss the essence, those great things that make a game dynamite. Let's say Leafs winger Fredrik Sjostrom taps the pads of his teammate goalie James Reimer. On live television, in real time, it goes by in a heartbeat. If we catch it and replay it in super–slow motion, it can be illuminating.

Grapes and I have a schedule. We talk on the phone every Saturday morning at 9:30. I refer to the notes I've made all week where I just theorize, jotting down ideas. Don makes a list of possible clips, too, and on Saturday morning we go over everything. And then I give the ideas to our producer at the CBC, Kathy Broderick, so she knows what's on tap for the show.

Finally, at 5 o'clock on Saturday afternoon, Don is in the building, and we look at clips and decide what is good.

When a player needs defending, it should come from Don. Who cares what a Junior B referee has to say? I understand that. But at those times, I certainly don't argue with him, which is, by default, my version of defending him too.

I try to make sure the guy isn't a jerk or a phony. But sometimes I go to bat for a guy I don't know. I remember when Bobby Clarke phoned me, all hot because Dave Babych, a player best known for his time spent with the Winnipeg Jets and a fine NHL defenceman, sued the Philadelphia Flyers' doctors. They had sent him back onto the ice with a bad ankle. I defended Babych's right to do that. And Clarke said, "Ron, what are you doing? The players don't like you for this position."

"I don't care what the players think, Bobby. Let me ask you a question. Is Dave Babych a good guy?"

And Clarke said, "Well, he's dumb."

"Is he a good guy?"

Clarke said, "Yeah, he's a good guy."

I said, "Well, then, he deserves defence." And Clarke got off my back. He understood that kind of dialogue.

Glen Sather got after me recently. He phoned me and gave me a hard time because I was on Colin Campbell for not suspending one of his rookies, Derek Stepan, over a head shot. He was worried the kid would be stigmatized. I said, "Glen, me showing his cheap shot on Mike Green is good for Stepan. Now everybody will know the kid's a little wingy. That's good."

And he said, "Ah, you're right."

On the air, I try to get from A to B to C as quickly as possible, but you can only prepare so much, because you have to adapt to what's happening. So at sign-on, I start by thanking the minor hockey team that opens the show—you know, "Thank you to the Oshawa Legionaires, great job, guys . . ." Meantime, whatever comes up grabs my attention. Say there is a dramatic shot of Carey Price blessing himself—that means talk about Carey Price. And before that thought is done, maybe Josh Gorges does something, so time to follow him. I stay absolutely in the moment, and most of what I thought I was going to say is lost. It's like dancing with an expert dance partner. You have to let the pictures lead.

One day during the 2005 Stanley Cup final in Anaheim, Grapes and I were driving from the hotel to the rink, and we were passing through a nice area with streets lined with palm trees. There was a homeless woman panhandling on the street. She looked to be in her fifties, blonde and pretty in a hippie-like way. I thought about her, so gorgeous but living a gypsy life. She reminded me of my favourite song lyric from the Eagles' "The Last Resort," which always made me think of my T-shirt shack/bar by the ocean. I told Don how I'd like to retire on the beach and then asked him, "What's your favourite song lyric?"

He said, "I like 'Put your camel to bed.'"

I said, "From 'Midnight at the Oasis.'"

He said "Yeah, because you know what's going to happen next."

I love it that he still has love on the brain. Don never plans to retire.

When I think about retirement, it usually leads to thoughts of my mortality. We all ponder it, I guess. I tell myself that when the diagnosis comes, I hope I deal with it well.

I don't have a one-size-fits-all solution for retirement. I might end up teaching broadcasting, but I don't plan anything and I don't expect anything, so there is no sense starting now. Something will fall my way, and that will be that.

Some days I daydream about doing a radio show like the one Jurgen Gothe did on CBC Radio 2 from 3 to 6 p.m. on weekdays. It was an eclectic mix of classical, jazz and some contemporary. He laced his show with anecdotes about his fondness for food, wine and locations that specialized in food and wine, like Tuscany. I liked that. It was a simple three hours of escape that I would catnap through.

If I were still a program director, I would program "vacation radio"—no traffic reports, no business reports, no headaches. A show from a different location each week. The listener would be on permanent vacation.

If all else fails, I can always open a little bar attached to a silk-screening T-shirt shop on the beach in the Caribbean and call it The Wherewithal. Then we'll see what happens next.

PHOTO CREDITS

Photos that appear in the interior sections are reproduced courtesy of the following:

1. Ron MacLean Sr.
2. Ron MacLean
3. Ron MacLean Sr.
4. Ron MacLean. NHL and NHL team marks are the property of the NHL and its teams. Copyright NHL 2011. Used with permission. All rights reserved.
5. Ron MacLean
6. Ron MacLean. Copyright CJL Collegiate.
7. Cari MacLean
8. Ron MacLean
9. Ron MacLean. NHL and NHL team marks are the property of the NHL and its teams. Copyright NHL 2011. Used with permission. All rights reserved.
10. Jim Pattison Broadcast Group LP
11. Ron MacLean
12. Ron MacLean
13. Jim Pattison Broadcast Group LP
14. Ron MacLean
15. Ron and Cari MacLean
16. D. J. Wright Photography Ltd.
17. Ron MacLean
18. Ron and Cari MacLean
19. Nancy Ackerman, *The Spectator*
20. Rob MacLean/CBC Sports
21. CBC/Hockey Night in Canada
22. CBC/Hockey Night in Canada
23. Ron MacLean/CBC Sports
24. Ron MacLean/CBC Sports
25. Ron and Cari MacLean
26. Copyright Dave Sidaway, *The Gazette* (Montreal)
27. Steve Carty/CBC Sports
28. Kirstie McLellan Day
29. Copyright Frank Gunn/Canadian Press
30. Ron MacLean/CBC Sports
31. Ben Flock
32. Ron MacLean
33. Copyright Kevin Srakocic/AP. NHL and NHL team marks are the property of the NHL and its teams. Copyright NHL 2011. Used with permission. All rights reserved.
34. Cari MacLean
35. Kirstie McLellan Day
36. Cari MacLean
37. Brad Dalgarno
38. Ron MacLean/CBC Sports
39. Gary Kennedy
40. Kirstie McLellan Day
41. Barry Erskine/Metroland Media Group
42. Peter Bregg/*Maclean's*
43. Copyright Liesa Kortman/Metroland Media Group
44. IPC Canada Photo Inc.
45. Ron MacLean
46. Kirstie McLellan Day
47. Ron MacLean
48. Larry Henderson
49. Copyright Canadian Forces
50. Kirstie McLellan Day
51. Copyright Gemini Awards
52. Patrick Festing-Smith
53. Ron and Cari MacLean
54. Kirstie McLellan Day
55. Ron and Cari MacLean
56. Ron and Cari MacLean. NHL and NHL team marks are the property of the NHL and its teams. Copyright NHL 2011. Used with permission. All rights reserved.
57. Kirstie McLellan Day

INDEX

INDEX